THE FRENCH REVOLUTION AND THE LONDON STAGE, 1789–1805

During the French Revolution most performances on the London stage were strictly censored, but political attitudes found indirect expression. New and popular genres like pantomime, Gothic drama, history plays, musical and spectacular entertainment, and, above all, melodrama provided metaphors for the hopes and fears inspired by the conflict in France and subsequent European wars.

George Taylor looks at how British drama and popular entertainment were affected by the ideas and events of the French Revolution and Napoleonic Wars. He argues that melodrama had its origins in this period, with certain Gothic villains displaying qualities attributed to Robespierre and Napoleon, and that recurrent images of incarceration and dispossession reflected fears of arbitrary persecution, from the tyranny of the Bastille to the Jacobin's Reign of Terror. By a cultural analysis of the popular entertainment and theatre performances of the eighteenth and nineteenth centuries, Taylor reveals issues of ideological conflict and psychological stress.

GEORGE TAYLOR is Senior Lecturer in Drama at the University of Manchester. He has written articles on Delsarte, Svengali, anti-slave trade plays and theatre production. He is the author of *Players and Performances in the Victorian Theatre* (1989) and *Plays by Samuel Foote and Arthur Murphy* (1984) published by Cambridge University Press in the series British and American Playwrights.

An anonymous cartoon of the production at Astley's Amphitheatre of *Paris in an Uproar; or, the Destruction of the Bastille* (17 August 1789) entitled 'An Amphitheatrical Attack on the Bastille'.

THE FRENCH REVOLUTION AND THE LONDON STAGE, 1789–1805

GEORGE TAYLOR

CAMBRIDGE
UNIVERSITY PRESS

PUBLISHED BY THE PRESS SYNDICATE OF THE UNIVERSITY OF CAMBRIDGE
The Pitt Building, Trumpington Street, Cambridge, United Kingdom

CAMBRIDGE UNIVERSITY PRESS
The Edinburgh Building, Cambridge CB2 2RU, UK   www.cup.cam.ac.uk
40 West 20th Street, New York, NY 10011–4211, USA   www.cup.org
10 Stamford Road, Oakleigh, Melbourne, 3166, Australia
Ruiz de Alarcón 13, 28014, Madrid, Spain

First published 2000

Printed in the United Kingdom at the University Press, Cambridge

Typeface 11/12.5pt Baskerville   *System* 3b2

A catalogue record for this book is available from the British Library

Library of Congress Cataloguing in Publication data
Taylor, George, 1900–
The French Revolution and the London Stage, 1789–1805 / George Taylor.
p.   cm.
Includes bibliograhical references and index.
ISBN 0 521 63052 5 (hardback)
1. Theatre – England – London – History – 18th century. 2. Theatre – England –
London – History – 19th century. 3. English drama – 18th century – History and criticism.
4. English drama – 19th century – History and criticism. 5. France – History – Revolution,
1789–1799 – Influence.
I. Title.
PN2596.L6 T39 2001
792′.09421′09033 – dc21   00-062141

ISBN 0 521 63052 5 hardback

To Anna and Chris

Contents

Acknowledgements

At a time when academics are being urged to set up collaborative research projects, and to use postgraduates to do the donkey work of literature searches, gathering statistics and even proofreading, I am somewhat reluctant to admit that this book is virtually all my own work. But, although I have little direct or practical assistance to acknowledge, I must record a debt to those whose insights have, over the years, informed my thinking about the content of this book. My fascination with the French Revolution dates back to undergraduate days, when the assiduity of Alfred Goodwin and the perspicacity of Brian Manning both inspired me to look behind the excitement of events to the driving forces of ideology and material interest. Similarly, Stephen Joseph, Peter Thomson, Martin Banham, Christopher Baugh and David Mayer, all from very different perspectives, fuelled my interest in the then disregarded genre of melodrama. Other scholars whose written work has subsequently enriched my appreciation of both history and theatre are acknowledged in the text.

However, the most stimulating recent influence on my thinking has been my wife, Anna Seymour. Not that she is a specialist in the history of my period, but our discussions about the different ways in which drama is created and effects both practitioners and audiences have given me many startling insights. Her firm grasp of the basic principles of theatre and of scholarship has also helped me maintain an integrity of analysis when occasionally overwhelmed by a wealth of anecdotes and examples.

Much of my primary work was done at the Henry Huntington Library, San Marino, California, where the delightful surroundings and generous assistance, as well as the richness of their eighteenth-century holdings, makes research there a particular joy. Nearer to home, the John Rylands Library of Manchester University provided comparable assistance, if not as beautiful a garden. I must also acknowledge the financial support of a Hayter Parry Award, awarded by the Arts Faculty of Manchester University, which made the assistance I was originally granted by the Arts and Humanities Research Board unnecessary for this particular project.

Particular thanks are due to Victoria Cooper of Cambridge University Press, whose advice, encouragement and editorial support were exemplary and highly valued by an often harrassed and anxious author.

Note on the text

Only modern editions of the plays are included in the bibliography. Plays cited in the text are referenced as either from the Larpent MS Collection in the Henry Huntington Library, San Marino, California, or from early printed versions.

Introduction

On 5 June 1783 the Montgolfier brothers launched a balloon that rose on a pillar of hot air above a bonfire in Annonay, central France. On 15 October their assistant, Pilâtre de Rozier, became the first man to fly. His balloon ascended above Paris, and, although the flight lasted only four and half minutes and rose only eighty-four feet, it provided its fearful occupant with an overview of a city which in the next ten years was to experience violent changes that have reverberated to the present day.[1] The development of aviation might be considered to have been more momentous, but the ideas and strategies hammered out in the forge of the French Revolution have just as decisively shaped the values and consciousness of the last two centuries. Like the Montgolfiers' balloon, the theatre of late eighteenth-century London may also appear to have been a gorgeous and flimsy package floating free above the city. But, like the balloon, it was more than just a fabulous spectacle to delight ignorant spectators; its flight provides us with a vantage point from which to view and analyse changes happening below, for, just as hot air kept the Montgolfiers' fragile craft afloat, so the shape and speed of theatrical change were invisibly determined by the heat of political and cultural conflict. This study will examine both the spectacle and the forces that shaped it. Examples of performance, drama and theatrical innovation will illustrate how public entertainment responded to the turbulence in the intellectual climate that socio-political changes induced, for, even though London did not suffer the traumas of Paris, it underwent a major cultural crisis.

By 'crisis' I mean that not only were there unprecedented material changes but that the ideologies available could no longer explain their development. The philosophies of the Enlightenment, which had originally inspired the revolution in France, were confounded by the excesses of the Terror and Napoleonic expansionism, while the benevolence of the Sentimental Movement was overwhelmed by harsh economic mechanisms that led to rural dislocation and urban deprivation across much of Europe. New material circumstances created both new audiences and new ideological opinions, thus causing a redefinition of both high art and popular entertainment to reflect changes in the values and expectations of all classes. In England the tension between repressive government, popular discontent and intellectual detachment was not as violent as in Revolutionary France, but the shock waves of revolution and war stimulated the most palpable class conflict in Britain since the Stuart period.

Finding it impossible to make sense of the inexorable mechanism of these political and economic juggernauts, many individuals in both France and England withdrew from social debate into individual angst and spiritual introspection. In time new debates and ideologies were to evolve, but in the meantime repression, reaction and disengagement were the preferred strategies of a culture in crisis. When artists can no longer represent the world in coherent patterns, the recognition of which engenders in the viewer a sense of identification and reassurance with the familiar, they may resort to the use of metaphor. They may rework experience into weird and intriguing patterns that distance the audience from reality, sometimes as a relief from its harshness, but often as an indirect subliminal means of making emotional, if not intellectual, sense of life's cruelties. In *Hard Times* (1854), written some forty years after the Napoleonic Wars, Dickens depicted the utilitarian industrialist Thomas Gradgrind, who believes only in facts, confronted by Fleary, manager of a travelling circus, who protests: 'You can't deny the people "Fancy".' This dichotomy between fact and fancy suggests a divorce between cultural expression and social reality. Yet theatre is a communal art addressing the experiences and concerns of a wide audience and must forge a link between the two. In the so-called 'great ages' of theatre the social or ideological homogeneity of audiences made a communal and cathartic experience of tragedy possible, but in the context of social division, like that of Dickens' Victorian mill town, mirth could not be unrestrained nor the ripeness of the tragic moment recognised – as the oppressed millhand, Stephen Blackpool, complained, ''Tis all a muddle!'[2]

The Victorian theatre produced no convincing tragedy and precious little intellectual comedy, and indeed throughout much of the century theatre itself was widely disparaged. Intellectual sophisticates, the socially fashionable, the religious, utilitarians and radicals condemned the theatre as trivial, extravagant, irrelevant, vulgar or immoral. The distribution of theatres fragmented into East End and West End; spectacular and intimate; circus, pantomime and opera. Each had its own establishment and each its own corner of the market. In the mid-eighteenth century there had been fewer theatres but they were more communal in their appeal. Although audiences were divided according to class between pit, box and gallery, all came to see the same shows, for within one programme there was a variety that not only satisfied the different groups but satisfied them all – mainpieces, comic or tragic; afterpieces, satirical, farcical, musical or spectacular; interludes of music, song and dance; the wit of prologue and epilogue and above all the attractions of the performers, all received plaudits from all corners of the house. Critics might make sharp comparisons, but little of the programme was dismissed as 'trash', or 'immoral', or irrelevant 'fancy'.[3]

Terms like 'rubbish' and 'nonsense' are particularly suggestive to the cultural historian. Disagreement as to what is trash and what is treasure suggests cultural crisis, when values are put under question by social stress or political conflict. The class divisions of the Victorian era were notorious for producing such stresses, and many of their cultural expressions have been condemned as hypocritical, pretentious or escapist. Although a period of relative stability, it was essentially a repressive stability, reform being gradually extracted by shrewd negotiation rather than by revolutionary confrontation. The Victorians knew power lay not in philosophy, nor even in faith, but in the inexorable machinery of market forces. Of course, there were idealists, moralists, mystics even, but orthodox Victorian culture marginalised them as 'unrealistic', fit only for fairytales and melodrama. The idealists themselves were tempted to hide their discontent behind a respectable front of conformity, recognising the importance of being earnest. In mid-eighteenth century England such deception was unnecessary. Tories despised Whigs; apprentices envied their masters; court fops, city merchants and country squires valued different lifestyles, they might mock each other and certainly enjoyed theatrical parodies of each other's class, but there was a cohesion and tolerance, a belief that the same motives drove courtier and highwayman, that parson and squire had the same interests, and that philosopher, scientist, scholar and artist were all in pursuit of different aspects of the same truth. They called it Enlightenment. As E. P. Thompson has shown in his *Customs and Practices* – which explored the period preceding that which he memorably categorised as *The Making of the English Working Class* – those on the 'lower' margins of society had not yet found a distinctive voice; their discontent found safe and symbolic expression in rowdy games and festive sports.[4]

Doubtless, my impressionistic sketches of the two mid-century periods are open to many exceptions, but I intend a more searching analysis of the age between Enlightenment and earnestness. At the turn of the century political upheavals, centred in France, affected the whole of Europe; economic developments, centred in the north of England, began to spread across the world; and the stresses of urban life, centred, for this study at least, in London but replicated in cities everywhere, led to feelings of displacement, alienation and social fragmentation. Historians have repeatedly considered how these revolutionary stresses shaped 'the modern world': defining class conflict as a clash of irreconcilable interests; undermining the accepted rationality of religion by revealing its dependence on faith rather than intellectual certainty; and setting the uniqueness of the individual against the generalities of society. Being of a century that has experienced many revolutions, we find it difficult to understand, even imagine, the preceding era and the unifying philosophies of the Age of Enlightenment, when a few scientific observations seemed to provided immediate access to 'universal principles', an autocratic monarch's 'enlightenment' seemed the route to social justice, and the rebellious colonials of New England felt confident enough to enunciate 'self-evident truths' as the basis of their constitution. And yet this 'unified' period produced a gallery of highly opinionated, original, even eccentric individuals – Samuel Johnson, Horace Walpole and Oliver Goldsmith; Lord North, John Wilkes and Charles James Fox; Quin, Garrick and Macklin – all in heated disagreement but, nevertheless, all engaged in a seemingly coherent discourse with a shared confidence that 'common-sense' was demonstrable and accessible to all humanity.

Of course, their individual disagreements and disputes were a rehearsal for the irreconcilable contradictions of the Revolutionary period, and a close examination of mid-eighteenth-century 'civilised stability,'[5] could well undermine its apparent coherence. Indeed there were several discordant voices that anticipated and prompted the violent clashes of the later age: John Wesley and Joseph Priestley, Thomas Paine and Lord George Gordon, Adam Smith and Thomas Arkwright. And there were shifts too in the position of women, who were beginning to question the male domination of the Enlightened Age – though it was not until the period of crisis that individual voices made their disruptive presence felt: Wollstonecraft, Edgeworth, Inchbald, Siddons. Perhaps these individuals still represented a minority of nonconformity, but in the 1790s individual voices became shriller and their ideas more persuasive to a different section of the population, thus contributing to social fragmentation and creating what today we call 'identity politics'. In retrospect one may dispute whether this concern for personal identity was the spume on the groundswell of fundamental class conflict, or whether it provoked of itself profound redefinitions of purpose and perception. In either case, the artistic culture of the Romantic period has long been categorised as one of introspection – individuals driven by persecution into exile or by misappreciation into a fantasy world of 'otherness'.

The discovery and exploration of Otherness is one of the most significant developments of the Revolutionary age.[6] Although pictures, poems and even interior decoration exploited the exotic East or the mysterious past for images to disturb and challenge the mundane and ordinary, it was in the theatre that the exhibition of the Other took on its most spectacular forms – scenic pantomimes, Gothic melodramas, fairytale ballets and antiquarian productions of Shakespeare. In the eighteenth century the past and the foreign had been generalised into a decorous classicism of stately pillars and nodding plumes, but on the Romantic stage whole new dramatic genres evolved in order to present barbaric or sublime images, and to unfold stories of unnatural violence and providential mystery. Consciously or unconsciously these dramas reflected the discoveries of the age, not only actual expeditions, such as that of Captain Cook to the Antipodes, or Napoleon's ill-fated invasion of Egypt, but the explorations of the mind in an age that tore down the Bastille, invented the guillotine, discovered the power of steam and the principles of electricity. Time too was being disrupted, traditions dying as unprecedented events took place. Sons could no longer expect to follow in their fathers' footsteps, inheriting their land, learning their trades. Some sank into undeserved penury; others achieved undeserved wealth. Kings and bishops had been overthrown in France, the king of England was mad, and his son, the regent, a grotesque voluptuary. Dr Mesmer could overrule the conscious will, and it was *almost* believable that Dr Frankenstein could reconstitute a living being.

All art functions on a metaphorical level, but at certain times, it is especially through metaphor that the complexities and mysteries of life can be apprehended. Politicians, philosophers and economists may have to hammer out rational interpretations of the seeming chaos of material reality, but for artists, and, more particularly, for their bewildered audiences, the naturalistic depiction of probability can seem inadequate. Only an evocation of the barely possible provides a satisfying response to the contradictions of a world which 'self-evident' principles can no longer explain. Thus we must tease out the metaphorical resonances of Grimaldi's clowning, Monk Lewis' maniacs and the passionate histrionics of Siddons and Cooke. A significance must be found for the 'fraternal' relationships in the plays of Holcroft (a committed radical), the besieging of castles in those of Colman (a patriotic manager), the mythological status of rapists (the monastic Ambrosio and the oriental Blue Beard), and the phenomenon of 'natural genius' as exhibited in the youth of Master Betty and in the skill of Astley's horses. Of course, it is unlikely that the significance that we might find was consciously intended by performers or even recognised by audiences at the time, but the elucidation of the resonance and possible meaning of cultural metaphors is integral to the methodology of the present study.

When analysing the statistics gathered for his invaluable work, *Theatre, Opera, and Audiences in Revolutionary Paris*, Emmet Kennedy argues that previous historians overstated the political content and influence of the theatre during the Revolution.[7] But, although 'uncommitted' plays far outnumbered those dealing with specifically political issues, his analyses of changes in emphasis and attitude show that the impact of events on theatrical taste was crucial – though indirect. Historians can fall into the same trap as political censors in trying to identify topics, stories and speeches that specifically refer to issues of the day, because the relationship is usually more subtle than specific precisely because it is unintentional. For instance, Pierre Desforges' *Le Sourd, ou L'Auberge Pleine* was the most popular French play of the period (1789–99), a comedy in which a man pretends to be deaf in order to gain accommodation in a crowded inn. Kennedy accurately summarises the plot and its reliance on conventional tropes and situations: 'Stock eighteenth-century themes are skilfully exploited here: marriage of love over marriage of interest, bourgeois frugality and prudence over aristocratic honour, testy master-servant relations in which money is the main factor, and the psychology of deaf-mutes . . . It has no political message, only a few social banalities.'[8] At first glance it does seem very traditional, and, no doubt, contemporary audiences read little into it. But all these 'stock themes' have implications in identifying the political sympathies of the audience, and some of the new situations or jokes had a more than stock resonance in the context of its first performance in 1790 – the legitimate travellers' room and the host's chair at table are 'usurped' by an outsider pretending to be deaf. Did the revolutionaries of 1790 seem 'deaf to reality'? Or just the provincial ones travelling to Paris? If their policies were a trick, should we admire their cunning or their effrontery? The play posed no such political questions directly of its audience, but its very popularity raises them for the cultural analysts. My own curiosity is raised particularly by the metaphor of deafness being adopted as a strategy for coping with a material problem – particularly as the number of dramatic characters who are deaf, mute or blind steadily increased during the period under investigation.

But understanding the Age of Revolution is not all a matter of 'dream interpretation' in which fears and aspirations find fantastic forms. The other side of cultural crisis is the desperate affirmation of ancient certainties – the reflex response of the conservative and reactionary. Edmund Burke's reading of history was not one that celebrated Otherness but proclaimed stability and tradition. The juvenile genius of the Younger Pitt was dedicated to political repression. Even if certain scientific developments were challengingly mysterious, such as Mesmer's 'animal magnetism', most were essentially rational and pragmatic. For instance Charles Bell's analysis of emotional expression was a far more objective approach to the psychological.[9] It found embodiment in the statuesque attitudes of Emma Hamilton and the passionate gestures of Sarah Siddons – whose son translated a treatise on rhetorical gesture.[10] In fact the techniques of acting were becoming more 'scientific', even as the effect of performance became more emotional. Perhaps the most mechanistic system to emerge from the period was the 'classical economy' of capitalist acquisitiveness, as developed from Adam Smith by Malthus and Ricardo, a system that made sense of cultural chaos and spiritual confusion by reducing everything to a commodity and its price – the harsh quantifiable facts of Thomas Gradgrind. This capitalist philosophy was to be the dominant ideology to emerge from the whole Revolutionary epoch, and it was manifested in the theatre by the increasingly exploitative management of both companies and buildings, which undermined the ensemble tradition and fragmented the market into exclusive audiences patronising specialised theatres. One protest against these market forces, the O. P. Riots of 1809, was a theatrical manifestation in its own right, a carnival of catcalls, costumes and rhetoric. Financial 'reality' won the day, but the O. P.s, representing the traditional liberty of 'free-born Englishmen', contested the liberty of a capitalist entrepreneur to 'do as he liked with his own property'.[11]

The theatricality of the O. P. Riots reflected the equally performative nature of the Revolutionary *journées* on the other side of the Channel, and this perception of the O. P. Riots as suggestive of wider political and cultural conflicts typifies my methodological approach to this study. In order to examine the relationship between the cultural activity of theatre and the unprecedented political and social developments of the Revolution, I will not unfold a seamless narrative of chronological 'theatre history'. Rather, a number of exemplary figures, events and performances will be described, and, by analysing why particular artistic choices and decisions were made, I will suggest how the material realities of the time affected both ideological positions and artistic forms. Although this runs the risk of imposing interpretations, rather than drawing out originally intended meanings, I believe that in scholarship transparent subjectivity is infinitely preferable to an illusion of objectivity.

My own method is fundamentally rooted in principles of historical materialism, which continually raise the question of in whose interest events take place, and look for the ways in which material conditions influence ideological explanations. But I would not attribute every particular development to a crude class conflict, especially as I will often be identifying bewildering contradictions between the intention of individual agents and the result of their actions or the effect of their cultural creations. When discussing theatrical production my focus will not always be on the most influential aspects of political or social change, but on how the apparently trivial minutiae of the entertainment business reflected ideological attitudes that were being determined elsewhere on the wide stage of the world. Thus I will employ some of the sensibilities of New Historicism to refine my essentially materialistic analysis. This might seem an uneasy combination of methodologies, but, as Catherine Gallagher suggests in her essay, 'Marxism and New Historicism': 'New historicism confronts Marxism now partly as an amplified record of Marxism's own edgiest, uneasiest voices. Those Marxists who listen carefully may hear many of their own unanswered doubts and questions. To dismiss such challenges as the mere echoes of a reactionary defeatism would be a serious mistake.'[12] In the current debates on historiography there have been insinuations that, on the one hand, Cultural Materialists are more concerned with a committed political stance than with 'real' historical analysis, while, on the other, New Historicists acknowledge no stance at all and indulge a dilettante fascination with the fragments and margins of 'real' history. Inevitably all histories, however 'new' their techniques, are deeply influenced by, even if not conscientiously engaged in, the political and cultural issues of their own time, and it is naïve to suggest that a concern for the byways, rather than the grand highways, of history is an apolitical, or even reactionary, exercise. As Stephen Greenblatt avers, a New Historicist's concern with minutiae does not replace analytical interpretation, but,

the interest lies not in the abstract universal but in particular, contingent cases, the selves fashioned and acting according to generative rules and conflicts of a given culture. And these selves, conditioned by the expectations of their class, gender, religion, race and national identity, are constantly effecting changes in the course of history. Indeed if there is any inevitability in the New Historicism's vision of history it is this insistence on agency, for even inaction or extreme marginality is understood to possess meaning and therefore to imply intention.[13]

However, whilst attracted by the oblique perspective of New Historicism, I will continually look to the ultimate shift in material power between social classes to explain the twists and turns of apparent contingency. This does not necessarily mean a search for some 'abstract universality' – indeed both terms were anathema to Marx himself. His was a dialectical analysis of material reality, in which individual consciousness is defined by an interactive process, in which both the canon of subjective masterpieces and the unselfconscious products of popular culture act as determinants and reflections, intimately involved in the wider fluctuations of political power and the creation of what Gramsci defined as the ideological hegemony. Without keeping a weather eye open for hegemonic developments, the recounting of ephemeral events and examples can easily lapse into a valueless positivism, or the unhelpful relativism of some of the New Historicists. In this revolutionary period traditions of morality and social status, the radical philosophies of the Enlightenment, and new feelings of inequality and oppression, were so chaotically thrown together in a kaleidoscope of events and arguments, that I find Raymond Williams' analysis of how ideologies change particularly valuable in assessing which certainties were crumbling and which were hardening into the new capitalist hegemony that was to dominate the nineteenth century.[14]

Two theatre historians whose work demonstrates vividly how social realities, critical discourses and cultural production interact, and who both deserve my acknowledgement here, are Joseph Roach and Bruce McConachie. Roach's analysis of how changes in scientific thinking, particularly biological and psychological perceptions, have effected the processes and appreciation of performance, will be much cited in chapter 5 below. But his whole approach to the creative interplay between ideas and practices has particular relevance to a period when ideas were continually being challenged. McConachie's own area of research is, unfortunately, later than my own, but his *Melodramatic Formulations* describes precisely how dominant social and political thinking finds expression in dramatic form, and conversely how the formulae of theatrical entertainment can itself effect the patterns of people's thinking about their own society.[15]

The sense of 'cultural crisis' arising from an ideological void, where no rational explanation can be formulated to fit the experience of social or political reality, has bedevilled historians. From generation to generation – even decade to decade – different explanations of the Revolution have been propounded. These inevitably reflect the political preoccupations and conflicts of the historians' own times. I can claim no freedom from such influences, but to identify my own position, I must express a distrust of those accounts of the 1970s and 1980s that tried to deny any explanation based on 'class interest'. François Furet's *Penser la Révolution Française* (1978), W. Doyle's *Origins of the French Revolution* (1980) and even Simon Shama's *Citizens* (1989), all tend towards the 'unpredictable chapter of accidents and miscalculations'[16] school of thought. Of course individuals disagreed, groups and classes were divided, and principles as well as policies were made up on the hoof under the pressure of circumstance. But I suspect that the detailed scrutiny of individual agents and their motivation can lead to myopic history and a confusion typical of the 1980s, when a 'radical' concern for individual and group identity became elided with 'reactionary' policies that prioritised consumers above citizens. On the other hand, by taking, as I have already attempted, an overview of before-and-after in order to identify the winners-and-losers, an inevitable conclusion must be that the Revolutionary period saw an increase in capitalist power and the emergence of a dominant bourgeois culture in both France and England, as is argued by Alex Callinicos:

> Bourgeois revolutions must be understood, not as revolutions made by capitalists, but as revolutions that promote capitalism. The emphasis should shift from the class, which makes a bourgeois revolution to the effects of such a revolution – to the class, which benefits from it. More specifically, a bourgeois revolution is a political transformation – a change in state power, which is the precondition for large-scale capital accumulation and the establishment of the bourgeoisie as the dominant class. This definition requires, then, a political change with certain effects. It says nothing about the social forces, which carry through the transformation.[17]

My study, of course, intends to explore the very specific cultural force of theatre production and how it was involved in 'carrying through the transformation'. But only by acknowledging the perspective of one's historical understanding, can individual agents, their achievements and aspirations, be properly analysed. So when describing specific examples of cultural production in the theatre, and considering questions of intention and effect, it will be with a continual awareness of the dialectics of class interest and with reference to shifts in socioeconomic power, as well as to declarations of political and ideological intent.[18] However, perceptive criticism is not solely a matter of hindsight, contemporary commentators too can recognise how apparently innocuous developments reveal changes of profound cultural significance. And so to conclude this introduction I will examine in some detail one such passage of criticism, which provides not only a particular perspective on theatrical changes but also one that will inform my whole analysis of the period.

George Colman the Younger's career as manager of the Haymarket Theatre coincided almost exactly with the period of the Revolution and the Napoleonic Wars. In the same month as the fall of the

Bastille he took over from his father, and in 1818, three years after Waterloo, he finally sold his controlling share in the theatre. In 1803, the mid-point of this career and two years before my own discussion closes, he produced his finest comedy, *John Bull.* Walter Scott described it as essentially realistic: 'The scenes of broad humour are executed in the best possible taste; and the whimsical, yet native characters, reflect the manners of real life.'[19] However an anonymous critic, 'E', writing in the *Literary Journal*, identifies a number of 'changes in manners', which precisely reflect changing cultural values:

Perhaps there is no better mode of estimating the comparative morals of two periods than a comparison of their popular comedies. Considering Mr Colman as eminent for comic merit now as his father was forty years ago, we will rest our investigation on the comedy before us and on the 'Jealous Wife'. The present comedy opens with the display of a romantic and dreary country, from which at first we can hardly think ourselves in England [it was set in Cornwall]; . . . One of the principle characters is a sentimental brazier, and the heroine, his daughter, a young woman seduced, and afterwards forsaken by a man greatly her superior in station; while the chief humour is derived from the blunders of an honest Irish landlord.

In the 'Jealous Wife', the chief characters are all gentlemen and gentlewomen, taking the world for what is, or perhaps we should say was its usual signification, and from their virtues, their vices, and their follies, the humour and the interest of the piece are derived. Sir Harry Beagle is a brutal country squire, but his conduct is not commented on by a virtuous groom; Captain O'Cutter is not accompanied by a sentimental boatswain; . . .

How is the distinction, which runs through most of the comedies as well as novels of the two periods to be accounted for? Not entirely from the change of manners . . . The universal practice of imputing every virtue to the lowest orders of society, and every vice and every folly to the wealthy and the noble; and the considering a breach in chastity as an essential requisite in an amiable female character, is certainly not derived from real observation on Modern British manners, but originates in the prevailing taste from that monstrous farrago of absurdity and immorality, the German drama. But there is one striking peculiarity of modern comedy which, it is to be feared, is derived from our Manners. The sole interest now turns upon poverty and wealth. We are no longer agitated by the various distresses and final successes of a generous passion. The Injuriae, Suspiciones, Inimicitiae, Induciae, Bellum, Pax Rursum of honourable lovers are banished from the stage; and distress arises from urgent creditors and sheriffs; and the happy catastrophe, from the intervention of fortune (like a god of the Greek tragedies) in the shape of an unexpected bequest or the detection of a forged will.[20]

Three elements are identified here, which the critic considers show a decline in both drama and manners, all of which are crucial in the ideological developments of the time. Firstly, a change in class values, for not only are there more lower-class characters than in *The Jealous Wife*, but the old metal-worker, his 'ruined' daughter, and the benevolent Irish publican provide the moral touchstones of the play – indeed old Job Thornberry's generosity and blunt-speaking categorise him as the 'John Bull' of the title. His final speech to the man who repents seducing his daughter typifies his amiable pragmatism and stubborn patriotism: 'I forgive you, young man, for what has passed; but no one deserves forgiveness, who refuses to make amends, when he has disturb'd the happiness of an Englishman's fireside.'

Secondly, Mary Thornberry's escaping punishment for her loss of chastity exercised the moral sensibilities of several contemporaries, and, although it was convenient to dismiss this lapse as un-English and influenced by the 'monstrous farrago of absurdity and immorality, the German drama', this suggestion raises two questions: how unacceptable was such behaviour when large and enthusiastic audiences applauded the play? And, what in fact were the influences from abroad? If the denouement engineered by the benevolent merchant and the gentleman Peregrine Rochdale was considered morally correct and not merely expedient, then Colman had depicted a widespread change in personal values, not one just associated with class interest. And finally, 'E' identifies what he considers to be the prevalent shift in subject matter, an increasing materialism in which 'the sole interest now turns upon poverty and wealth'. His earlier concerns for the morality of class and personal identity are here subsumed in a recognition of market forces. If Colman was accurately addressing the interests and values of his audience, which his own material success confirms, then it was no longer the gentry of his father's day, but the business-, crafts- and tradesmen, and their families, of the increasingly mercantile city. Although his own theatre, the Haymarket, held a summer patent, so perhaps the theatre-going gentry had retired to the country, his practice of offering his plays to the larger winter houses suggests that the new materialism spoke to audiences of all classes.

But, crucial as material circumstances are in determining artistic policies, then as now, it was not only in 'realistic' comedies, like *John Bull*, that Colman and other playwrights and managers indicated the increasingly commercial attitudes of their age. They gave expression to their hopes and fears in more fantastic productions, set in other times and among other races, and in more overtly populist genres than that of social comedy – musical romances and spectacular pageants, pantomimes and farces. As shall be seen, throughout this period of cultural crisis, the popular theatre embodied and reflected in many forms not only the material concerns but also many of the wider, less tangible, anxieties of its audiences.

CHAPTER I

England and France in 1789

While the mobs that had stormed the Bastille were still rejoicing their audacity on the night of 14 July, the audience at the Haymarket Theatre, London, gathered to see *Inkle and Yarico* by the theatre's manager George Colman the Younger. First performed on 8 August 1787, this comic opera had dominated the Haymarket's last two summer seasons and between October 1788 and June 1789 had also been performed twenty-four times at Covent Garden. Its 164 patent theatre performances by 1800 were a record for the last quarter of the century beaten only by *The School for Scandal*.[1] Unlike Sheridan's play, a classic example of classic comedy, *Inkle and Yarico* was of a new genre rather vaguely defined as 'mixed'.[2] Containing thirteen songs, it was published as an 'opera', and, while its tone was essentially comic, its potential for tragedy locates it in the Sentimental tradition, with topical references to the anti-slave trade movement. This hybrid entertainment is indicative of what Alan Sinfield has described as a 'cultural faultline': 'Faultline stories are the ones that require most assiduous and continuous reworking; they address the awkward, unresolved issues, the ones in which the conditions of plausibility are in dispute [and which] comprise within themselves the ghosts of the alternative stories they are trying to exclude.'[3] Despite her having saved his life, the merchant Inkle attempts to sell Yarico, a Native American, as a slave. And, although the benevolent Governor of Barbados thwarts his plan, the play challenged the ideological complacency of the mid-eighteenth century. It dramatised the conflicts between slavery and liberty, moral principle and commercial self-interest, the generous instincts of 'the savage' and the hypocritical sentiments of the imperialist entrepreneur – as well as the question, that was the point of Richard Steele's earlier version of the story, of which sex is the more constant.[4]

To appreciate the faultline nature of this play we need to consider the apparent stability of its social context. Certainly it seemed that in the 1760s and 1770s England had enjoyed a 'civilised security'. The Seven Years' War had expanded the Empire in both hemispheres, George III's declaration that he 'gloried in the name of Britain' had signalled an end to the Jacobite threat, and London was the commercial centre of the world – confirmed by the handsome new squares around Hyde Park and the network of turnpikes providing unprecedented access to and from the capital. The sixties and seventies saw the beginning of the Industrial Revolution, with Watt's steam engine, Hargreaves' spinning jenny, the Bridgewater Canal, the Carron steelworks and Wedgwood's pottery, and a lowering of food prices due to the agricultural improvements of land enclosure, which, by the loss of small-holdings and common land, was driving the rural population into the growing conurbations. The social problems created by these economic developments were as yet not critical, so that, particularly when viewed from the Continent, Britain seemed a model of material prosperity, political stability and cultural enlightenment.

Indeed English ideas, experiences and culture provided substantive models for the 'Age of Enlightenment' across Europe. During the 'Scots Renaissance' of the 1760s Edinburgh and Glasgow were rebuilt in the English classical style, and Scottish artists, philosophers and politicians headed for London. Similarly, the French *philosophes* developed their ideas and their art with continual reference to English models – the philosophers Newton, Locke and Hume, and artists Shakespeare, Richardson and Lillo. The '*style-anglais*' was the rage in clothes, landscape gardens and theatrical performance. It was a style of thought, behaviour and art that seemed rational yet relaxed, innovatory yet respectful of tradition, materially successful yet inspired by sentiments of generosity, and all apparently underpinned by principles of toleration and equality before the law. It had precisely the qualities that Sinfield attributes to an ideological hegemony:

The strength of ideology derives from the way it gets to be common sense, it 'goes without saying'. For its production is not an external process . . . ideology makes sense for us – of us – because it is already proceeding when we arrive in the world, and we come to consciousness in its terms. As the world shapes itself around and through us, certain interpretations of experience strike us as plausible: they fit with what we have experienced already, and are confirmed by others around us . . . The conditions of plausibility are therefore crucial. [5]

The culture of England in the 1760s was extremely plausible, not only for the English, but for much of 'cultured' Europe – and, of course, for the expatriate inhabitants of America.

In her study of the development of patriotic identity, *Britons: Forging the Nation*, Linda Colley argues that the successes of the Seven Years' War paved the way for the rebellion of the American colonies – now that Canada was ruled by Britain, why should they pay taxes for an army to protect them from the French? In turn the rebellion prompted internal challenges to the political establishment from the radicalism of John Wilkes, the fanaticism of the Gordon Riots and the cynical hedonism of the 'dandies'.[6] Success bred complacency as well as confidence, inspired envy as well as respect, and, with the loss of the colonies in 1783, eventually led to national humiliation followed by an aristocratic reaction that intensified throughout the period of the Revolution and the Napoleonic Wars. As Colley argues, the élite of 1815 may have been no more powerful than that of 1760, but it was more aware of its power and thus more intentionally oppressive:

Even though attacks on their exclusivity, rapacity and overweening power continued in some quarters after Waterloo, the men who dominated Great Britain still had substantial cause to congratulate themselves. They had bounced back from the humiliation of defeat in America. They had resisted French republicanism and quashed any attempt to imitate it at home. They had destroyed Napoleon Bonaparte's military machine in Continental Europe. And in the process, they had dramatically increased the size of Britain's empire. They had done something else as well: assumed many of the characteristics of a service élite . . . Without opening the upper echelons of power and rank to more than a limited number of self-made men, a far more self-conscious rhetoric and appearance of service to the public and to the nation had been broadly adopted which proved remarkably effective.[7]

This book will chart how theatrical culture contributed to, and disputed, this élitist development, for the faultlines revealed in Colman's apparently light-weight musical were eventually to become gaping fissures.

Inkle and Yarico's original 1787 production had coincided with the agitation by opposition Whigs, led by Fox, Burke and Sheridan, for the prosecution, on charges of corruption, spoliation and cruelty, of Warren Hastings, who had been Governor General of India since 1771 and had greatly expanded the East India Company's power during the previous three decades. Indeed, leaving the government of a subcontinent to a commercial trading company had long been questioned, and 'Nabobs' returning with ill-gotten fortunes had inspired much criticism, including a dramatic satire from Samuel Foote.[8] Hastings' impeachment eventually began on 13 February 1788, and his prosecutors, many of whom had championed the American colonists ten years before, hoped to humiliate both the East India Company and the Tory government for their ruthless expansionist policies. Although Colman's story is of individual betrayal, its application to imperialist exploitation is clear when Inkle is described by Medium, a more amiable fellow merchant, as 'a schemer, a fellow who risks his life for a chance of advancing his interest! Always advantage in view! Trying, here, to make discoveries that may promote his profit in England. Another Botany Bay scheme, maybe' (Act 1, scene 1).[9]

Inkle's heartlessness is attributed to the principles of his commercial class as instilled by his father – a class for whose benefit the Elder Pitt had waged war and the Younger Pitt was manipulating the economy. But a more subtle association between commercial interest and the philosophical pragmatic tradition of Newton, Locke and Bentham is suggested by Inkle's preoccupation with mathematics: 'I have been comparing the land, here, with that of our own country . . . and calculating how much it might produce by the acre . . . I was proceeding algebraically upon the subject, and just about extracting the square root . . . I was thinking, too, if so many natives could be caught, how much they might fetch in the West Indian market' (Act 1, scene 1). The issue of slavery is, of course, the central theme of the play, as Inkle decides to sell the Indian maiden, Yarico, to a Barbados sugar planter, even though she, like Pocahontas, had saved him from the warriors of her own tribe. In 1787, the year of Colman's play, William Wilberforce became leader of the anti-slave trade movement, and in 1788 he introduced his first Abolition Bill. As several other works condemning slavery appeared at this time we can conclude that Colman was well aware of addressing this particular political issue.[10]

However, if Colman was consciously writing against commercial and imperialist trends, he also suggested, unconsciously, Sinfield's 'ghosts of an alternative story'. If responsibility for the slave trade could be attributed to calculating self-interest, the reverse proposition deserves attention. Why should the impulsive generosity of Inkle's clerk Trudge, and the brash ebullience of Governor Sir Christopher Curry, be considered more trustworthy than the rational logic of planters and traders? Colman has absolutely no doubt as to the validity of their instinctive virtue, but that very certainty, which seems to 'go without saying', suggests a 'plausible' preconception:

MEDIUM. Well, it is not for me to boast of virtues . . .
SIR CHRISTOPHER. Your virtues? Zounds, what are they?
MEDIUM. I am not addicted to passion. That, at least, Sir Christopher –
SIR CHRISTOPHER. Is like all your other virtues, a mere negative . . . Ouns,
　　if you want to be an honest fellow, act from the impulse of nature! . . .
　　　　Oh, give me your plain-dealing fellows
　　　　Who never from honesty shrink,
　　　　Not thinking on all they should tell us,
　　　　But telling us all that they think.　　　(Act 2, scene 2)

For Sir Christopher, who is the play's crucial force of benevolence, morality is instinctive and common sense. So it is for Trudge, when a Planter proposes to buy his Indian preserver Wowski. His 'natural impulse' is one of gratitude and constancy. As 'natural' indeed as the prejudice against her blackness, which is shared by both the slave owner and the poor girl's lover – though the latter nobly tolerates it!

TRUDGE. Sell Wows? My poor, dear, dingy wife?
PLANTER. . . . Your wife, indeed! Why, she's no Christian!
TRUDGE. No, but I am, so I shall do as I'm done by, Master Black Market.
　　And, if you were a good one yourself, you'd know that the fellow-
　　feeling for a poor body who wants your help is the noblest mark of our
　　religion . . .
PLANTER. Hey-day, the booby's in love with her! Why, sure, friend, you
　　wouldn't live here with a black?
TRUDGE. Plague on't, there it is! I shall be laughed out of my honesty, here.
　　But you may be jogging, friend! I may feel a little queer, perhaps, at
　　showing her face, but damme if ever I do anything to make me
　　ashamed of showing my own . . .
PLANTER. Pshaw, the fellow's a fool! . . . He ought to be sent back to the
　　savages again! He's not fit to live amongst us Christians!
TRUDGE. Christians! Ah, tender souls they are to be sure!　　(Act 2, scene 1)

Religious hypocrisy is suggested again when a second planter offers to buy Yarico from Trudge's master:

> What return can the wench wish more than taking her from a wild, idle, savage people and providing for her, here, with reputable hard work in a genteel, polished, tender, Christian country? (Act 2, scene 1)

Although the idea is not developed by Colman, the implication of the contrast between Inkle and Trudge, master and servant, between the sensible Medium and the impulsive Sir Christopher, and between the native girls and their civilised captor/suitors, is that the natural and the intuitive is morally superior to sophistication, civilisation and even religion. Nor was this belief that goodness is stimulated by inherent impulses of sensibility restricted to a single play; it informs most of the literature and particularly the drama of the period. It elevates the brash Charles Surface over his hypocritical brother Joseph, makes the unselfconscious Young Marlowe more attractive to Kate Hardcastle than his bashful alter ego, and is the redeeming feature of Cumberland's 'West Indian' – a colonial merchant whose impetuosity is the antithesis of Colman's calculating Inkle. That so many popular plays of the period propagate these ideas suggests that audiences shared an unproblematic scale of values, a morality that need not be argued but merely demonstrated as 'natural'. The failure of the Hastings impeachment, after seven years of trial, the rejection of Wilberforce's anti-slave trade bills year upon year, and above all the revolution in France, made issues of human rights, of constitutional change, of the primacy of nature over nurture, and of the efficacy of religion questions that needed arguing and fighting for. Such questions might have been debated in London in 1789, but they were not yet issues of life and death – except of course for the slaves who inspired the sentimental impulses of Colman's opera.

That Colman failed to question the benevolence of intuition is perhaps surprising, because he had become manager of the Haymarket in 1788 when his father, Colman the Elder, had to be committed to a madhouse after a stroke. The wider public too might have reflected on the question of rationality when the king himself became deranged for three months in November 1788. Indeed the *Morning Post* of 12 August 1789 remarked that Colman 'at present stands in the same predicament that the Heir Apparent did some months ago'.[11] But, whereas Colman succeeded smoothly with the approval of his demented father, the animosity within the royal family, exacerbated by the rivalry of the politicians, dominated public affairs throughout the Regency Crisis. Pitt was fighting for survival as the Whigs demanded that all prerogatives, including the choice of ministers, should pass unchecked to the Prince of Wales. Sheridan, proprietor of Drury Lane, was the prince's closest advisor, and had dreams of ministerial power once Fox was installed in Downing Street. The king's recovery forestalled such hopes, and, once he learnt of the scandalous behaviour of his sons and their cronies in Carlton House, the chance of a Whig administration during his lifetime virtually disappeared. Sheridan, however, undaunted in radical zeal, rededicated his rhetoric to the prosecution of Governor Hastings.

Such were the political issues that dominated London as Paris slipped closer to revolution. Not that anyone in France could foresee the drama that was about to unfold. In 1787 Louis XVI, faced by a budget deficit that had never recovered from France's victories in the War of American Independence had called an Assembly of Notables, whom he hoped to persuade to the fiscal policies of his chief minister Calonne ending the feudal privileges of aristocrats and the church. When the Notables rejected the reforms, the call came to reconstitute the Estates General that had not met since 1614. As there was no parliamentary opposition in France to initiate radical action – such as the Whig's impeachment of Warren Hastings – the financial crisis, and the possibility of more representative institutions, raised the political temperature in the salons, clubs and even theatres of Paris. In autumn 1788 the first political clubs were formed: the Club de Valois, organised by the Duc d'Orleans, was comparable to the Prince of Wales' circle at Carlton House, while Brissot's Société des Amis des Noirs corresponded to the anti-slave trade pressure group of Clarkson and Wilberforce. Nevertheless, although changes were imminent, there was little expectation that the common people of Paris would be involved – nor would they have been but for food shortages in 1789 – or that in a few years the whole structure of monarchy would be in question. The naïveté of Louis XVI and even the scandals surrounding 'la Autrichienne', Marie Antoinette, were apparently less constitutionally dangerous than the madness of George III, but when Calonne, and later Necker, wanted to introduce fiscal changes that British ministers, Tory or Whig, would have considered economic common sense, it sparked off an extraordinary chain reaction.

The essential ideological conflict of the whole Revolutionary period – although its forms varied greatly between 1789 and 1815 – was between the 'common sense' of the merchant classes and the 'irrational' protectionist tradition of privilege. Although by definition privilege meant institutionalised oppression, it also implied certain values of communality and responsibility, as Emmet Kennedy explains:

The old regime was a hierarchy of honor and birth. It was also a corporate society; members of a profession or of a social order, like the nobility and the clergy, enjoyed privileges peculiar to that order. Privilege by definition was inegalitarian and accorded to some what it denied to others. But the old regime did countenance equality in two ways. Within orders and among corporate bodies members were equal. Carpenters felt close to and supported one another – in their work, services and prayers. The *ancien régime* corporation was as much a moral as an economic entity. In addition, all members of the old regime, from princes to paupers, enjoyed a spiritual or moral equality in the sight of God, regardless of the functional and honorific inequality that separated them for the good of society. This Pauline medieval image of society was patterned after the human body; the king is the head, the plowman the feet, the administrators the hands and arms. All occupied different places, with different degrees of honor, but the cooperation of all was essential to the good of the whole.[12]

These principles, dating back to feudal times and reinforced by the regimentation of Louis XIV, were the antithesis of the variously defined 'social contracts' of Locke, which had validated the Glorious Revolution of the British Whigs, of Montesquieu, which had informed the American constitution, or of Rousseau, which was to inspire the Jacobins' Reign of Virtue. Just as the British government reaped humiliation after the successes of the Seven Years' War, so the French monarchy was to regret their victorious alliance with the new America. Not only did the War of Independence increase an already massive national debt, but it also made fashionable ideas that were incompatible with traditions of corporate privilege.

The practical implications of this ideological reassessment can be seen particularly clearly in the reorganisation of Parisian theatre between the American War and 1789. The relationship between theatres, which had been defined by privileges granted under Louis XIV, was now being challenged by changes in audience demand. But, rather than allowing commercial pressures free reign, the bureaucrats of court, government and municipality struggled to control the competition by the old means of granting corporate rights according to categories of theatrical genres. Between 1716 and 1770 theatrical provision remained more or less as decreed at the accession of Louis XV: three royal theatres, the Comédie-Française, for classic spoken drama, the Comédie-Italienne, for pantomimic *commedia-delle'arte*, French farces and musical comedy, and the Opéra, or Royal Academy of Music, responsible for ballet as well as Italian opera. Other non-dramatic entertainments were performed in booths at the great city fairs, though, from the middle of the century, several fairground companies tried to establish permanent homes. In theory this policy of cultural categorisation reflected, and to an extent controlled, social differences:

Contemporaries recognised at least three broad theatrical publics: persons of high estate, the middle bourgeoisie, and the people. Each of these three publics was supposed to frequent a separate tier in the hierarchy of theatres. The upper class was to attend the royal theatres, the middle class the Variétés-Amusantes and other small stages of the Palais-Royal and the people the little theatres of the boulevards and fairs.[13]

Officially each 'popular' troupe was licensed for the privileged performance of a specific category of entertainment, just as the royal theatres specialised in their own genres; however, each managed to extend the scope of their specialisation. In particular, fairground troupes found ways of introducing dramatic narratives into their repertoire, even though they were officially restricted to acrobatics, mime, puppetry or child performers. The first troupe to have a significant existence beyond the fairs was the Opéra-Comique under Jean Monnet, who in 1743, at the fairs of St Germain and St Laurent, employed such established artists as Favart to write, Rameau to compose, Boucher to design and Dupré to choreograph elaborate musical pantomimes. Amongst the dancers was the young Jean-Georges Noverre, who was to develop a new genre of narrative ballet, at first with Monnet but later at the Opéra itself. Arguing that the Opéra-Comique infringed the royal theatres' privileges, Monnet was closed down in 1745. He moved his activities to Lyons and then to London, until in 1752 a new formula was found to allow the Opéra-Comique to reopen in Paris.[14] Eventually, in 1762, the problem of reconciling their output with the royal theatres was resolved by amalgamating the company into the Comédie-Italienne.

Of a very different class of entertainment, Jean-Baptiste Nicolet had by the 1760s established his fairground troupe of rope-dancers and performing animals permanently on the Boulevard du Temple to the north-east of the city. In 1767 Nicholas-Médard Audinot set up a marionette theatre, later known as the Ambigu-Comique beside Nicolet's Grands Danseurs du Roi and from the 1770s several troupes, which had performed irregularly at the fairs, established permanent theatres on the Boulevard du Temple. The Paris police authorities, as well as the royal Intendent des Menus Plaisirs, were happy to encourage these permanent establishments, firstly because they were more easily monitored than irregular fairground events, and secondly because they could be made to pay for the privilege of their existence. So in 1773 the municipal authorities imposed a poor tax, officially set at 24 per cent of takings, to help finance the Paris hospitals, and from 1769 the royal theatres were authorised to examine any script before performance to identify infringements of privilege. Thus actors from Comédies-Française and Italienne could censor the performances of their illegitimate rivals, and charge them a fee for the service.

In 1784 the patronage of the Duc d'Orleans provided auditoriums within the Palais-Royal for the Variétés-Amusantes and Beaujolais companies. In the same year, in order to lessen their claim on royal finances, Louis XVI handed over the actual licensing of fairground and boulevard performances to the three royal theatres, so they could extract registration and performance fees directly. As it generated much needed revenue, the Opéra was very happy to licence the boulevard theatres the use of its music – as long as they did not emulate Opéra performances exactly. Eventually the fees brought in 100,000 livres a year, which suggests it made good business sense to Nicolet, Audinot and other boulevard managers to pay for the privilege of extending their legally restricted repertoire.[15] In all these arrangements commercial competition was being regulated by a complex of licences, privileges and monopolies, rather than by the free-for-all of market forces.[16]

Thus in the years preceding the Revolution, control of the theatrical market, through a system of decrees to categorise genres, restrict rights and bestow privileges, became elaborated into the absurdity described by Michèle Root-Bernstein:

Monopolies of dramatic genre no longer distinguished the great from the popular stage. Differences between one minor spectacle and another, between the great and the little theatres, were, rather, maintained by arbitrary device. Since the late 1760s, for instance, comic opera had been exploited solely by the Comédie-Italienne, which held the right to this genre from the Opéra. In 1784 the Opéra leased the same genre to a small theatre in the Palais-Royal, but with the stipulation that the young actors of the Beaujolais mimic on stage what others sang for them in the wings. Given these simple restraints comic opera performed by the minor theatres was judged different from that performed by the royal company. Two years later a new boulevard theatre, the Bluettes established by Clement de Lornaizon, began to perform comic opera in the manner of the Beaujolais, but in order to separate these minor enterprises from each other, the

Bluettes was forced to place a gauze curtain or scrim between the audience and the stage. Colon's Déclassements-Comiques adopted this scrim to differentiate itself from the [Théâtre des] Associés, which in turn opened its show with marionette skits that symbolically bound to the fair its forays into the élite genres of tragedy and comedy.[17]

As critic Millin de Grandmaison wrote in 1790: 'An understanding of the dramatic hierarchy was truly a science difficult to acquire; one learned to admire greatly the fecund genius of the minister of Paris in finding means of granting new privileges without infringing the old.'[18] Thus it was no surprise that in January 1791 the National Assembly swept the whole hierarchy away: 'Any citizen will be able to open a public theatre . . . by making prior to the establishment of his theatre a declaration to the municipality.'[19] Chapelier, who had drafted the decree, adopted the classic arguments of economic *laissez-faire*: 'When . . . despotism takes upon itself the task of encouraging the arts, competition in theatre can become a greater cause for quarrels than a means to perfection; there are only protectors and protégés; and the protégés have talent only in proportion to the influence of their protectors. Under liberty, it is merit which prevails, and competition only stimulates it'.[20] Before considering whether this sanguine trust in free competition actually benefited the Parisian theatre, we must compare the pre-Revolutionary theatrical scene with that of London.

At first glance the London Patent Houses seem exactly equivalent to the Royal Theatres of Paris, but their legal status was crucially different, and so therefore were their artistic policies. Officially both were extensions of the royal court – created to entertain their monarch but authorised to perform to a paying public – but the London Theatres Royal had always enjoyed greater autonomy than those of Paris, because Charles II granted the patents as a form of property rather than privilege. Even the apparently individual patent for summer performance at the Haymarket, obtained in 1767 by the Duke of York for Samuel Foot in compensation for a physical injury, was a personal property that he sold to Colman the Elder, who then bequeathed it to his son. This also meant that questions of disputed ownership were settled in the law courts rather than by direct appeals to the king or to the head of his household, the Lord Chamberlain. For example, after the fires that destroyed the King's Theatre in 1789 and Covent Garden in 1808, there were legal wrangles over whether the monopoly right to perform was essentially the same as the ownership of the theatre buildings. That the patent right was legally a property – which could be divided into shares, just as the building might be owned by partners or a syndicate – ensured the ultimate victory of the management of Covent Garden over the O. P. rioters of 1809. However, because the King's Theatre was not patented but performed by annual licence of the Lord Chamberlain, the rivalry between the *owners* of the rebuilt Kings Theatre and the displaced *management*, led by Giovanni Gallini, for whom Lord Chamberlain Salisbury was minded to change the annual licence into a patent right to perform at the Pantheon, led into a legal minefield with the Lord Chancellor, head of the judiciary, in conflict with the Lord Chamberlain, head of the king's household.[21]

Although the King's Theatre's licence obliged it to specialise in Italian Opera,[22] no similar injunction differentiated the other three Theatres Royal, so their rights to a particular genre were far less rigid than under the French bureaucratic definitions of privileges. Competition was thus a matter of managerial policy, with actors, playwrights and other artists enticed from one theatre to the other. As with the ownership of the right to perform, the rights over a particular script were controlled by contracts between author and manager, though disputes seldom came before the courts. Covent Garden and Drury Lane could therefore compete with plays in the same style and on similar subjects. In the case of Shakespeare, on whom there was no copyright restriction, they could perform the same play on the same night, as with the rival Romeos of Garrick and Barry, or when Edmund Kean's Othello demolished that of Junius Brutus Booth. Nevertheless, because the Royal Theatres' patents stipulated their right to 'spoken drama', their written scripts were answerable to the authority of the Lord Chamberlain, and, through his Licenser of Plays, he – and thus the government – maintained a strict censorship over the content of new plays. The monopoly patent rights also meant that there were genre restrictions on non-patent theatres similar to those on the boulevard theatres, though not as absurdly precise. The London Minor Houses performed under licences from municipal magistrates with the stipulation that they could not perform 'legitimate drama'. The long and complicated struggle to establish the difference between the legitimate and the 'burletta' – which was officially the only dramatic form allowed to the minors – was only resolved in 1845 with the abolition of the Theatres Royal monopoly and the creation of a 'level playing field' for commercial competition.[23]

In 1785 'Plausible Jack' Palmer, a regular actor for both Colman and Sheridan, made the most blatant attempt to subvert the patent rights before the Revolutionary period, by opening a new theatre in the East End of London. He could have done this on the authority of a magistrate's licence, had he emulated the long-established Sadler's Wells, which, although seating 2,000 and employing fine actors and expensive scenery, restricted itself to pantomime and other illegitimate spectacles. But Palmer wanted a repertoire comparable to that of the Haymarket, and to repeat the success of the adjacent Goodman's Fields Theatre, where, in the 1730s, Henry Giffard had presented the legitimate repertoire with impunity, until David Garrick's debut in 1742 drew fashionable audiences and led the patentees to take legal action. Palmer's Royalty Theatre opened with a gala on 9 June 1787, when he announced a programme of regular drama would start on 20 June. At this the patent managers, Harris, Lindley and Colman, published a threat to evoke the Vagrant and Vagabond Acts against Palmer's company. In a move to increase the support of local magistrates – just as the Poor Tax had won municipal support for the boulevard theatres – Palmer announced his first night to be a benefit for the London Hospital. It opened with a provocative prologue by Arthur Murphy:

> Yet some there are who would our scheme annoy;
> 'Tis a monopoly they would enjoy.
> Th' Haymarket, Covent Garden and Old Drury
> Send forth their edicts 'full of sound and fury' . . .
> But wit, like day-light, nothing should restrain,
> The same in Goodman's-fields and Drury-lane.
> And if the Drama list on Virtue's side,
> Say – can the moral be diffus'd too wide!
> If the sun gild yon *West* with golden ray,
> The *East* may feel the beam of rising day. . .
> Fines and imprisonment no more proclaim,
> But praise the soil from which our Garrick came.

Just as the Royal Theatres of Paris used their privileges to restrict competition, so the patentees evoked their rights to close Palmer, which, after an acrimonious exchange of letters and articles in the press, was the inevitable outcome of his attempt to encroach their monopoly. But Palmer's attempt at free competition had appealed to the 'enlightened' spirit of liberty, which was becoming as fashionable as the craze for amateur theatricals:[24] 'Does it not imply some little inconsistency in a well-regulated State, for one subject to be punished as a rogue and vagabond for doing in publick, which another, perhaps the first peer in the realm, is proud to do with applause within the walls of his own house!'[25] Indeed, in his final attempt to rescue the Royalty by an appeal to introduce a bill in parliament, Palmer gathered 5,000 signatures from the inhabitants of Middlesex. The petition had no chance of success, but the episode gave warning that patented privilege was challengeable – a challenge that was taken up by the aristocratic patrons of the Pantheon opera scheme, the 'democratic' O. P. rioters of 1809, and the campaigners for a Third Theatre in 1809–11.[26]

Given his obvious contempt for the royal privilege that had closed his theatre, it is hardly surprising that Palmer warmly welcomed the triumph of liberty across the Channel. In 1789 he directed John Dent's celebratory burletta *The Triumph of Liberty; or, the Bastille* at the Royal Circus, where, according to its dedication to the Duke of Orleans, 'Mr Palmer has proved it possible to have represented at the Royal Circus, even limited and restricted as he was, an entertainment capable of bringing *crowded* and *brilliant* audiences for SEVENTY NINE NIGHTS *successively*'.[27] Details of this production will be considered in the next chapter, but in the light of Palmer's persecution it is not surprising that pro-Revolutionary material found a ready home in the minor houses. Although the three patent houses were the only venues for serious plays, their monopoly of literary drama did not give the revolutionary spirit its most effectual theatrical expression. The excitement of revolution and the anxieties of war were more effectively embodied in images, music and ritualised patterns of action rather than the specificity of words, particularly in the dialogue of traditional social comedy and heroic tragedy. Ironically, the oppression of privilege, by denying popular minor theatres access to generic drama, forced them to create new and highly conventionalised forms in which the narratives essential to formulating ideological plausibility could be enacted.

Stories can provide metaphorical interpretations of the powerful currents of social change, by reasserting communal values or giving shape to the threat of an unknown future, and there was a burgeoning of narrative even in areas of non-theatrical cultural expression. This need for stories was manifest not only in the popularity of novels and circulating libraries, but also in the visual arts. Fashionable pastoral landscapes and society portraits gave way to climactic scenes of narrative painting. In France moments of crisis in village life and Republican Rome were depicted respectively by Greuze and David, whilst in England Copley, Hamilton and West virtually created the genre of history painting.[28] Burke proposed that the emotional impact of the 'sublime' in art was in its suggestion of immanence – threatening or transcendent. Lessing analysed the sculpture of Laocoon as a frozen moment in an on-going struggle. Even interior decoration and architecture suggested a changing of environments – to India or China or to a Etruscan or Gothic past. For centuries the stories illustrated in the visual arts had been drawn from the Bible or Greek mythology, but now the stories were of secular heroism, depicting psychological rather than spiritual journeys, and were loosely metaphorical rather than strictly allegorical.

Similarly the creation of narratives was prioritised in boulevard entertainment. For instance, the equestrian Philip Astley, popular on both sides of the Channel, introduced stories into circus performance. The public demonstrations of horsemanship at his Lambeth riding school started in 1768, but by 1771 they had been dramatised into *The Tailor Riding to Brentford; or, The Unaccountable Sagacity of the Tailor's Horse*. Astley developed such narratives for both his amphitheatres in London and Paris, where they became known as *scènes de manège*. An account of *Le Tailleur anglais* has survived as performed by Antonio Franconi in Paris 1795 under the title *Rognolet et Passe-Carreau*. The tailor Rognolet, with the bungling assistance of his servant, attempts to ride several different horses, which 'act' either exhausted or wild, refusing to move or throwing their rider. Eventually when the tailor insults a new mount offered him by the Post Master, the horse, 'furieux, comme s'il comprenoit ce language,'[29] chases Rognolet around the ring, overturns his tailor's bench and pursues him off stage by jumping through the scenic shop window. This simple drama survived in various forms for at least sixty years, for its characterisation not only displayed the tricks of the horses and the skill of the riders, but its plot mocked the stupidity of the petty-bourgeois compared to the 'natural sagacity' of the dumb animals.

Eventually a whole new genre of equestrian drama developed. Sometimes the horses were employed naturalistically, pulling exotic chariots or providing cavalry for re-enacted battles – French defeats in Astley's London Amphitheatre, French victories in Franconi's Cirque Olympique. Horses were trained to display their own 'characters' and express their own 'emotions'. And, as the show-man's patter in praise of the performing horse in Büchner's *Woyzeck* suggests, animal intelligence not only astonished simple spectators, but exercised romantic philosophers: 'His message is: Man, be natural. You are created from dust, sand and slime. Would you be more than dust, sand and slime? Look here if you want to know what reason is; he can do arithmetic but he can't count on his fingers. Why? He just can't express himself, can't explain things. He's a transmogrified human being'.[30]

A similar desire to contextualise through narrative the physical expertise of human acrobats is apparent in the pantomimes created at Sadler's Wells and for Nicolet's 'rope-dancers' on the Boulevard du Temple. However, these dramas risked opposition from their respective Royal Theatres, as the demarcation between mute mime, spoken pantomime, musical burletta and legitimate drama was less obvious than the presence of horses in a hippodrama. In Paris these distinctions were settled by royal decree, but in London the principle of precedent, as in English Common Law, provided increasingly larger loopholes in the definition of legitimate drama. Because of their popularity, pantomimes and musical burletta were also pro-duced by patent theatre managers. However, once the major houses advertised a play as a 'burletta' and it had prose dialogue, or a limited number of songs, or even no musical accompaniment at all, then it became impossible to prosecute minor house entertainments that adopted the same pattern.[31] Nevertheless, conventionality typified the illegitimate repertoire, performances in mime or rhyming couplets, interspersed with songs and with more or less continuous musical accompaniment.

Precision of definition was further undermined by the loose descriptions applied to English opera as presented in the Theatres Royal. In her study of Stephen Storace, Jane Girdham devotes a chapter to 'Questions of Genre' and suggests the descriptions 'opera', 'comic opera', 'musical entertainment', 'musical romance', 'musical spectacle' and even 'play with music' were used fairly indiscriminately on playbills and published versions, and quotes John Adolphus' 'sweeping generalisation' from his *Memoirs of John Bannister* (1839) that 'an English opera is, properly, a comedy enlivened by music'.[32] Just as predominantly musical genres were developing narrative structures, so narrative-based dramas were incorporating musical elements, not only songs in the tradition of the 'ballad opera' (itself a rather vague generic term) but overtures and incidental music to tableaux of scenic spectacle. Most of the plays discussed in the present volume had considerable musical elements, from Colman's *Inkle and Yarico*, 'an opera in three acts', to his *Blue Beard*, 'a dramatic romance', and his *Iron Chest*, 'a play with music'. Although Walter White's term '*pasticcio*'[33] is more properly applied to Italian opera, it accurately reflects the normal practice of the composers of English opera to arrange music from many sources rather than rely entirely on their own composition, especially in works tending towards the 'play with music' definition. The technique of breaking up scenes of dialogue with songs to melodies popular from other sources emphasised the artificiality of, and helped blur the distinction between, legitimate and illegitimate genres. The music, particularly comic songs, helped to 'distance' legitimate dramas by emphasising the conventionality of their performance, though later the emotional appeal tended to be intensified as they moved towards the more fully integrated genre of melodrama. Such a development is suggested in Girdham's comparison between Storace's *The Haunted Tower* (Drury Lane, 24 November 1789) a Gothic 'opera', in which the potentially terrifying ghost scene is comically subverted by being merely a drunken misapprehension, and his *The Pirates* (Drury Lane at Kings, 21 November 1792). This was a complicated 'escape opera', which included ensembles that advanced the dramatic narrative and an overall musical development in the style of an Italian *opera buffo*.[34]

The most conventionalised illegitimate genre long established in the popular theatre was pantomime. Those in which John Rich performed Harlequin in Covent Garden around 1715 were short silent sketches combining gymnastic skills and physical comedy. In 1723, to compete with Rich's acrobatic mime, Drury Lane developed a more complex narrative structure with dialogue. This form of pantomime was to become the speciality of Sadler's Wells, the minor theatre on the outskirts of London that most nearly resembled Nicolet's on the Boulevard du Temple. The Wells presented shows throughout the summer season, and in winter their artists were employed to perform in patent house pantomimes. In this respect there was never as clear a division of genre as in Paris. In the 1750s the Sadler's Wells company had been exclusively singers and acrobatic entertainers, and even in the 1770s their programme, like Nicolet's, consisted predominantly of variety acts. The attractions on the night of Easter Monday 1781 – when Joey Grimaldi made his first appearance at the age of three – were the slack-wire artist Billy Saunders, who 'performed a continual Summerset on the Wire, whilst Fireworks are playing from different parts of his Body'; the rope-dancers Signor Placido and the Little Devil; *The Medley; or, a Masque in Masquerade*; a 'new Serio-Comic, Prophetic, Political, Musical, Piece, consisting of Songs, Choruses, Dancing, etc.'; and finally at the top of the bill the pantomime, *The Wizard of the Silver Rocks; or, Harlequin's Release*.[35]

Young Grimaldi was eventually to develop the pantomime clown into a great satirical creation, and his genius will be examined in a later chapter, but already the narrative structure of pantomime can be seen as open to metaphorical interpretation. A stock of characters is introduced – patriarch, maiden and lover, each with their respective servants – who are transformed magically into Pantaloon, Columbine and Harlequin, with Clown as the main comic servant. Harlequin is entrusted with a magic sword, or slapstick, which can transform props and scenery before our very eyes. The characters chase each other from scene to scene – providing the painters ample scope for invention – until the 'Dark Scene' when the forces of evil are overcome and the pantomime characters are restored to their original roles. This archetypal plot of young love frustrating senile lust could reflect many relationships, the magical variety of settings could conjure up the past or present, exotic or familiar, and the forces of good and evil be given many different fantastical shapes. While mainly reproducing the psychological patterns of generational conflict, the harlequinade could also embody class conflicts – Pantaloon the merchant with his lower-class servant Clown, who commonly betrayed his master, confronted by Harlequin, whose elegant patches could as well represent a distressed aristocrat as an upwardly mobile artisan. David Mayer, in his study of pantomime during Grimaldi's pre-eminence, suggests that 'the greatest of its faults was a refusal to discriminate between the worthy and the paltry', and 'when confronted with more complex issues it became tentative and hesitant'.[36] As popular entertainment this may seem inevitable, particularly under the Lord Chamberlain's censorship, however, as Leigh Hunt pointed out in 1817, the suggestive image may be as powerful as the didactic message: 'The absence of dialogue in pantomime . . . leaves the spectators, according to their several powers, to imagine what supplements they please to mute caricatures before them.'[37]

This freedom to interpret meaning into a narrative pattern devoid of explanatory dialogue could equally apply to the ballet, whose dancers performed in both England and France. The development of the narrative *ballet d'action* is traditionally attributed to Jean-Georges Noverre, but he may have been influenced by John Weaver, who helped John Rich develop English pantomime at Covent Garden, where as ballet-master in 1717 he had choreographed *The Loves of Mars and Venus*. This, like many subsequent musical after-pieces, developed the conventions of the court masque for the public stage, alternating set dances and mimed action. Noverre's particular contribution to narrative ballet was in combining demonstrative gesture with the formal footwork, so that individual emotions could be expressed and dramatic relationships developed within the actual dances.[38] In the 1780s and 1790s French ballet was a mainstay of the King's Theatre, where leading dancers were brought over from Paris every year,[39] but originally much of Noverre's work had been developed in the London Theatres Royal as well as in Paris. He was first employed in 1743 as a dancer at the Foire de St Germain by Jean Monnet of the Opéra Comique. The Paris authorities closed down this theatre, but in 1749, after the treaty of Aix la Chapelle, Monnet's company was invited to perform at the London Haymarket. Unfortunately, when the French company opened they were greeted by catcalls and whistles for two nights until the subscribers hired a 'contingent of Thames boatmen and Smithfield butchers who cleared the gallery'.[40]

That both Rich and Garrick had encouraged Monnet's visit suggests that theatre professionals were more Francophile than their audiences. Garrick's second attempt to bring French ballet to London in 1755 was equally disastrous when he engaged Noverre himself to present *La fête chinoise*, which he had created the previous year for the reopened Opéra Comique. The first performance at Drury Lane was a royal command, which kept hostility at bay, but on the next night the presence of French dancers inspired a riot. 'Several innocent paid for the guilty. The Nobles lost patience and struck at all without distinction; they broke arms and heads, blood flowed on every side; finally the Nobles drove the disabled rioters out of the theatre.'[41] Eventually Garrick agreed to cancel when both sides threatened to destroy his theatre. The ballet's supporters were generally aristocrats, and the opposing rioters 'cits' and tradesmen whose hostility was as much economic as chauvinist. This social division suggests that prior to the French Revolution cosmopolitan attitudes in England were exclusive to the 'cultivated élite', and were derived from a sense of shared international class interest – even solidarity once the French aristocrats began to arrive as émigrés. This cosmopolitan taste was to survive the Revolutionary Wars into the early nineteenth century, when notoriously the English upper classes deserted the dramatic theatre for the exclusivity of Grand Opera.

Noverre did not return to London until 1781, when he was appointed ballet master at the King's Theatre for a season, by which time he had created ballets in Paris, Vienna, Milan and Naples. That ballet was as international as Italian opera in both its production and appeal is demonstrated by the fortunes of a French drama, *Le Déserteur*, which took many forms, but was particularly successful in London as a *ballet d'action*. Originally written in 1769 as an *opéra comique* by Michel Sedaine, with music by Monsigny, it was translated by Charles Dibdin into a two-act musical farce in 1773. In 1779 Alessandro Zuchelli, an Italian dancer at the King's Opera House, adapted it as a ballet, *Il Disertore*, and in 1784 the King's Theatre presented *Le Déserteur; ou, La Clémence Royale* as a 'Tragi-comic Pantomime Ballet' created by the theatre's ballet master, Jean Bercher Dauberval, who had worked under Noverre at the Paris Opéra.[42] Spire Pitou's *Encyclopaedia of the Opéra* suggests that Dauberval created it for le Grand-Théâtre de Bordeaux in 1785, and that yet another ballet with the same title was created by Maximilien Gardel in Fontainbleau in 1786 and performed at the Paris Opéra in 1788. Whether all these versions were identical in libretti, choreography or music is highly unlikely, but the proliferation of versions of this one plot on both sides of the Channel suggests that in dance, music and pantomime there was a considerable two-way traffic of performers, pieces and techniques.

Dauberval's 1784 London version, which remained in the repertoire for the next ten years, was reviewed in the *Public Advertiser*:

The Ballet was founded on the French piece of *le Déserteur*, of which was retained a good deal of the music. The Dancers, incomparably the best Groupe in Europe, exerted themselves very successfully; D'Auberval's Drunkenness was well managed, Rossi's Fainting Fit, her Agitation preceding it, and her Revival from it; Lepicq's hovering over Rossi when in her Swoon and in his Separation from her, were all told very expressively indeed. Lepicq is the most graceful dancer in Europe, and excels every competitor in the Narrative and Pathos of Gesticulation.[43]

Clearly the choreography, following the conventions of Noverre, conveyed both the story and the emotions. However, new conventions are always open to parody and on 7 February 1784 the Italian Delpini created a burlesque at the Haymarket, in which he danced the heroine, and on 18 September a 'Theatrical Comic Company of Dogs' trained by Signor Scgalioni performed a version of the ballet in the Military Room in the Strand. In 1786 Sadler's Wells presented another canine version with Signor Costello's performing dogs – unless Frederick Reynolds' memory confused this with Scgalioni's:

Simpkin, Skirmish and Louisa were so well dressed, and so much in earnest, that, in a slight degree, they actually preserved the interest of the story, and the illusion of the scene. But Moustache, as the Deserter! I see him now, in his little uniform, military boots, with smart musket and helmet, cheering and inspiring his fellow soldiers, to follow him up the scaling ladders, and storm the fort. The roars, barking, and confusion which resulted from this attack, may be better imagined, than described.[44]

Finally in 1788 John Palmer created *The Deserter of Naples; or Royal Clemency* for his newly opened Royalty Theatre, with music by William Reeve. Although the cast list was the same as for Dibdin's play, it introduced the scenic spectacle of Vesuvius erupting at the end of the first act.

This catalogue demonstrates not only, as Roger Fiske noted, that 'the theme of The Deserter was strangely popular for a long time',[45] but that the effectiveness of these various pieces had little to do with the written dialogue, for although the operatic versions had both dialogue and lyrics, the wordless ballets retained only the essence of the plot. Yet the subject matter involved a real political issue. Just as the anti-slave trade agitation informed *Inkle and Yarico*, so there was active concern in France over the fate of peacetime deserters. The plot of Sedaine's opera, Dibdin's farce and Dauberval's ballet was that a soldier (Alexis in Sedaine, Henry in Dibdin) leaves his regiment when he hears that his fiancée is going to marry another. In fact this is a hoax arranged by Louisa's father to test the hero's fidelity, but while the mock wedding is underway, he is arrested for desertion. The second act is set in the prison where Alexis/Henry is awaiting execution. However Louisa begs a pardon from the king, who releases him to marry her.[46] That the issue of desertion was not as trivial as appears in this bare outline, is illustrated by yet another play with the same title. Louis-Sébastien Mercier wrote his *Déserteur* in 1770, the year after Sedaine's opera. Perhaps provoked by the opera's superficiality, Mercier's play argued aggressively against the death penalty.[47]

In Mercier's plot the deserter, Durimel, has settled over the border of France. When the French army advances through the area, two officers of his old regiment are billeted in his home and Durimel is identified as the deserter of seven years before. One officer, Saint-Franc, is in fact his father, and the old soldier now becomes the central character. Ever since his son's desertion he has argued against capital punishment, but now he sees no choice but to do his duty and accompany his son to his execution. Possibilities of escape and appeal are considered but rejected as dishonourable by either father or son, and eventually the old soldier has to watch his son be shot. In contrast to the pardon extended to Sedaine's Alexis, this tragic denouement demonstrated with emotional intensity the injustice of the present law. Apparently Marie Antoinette specifically requested Mercier to rewrite the ending so the Colonel of the Regiment was moved to pardon him by Saint-Franc's passionate outcry before the firing squad: 'Apprenez tous qu'il est mon fils . . . Oui, mon fils. – Frappez deux victimes!'[48] Whether either Mercier or Marie Antoinette should take any credit, the severity of punishment for desertion from the French army was relaxed by decree in 1775.

This *drame larmoyante* followed the principles of Mercier's friend Diderot with scenes of great pathos – recognitions, reunions and farewells – and in Saint-Franc an eloquent spokesman for benevolence and enlightenment. It expressed real concern and may have contributed to a genuine redress, yet it was Sedaine's comic version that was more often redramatised, and in ways that precluded discussing the actual law. But, perhaps the very artificiality of poetic justice provides a critique of real injustice. Even before Mercier wrote his own happy ending, they were provided in pirated provincial versions of the play.[49] The first English-language version of Mercier's play, by John Henry, *A School for Soldiers; or, the Deserter*, was published in 1783 in Jamaica, which suggests a military audience. The title page asserted that 'this piece is now performing in America (with many alterations) adapted to the Meridian of the US and the scene laid in Philadelphia'. All Mercier's didactic arguments against the death penalty are removed, and its ostensible message is more in support of discipline than honour. Major Bellamy exhorts his son:

> The law must have its course, to complain is useless – If thou had'st fallen in the field of honour, thou would'st have died without regret; but your death may now be heroic; think it will be more useful than thy life, as thy suffering will deter many imprudent young men from quitting their country's colours – embrace this idea worthy of a citizen, say to thyself – 'if I have offended against the laws of my country, it shall have nothing to reproach me with, I will cheerfully submit to their punishment.'

Indeed Young Bellamy's final appeal is: 'My fellow soldiers! Take this warning from a dying man! Let no consideration tempt you to desert the service of your king!' As this version, and probably the provincial French ones, was more celebratory than critical, father and son are rescued from the firing squad by a sentimental change of heart in their commanding officer.

Yet, regardless of the variety of denouements to Mercier's story, and the comic tone of those developed from Sedaine's, the popularity of the central predicament suggests that *The Deserter* was another 'faultline' story like *Inkle and Yarico*. However emollient its outcome, it inevitably touched political sensibilities because it dealt with the individual as victim of the state. The impressing of petty criminals and the unemployed was legal and the recruiting sergeant's cunning was legendary, yet the aims of war in the eighteenth century were almost entirely economic and imperialist. The ideological wars of religion had passed, and revolutionary politics had yet to come. A soldier's loyalty was to his pay under a discipline of vicious punishment. The royal clemency of the musical versions was obviously unrealistic, but if clemency might reward the passionate pleas of the deserter's fiancée, the question remained: on whose behalf would he have been executed? A popular entertainment, *The What Is It* at the Royal Circus in St George's Fields, suggests a radical answer. This burletta is based, almost verbatim, on John Gay's satirical *The What de'ye Call It* of 1715. In it Thomas Filbert is drafted into the army by heartless magistrates, and Timothy Peascod is sentenced to death for desertion. As in Gay, they are both farcically reprieved, but one speech added by the anonymous adapter compares the fate of Filbert with that of the Squire:

But conscience and power are no ways a kin;
What was heinous in Filbert, with *him* is no sin.
The poor man's the weakest, and goes to the wall;
But the culprit, if rich, is no culprit at all.[50]

That there were at least two versions of the Deserter story confirms Sinfield's contention: the realistic, radical and, less popular version by Mercier is 'the ghost of the alternative story' which that of Sedaine, Dibdin and Dauberval is 'trying to exclude'.[51] It provided a dialectic, such as Brecht sought when he wrote *Der Neinsager* to complement *Der Jasager*, or exhorted his actors to reveal what might, but does not, happen: 'Now "he did this" has got to become "he did this when he might have done something else," . . . a counter-experiment should now and then be conceivable.'[52] So, in this case at least it would seem that the 'artificial' operas and ballets were the socially *positive* – saying 'No' to oppression by subverting injustice – whereas the five-act tragedy was critically *negative*, in that its victims submit to their realistic fate. In the Revolutionary period, which was overwhelmed with 'topical issues', the artificial drama with its 'unrealistic' solutions was to prove the dominant form.

Of course there were English equivalents to Mercier, playwrights who used legitimate drama to propagate ideas, enlightened optimists who, like the *philosophes*, believed that exposing injustice would lead inevitably to its correction. Although patent houses were subject to the Lord Chamberlain's censorship, they could present 'moral' dramas as long as the contemporary relevance was not too apparent. In the 1760s the satirist, Samuel Foote, had been censored for personal caricatures rather than for his politics, and sensitivity to reputation continued to preoccupy the Licenser.[53] However, Elizabeth Inchbald's successful *Such Things Are* (Covent Garden, 10 February 1787) combined radical content with an identifiable portrait, though unlike Foote's, Inchbald's characterisation was complimentary, even idealised. Haswell was, as a benevolent prison visitor, a thinly disguised portrait of John Howard the penal reformer. Imprisoned himself in France during the Seven Years' War when on his way to assist survivors of the 1755 Lisbon earthquake, Howard wrote four reports on British and foreign prisons between 1774 and 1784, denouncing their inhumanity and their inefficiency. As a Bedfordshire magistrate he improved establishments under his own jurisdiction, and as a true exponent of the Enlightenment he travelled to Russia to investigate their gaols. There he died of camp-fever in 1789.

Haswell's scenes in prison conformed to the pathos and didacticism of the *drame larmoyante* – the repentant criminal returning Haswell's stolen wallet moved the theatre to tears and applause:

HASWELL. What's this?

ZEDAN. I meant to gain my liberty with it – but I will not vex you.

HASWELL. How came you by it?

ZEDAN. Stole it – and wou'd have stabb'd you too, had you been alone – but I am glad I did not – Oh! I am glad I did not.

HASWELL. You like me then?

ZEDAN. [*Shakes his head and holds his heart*] 'Tis something I never felt before – it makes me like not only you, but all the world besides – the love of my family was confined to them alone; but this makes me feel I could love even my enemies.

HASWELL. Oh nature! grateful! mild! gentle! and forgiving! – worst of tyrants they who, by hard usage, drive you to be cruel.

Haswell's exclamations demonstrate the same belief in natural benevolence as Colman's *Inkle and Yarico*, and typify the optimistic philanthropy of pre-Revolutionary radicalism. Yet, however recognisable Inchbald's flattering depiction of Howard, she adopted a dramatic strategy that was to become increasingly common. The play was set not in a British gaol, but in Sumatra, where the sultan responds to Haswell's pleas on behalf of innocent prisoners first with barbaric indifference, and then with the incredible disclosure that he is himself an exiled Christian. This of course opens the way to a contrived happy ending, but as with the 'illegitimate' examples discussed earlier, the artificiality to the ending cannot entirely negate the emotional impact of the play's didactic purpose. It is perhaps only in hindsight from our more explicit age that the distancing technique of staging topical issues in an exotic orient seems a betrayal of any serious intent.

Although the plot of *Such Things Are* was original, Inchbald adapted many plays from the French, and most of her sources, like Patrat, Dumaniant and the comtesse de Genlis, were *habitués* of the more liberal salons. However, the last pre-Revolutionary play I wish to consider, also taken from the French, caused a far greater stir in Paris than did the England version. This was not because the translator, Thomas Holcroft, was unaware of the subversive intent of Beaumarchais' *Mariage de Figaro*, for not only was its French production a *cause célèbre*, but Holcroft was a committed political radical whose own biography seems to confirm all the optimism of the Enlightenment. Born in 1745, the child of a peddler, his first job was as a stable-boy at Newmarket. In 1760 he became an apprentice cobbler in London, and then a schoolmaster in Liverpool. Being thus acquainted with life on the road, the industrial north, aristocrats gambling at the races and a class of metropolitan artisans who were becoming increasingly politicised, he had a wide experience of English society, and this taught him a 'class consciousness' that informed the rest of his life and works. From the time he learnt to read the Bible, Holcroft engaged in a process of self-education, which led him to take up 'spouting' as an amateur actor, and in 1770 he was employed as an actor/singer by Macklin for a season in Dublin. This engagement led to provincial strolling during which he became friendly with Mrs Inchbald. He was employed at Drury Lane as a chorus member and in minor 'character' roles, but the success of his first play, *Duplicity* (Covent Garden, 1780), allowed him give up acting for writing. Already his journalism, a novel *Alwyn* (1780), and a 'philosophic poem' *Human Happiness, or the Sceptic* (1783) – which argued his lifelong atheism – brought Holcroft to the attention of William Godwin, who was the intellectual leader of radicalism as Tom Paine was its propagandist.

In 1783 Holcroft was sent to France as correspondent for *The Morning Herald*, with an introduction to, amongst others, the playwright Mercier. Here he began translating a number of progressive authors.[54] In September 1784, having returned to London, he dashed back to Paris to watch enough performances of *Le Mariage de Figaro* to be able to write his own version on the way back to London. However *The Follies of a Night* failed to have the impact of Beaumarchais' original, which had been banned for several months, despite the author giving readings in various salons, and even at court. Louis XVI commented, with unconscious irony: 'The Bastille would have to be torn down before the presentation of this play could be anything but dangerous folly.'[55] By adopting the usual translator's strategy of concentrating on plot and curtailing the dialogue (which eventually enabled its performance as a two-act afterpiece), Holcroft removed much of Beaumarchais' satirical comments. And because Holcroft left the play's setting as Seville, neither anglicising it nor indicating its French origins, perhaps for once the distancing effect actually neutralised the political attack on the aristocratic oppression of Count Almaviva's *droit de seigneur* to sleep with Figaro's bride Suzanna. Such behaviour may have seemed unexceptional when seen in the tradition of Spanish intrigue from Beaumont and Fletcher, Mrs Centilivre and Sheridan's *Duenna* (1775). Certainly the Licenser passed Holcroft's version as inoffensive. But perhaps the main difference between the two versions was that the story lost its subversive effect in a theatre that had grown to expect the triumph of intuitive benevolence, and in a country that was less hidebound by feudal privileges and whose cultural élite did not share the fragility of the *ancien régime* of France.

CHAPTER 2

The Revolution

The speed with which Holcroft was able to bring a version of Beaumarchais' play to the London stage – seen in September produced in December – indicates the time lapse between events, news of the events and their depiction or reflection in cultural production. In an age of electronic communication topicality is measured in days, but with handwritten reports, horseback couriers and movable-type newspapers, topicality was more a matter of months. Nevertheless, the arrival of news occasioned not only discussion in coffeehouses and journalistic commentary, but also, as Frederick Reynolds recorded, media exploitation:

The French Revolution . . . had for some time excited the public attention in a considerable degree; but it did not cause a general and alarming sensation until the memorable fourteenth of July, 1789, when the Bastile [*sic*] was destroyed. Then, as is usual in these cases, every man began to consider how the consequences might affect himself . . . The loyalist saw the revolution in one light, the democrat in another; and even the theatrical manager had also his view of the subject. The *Bastile* must bring money; that's the settled point; and a piece of that name must be written.

At least three theatrical representations of the fall of the Bastille went into rehearsal. The one at Covent Garden ran into problems with the censor, as Reynolds continued: 'A piece under that title was written, and put into preparation at Covent Garden Theatre. But, when the parts were studied, the scenery completed, and the music composed, the Lord Chamberlain refused his licence.'[1] However, the Lord Chamberlain had no direct control over pieces presented at Sadler's Wells, the Royal Circus and Astley's Royal Grove Amphitheatre.[2]

Astley presented *Paris in an Uproar; or, the Destruction of the Bastille* (17 August 1789) inspiring a revealing cartoon 'An Amphitheatrical Attack on the Bastille' (see frontispiece). This illustration suggests

42

that the scenic spectacle was less impressive, at least in this minor theatre, than the playbills claimed. The use of 'speech banners' and disproportionate scenic pieces reveal the origins of such popular theatre in the fairground and to modern eyes has more in common with a Blue Blouse agitprop sketch or Worker's Pageant of the 1920s than the cinematic realism that is evoked by some of the extravagant descriptions of the time.[3] The Bastille entertainment at Sadler's Wells (31 August) was enthusiastically entitled *Gallic Freedom; or, Vive la Liberté*, but nothing more than a playbill synopsis has survived, including, 'The Cannonade and general Attack . . . The Skirmish with the Garde Criminelle . . . The actual Descent of the Soldiers and Citizens by Torch Light, into SUBTERRANEAN DUNGEONS . . . And the plundering and final Demolition of the Bastile by an exasperated Populous.'[4] Significantly however these scenes of revolution were followed by *Britannia's Relief*, representing the procession to St Paul's in thanksgiving for the recovery of George III. John Dent's *The Triumph of Liberty; or, The Bastille* at the Royal Circus under the management of Charles Hughes (5 August), was possibly the same play that the censor had banned at Covent Garden, for it was not unknown for banned plays to be transferred to minor houses outside the Lord Chamberlain's jurisdiction. According to the published address, it was directed by John Palmer, who since the suppression of his Royalty Theatre in 1787, had been acting at Drury Lane, and designed by William Capon, who was to become a scenic artist at Covent Garden in 1792. The play was dedicated to the Duke of Orleans and was so popular it received seventy-nine successive performances. Although a Mr Miell, described as the only real actor in the company, played the leading role of Henry Dubois for the first five nights, it was taken over by Palmer himself. Frustrated by his previous struggle against theatrical privilege in London, and no doubt inspired by the declaration of theatrical liberty in Paris – the director of the Délassements-Comique, Paul Valcour, tore down the gauze curtain imposed by the authorities with the cry 'Vive la Liberté!'[5] – Palmer vocalised his own feelings in prose and was prosecuted for it, as actors in the Circus were only allowed to speak in verse.[6]

As a burletta the piece depended more on visual symbolism than dialogue, although there were several songs, and a certain amount of doggerel verse. Matilda's opening speech is typical in style and sentiment:

May gracious Heav'n aid great Freedom's cause
And make us happy in our country's laws. [*Shouts heard*]
That Patriot shout proclaims the public voice,
And Liberty shall make this day her choice;
Despotic sway from hence for ever fled,
Happiness shall on all its comforts spread.[7]

Fearing that her old father is imprisoned in the Bastille, she awaits her fiancé, Henry Dubois, to join in the attack on the fortress. In the second scene peasants join the assault because 'this season our crops have prov'd so bare'. In the third the governor of the Bastille plans to trap the besiegers by letting them in and then raising the drawbridge. In scene four the attack takes place:

> *Troops enter in military order, and are drawn up before the Bastille, on which the white flag is displayed; the Drawbridge is let down, and the officer, sent to demand the Surrender of the Fortress, is seen to return over it in his way back to the Citizens; a party of Soldiers then immediately pass the Drawbridge as agreed on for taking Possession, which having been done, it is suddenly drawn up; the Report of Guns are then heard, with various Cries and Groans.* [At this point Henry Dubois urges an attack by the civilians.] *The Bastille, defended by the Garrison, is then seen attacked, when Bombs are thrown into it for a considerable Time; a Breach is made, and entered, Henry first mounting the same.*

The sixth scene then presents a '*Picturesque view of the inside of the Bastille with the various Instruments of Torture*'. This scene was to be reproduced in play after play over the next few years, as the images of imprisonment and release became the conventional symbols of oppression and revolution. '*Several Miserable Objects are released, and taken from the Cells, and a Skeleton is brought to the Front of the Stage*'. Henry discloses that the dead man's only crime was:

> a lampoon on French ministry.
> O! Happy England, be thy courts rever'd
> Where no man's punish'd till he first is heard;
> Where Magna Carta checks despotic fury,
> And every crime's determined by a jury.
> > *The Skeleton of a Man with the Face in an Iron Mask*
> > *is then brought forward.*
> A mask contriv'd by such ingenious means,
> To put the very face of man in chains!

In the final scene, after reuniting Matilda with her emaciated father, Henry delivers his final exhortation. Its being in prose was not only in defiance of theatrical privilege, but gave it a rhetorical immediacy far more effective than the preceding sentiments delivered in verse:

> France quits her chains, emerges from her darkness, and is warmed to animation by the bright beams of the *Sun of Liberty* . . . With minds enlightened, and with hearts sincere, we have long groaned in bondage, and been treated with ignominy. Brave in character, generous in disposition, magnanimous in exertion, we have yet been SLAVES; but even then were PATRIOTS . . . The patriotism of France is no longer *prejudice*, it is now founded in reason, it is now fixed on truth . . . Yet let the remembrance of the tyranny of that state prison live for ever in your bosoms; recollect that its miserable victims were sacrificed, with a shameless secrecy, at the altar of private malice . . . The enemies of the people deserve punishment; but as MEN they have a right to a fair trial. The administration of the laws of England is the first boast of the inhabitants of that island . . . we shall henceforth share the palm of glory, and the blessings of liberty with the immortal sons of freedom – Englishmen!
> *Low Music,* BRITANNIA *descends, seated in her Triumphal Car, supporting two great transparent Portraits of the King and Queen of Great Britain.*
> BRITANNIA. From Britannia you caught the Patriot flame,
> On Britain's plan then build your future fame . . .
> *The Statue of Liberty trampling on the Figure of Despotism is seen to ascend.*

The ambiguity between praise of Britannia and the attack on despotism, was to become typical of all plays that touched on the struggle for liberty in France. Many of those who welcomed the Revolution did so in the belief that France would emulate the British rule of law, but, as even British law did not preclude the threat of censorship or prosecution, theatres were well advised to distance themselves from any hint of sedition. British audiences, moved by the injustices of France, might well recognise injustice in their own circumstances, in which case patriotic tableaux could not entirely defuse the incendiary rhetoric of the French Revolutionists.

In an interesting exchange of genres, Covent Garden next attempted to exploit the topicality of French politics by reviving Charles Dibdin's pantomime *Harlequin Touchstone*, first produced in 1778 and last performed in 1782. A Grand Spectacle was added: 'the procession of the three estates from the church of notre dame, to that of St Louis', described as 'a vision of our neighbouring nation . . . emulous of our Laws and Liberty, met in solemn pomp to implore from heaven blessings similar to those heap'd on this favoured Isle', accompanied by a hymn in praise of Liberty and Fraternity. Even though the programme pointed out that this procession took place 'in May last, long pervious to any troubles in the Metropolis', the Licenser took exception to some sentiments in the hymn:

> Oh, let the noble, rich and free
> The poor man's griefs alleviate
> Nor be the Yeoman or his lord
> A Slave or proud Dictator,
> Alike for ever be abhor'd
> The Tyrant and the Traytor [*sic*][8]

When after correction the pantomime was eventually presented on 30 November, the finale had been relocated as 'a Representation of a Jubilee Procession of the Nobles, Clergy and People at Rome'.[9] Possibly the audience knew about the censor's involvement and failed to appreciate the alteration, for at the next performance 'The pantomime has undergone some curtailment. The last scene was omitted . . . certainly for the better.'[10] After this performance it disappeared from the repertoire.

Meanwhile Drury Lane had adopted a similar distancing strategy to exploit topicality. They presented Hon. John St John's ballad opera *The Island of St Marguerite*, on 13 November 1789, set in the Mediterranean island off Cannes. The tyrannical governor fears the populace may storm his castle and free a prisoner locked in an iron mask like the one depicted in John Dent's *Triumph of Liberty*. The Licenser let these similarities pass, but excised references to the Rights of Man. A verse including

> Generous Hearts Assert your Freedom
> Vindicate the Rights of Men.

was replaced by

> Then Join the Chorus, Lads rejoice
> The Day is all our own
> Hark to the Call. 'Tis Freedom's Voice
> And Liberty we'll Crown.

Although the evil commander is defeated, Larpent also cut references to his execution and the death march as he is led away. In the denouement the heroine, discovering that the Iron Mask is a prince, renounces his love with an appeal to Equality, the sophistry of which could hardly be condemned as revolutionary:

> That bless'd Equality, which can alone
> Ensure a genuine passion clear of all

> Suspicion of ungenerous Views – No, never
> Never will I consent that my free Love
> Shall seem to flow from Gratitude – Farewell . . .
> You are a prince
> And I a Peasant, sir.[11]

She is extricated from the painful logic of this equivocation by the revelation that she is herself of noble birth, and so an 'equal' betrothal can be accomplished. If the parallel between St Marguerite and the Bastille was actually recognised, there was little danger that St John's aristocratic sentiments could be confused with the incendiary politics of the Paris mob. I suspect Drury Lane manager Sheridan's own principles were equally confused; as a Whig he stood for Liberty, but as confidant of the Prince of Wales he could hardly espouse genuine Equality.

That the fall of the Bastille inspired a more radical reaction from the minor houses, similar to that of the deprivileged theatres of Paris, is hardly surprising, but the London Patent Houses were keener to dramatise the event than to adopt the politics. Drury Lane had removed the storming from Paris to an island off the South of France, and when Covent Garden's version of *The Bastille* ran into political problems, Harris adopted a similar strategy to distance the event. He called in Frederick Reynolds, whose comment on the commercial attractions of a 'Bastille' play opened this chapter, to transfer the action into the past:

> In this dilemma, Mr Harris called on me, requesting to know whether all the magnificent preparations intended for the *Bastile*, might not be introduced into the opera I was then writing, called the *Crusade*.[12]

Writing in 1827, Reynolds acknowledged the 'horrible incongruity' of the anachronistic settings, but their acceptance in 1789 by both manager and author suggests a 'ghostly' relationship between Reynolds' historical romance and contemporary events similar to that between the romantic and didactic versions of *The Deserter*. It is difficult to identify precise parallels, but the symbolic imagery of Christian knights regaining Jerusalem from the barbaric Saracens[13] not only suggests a popular attitude towards the conflict in France, but also an ideological assumption that historical narrative, whether fictional or scholarly, provided a way of explaining and containing events that themselves threatened to change the course of history.[14]

As with many of the cultural developments associated with the

Revolutionary period, a reassessment of the nature and significance of history itself was already underway. In Edward Gibbon's *Decline and Fall of the Roman Empire*, first published in 1776, the Romans, like characters in heroic tragedy, behave extravagantly but are motivated by fears and ambitions uncannily like those of the mid-eighteenth century intelligentsia. Gibbon's rationalist scepticism of the 'enthusiasm' of the early church, and his urbane contempt for the 'sophistication' of the élite of Imperial Rome, were both attitudes shared by Enlightenment scholars when contemplating contemporary society. On the other hand, Burke's *Reflections on the Revolution in France* of 1792 suggests that historical change has a less rational basis and that societal values are more culturally determined. His classic exposition of the 'organic development' of national institutions argued that the French revolutionaries ignored their historical roots at their peril, and that tradition had what Gramsci was to describe as hegemonic authority over attitudes and actions. Ironically, political radicals like Paine, Priestley and Price also looked back to pre-Norman institutions as models of a more active local democracy and less chauvinistic international relations. This range of ideological interpretations of history as precedent, determinant and inspiration helps explain the appeal of historical dramas, of which, as Reynolds had said of the historical events of July 14th, 'every man [could] consider how the consequences might affect himself'.

Less self-consciously ideological than either Paine or Burke, the antiquarians Stukeley, Percy, Ritson and Walpole pursued a 'purely scholarly' fascination with the strangeness of the past.[15] They felt that they could recapture something of its exoticism, not only by collection and description, but also by reconstruction. Some forms of reconstruction were long established, as in the use of classical motifs in the visual arts, classical forms in literature, and classical references in philosophical and rhetorical argument. However, the new interest in the non-classical past – the humanism and artistry of the Renaissance, the faith and chivalry of the Gothic era and the noble savagery of the Dark Ages – made reconstruction a more self-conscious practice than the conventional borrowing from, and elaboration of, Roman models by baroque artists. One remarkable offshoot of antiquarianism was the forgeries of the antique poems of 'Ossian' and 'Rowley' by Macpherson and Chatterton. They indicate an irrational desire for personal identification with the ancient world that would not have affected the Augustan writer of epics, odes or eclogues, however meticulous their emulation of Virgil or Juvenal. There was now a deeper awareness of the differences between ancient and modern, not just of form but of feelings and sensations – the attraction and the threat of the Other. Heroes and heroines in the Gothic novels of Walpole, Beckford and Radcliffe explored the world of the past with all the sensibilities of modern times. Indeed, the medieval castles and cloisters, where they were so often entrapped, appeared as already in ruins although newly built in the period of their narratives. This sense of history as a distorted mirror of the present is thus equally apparent in scholarly, didactic and fictitious history. Like science fiction in the cinema of the 1990s, it suggests a need to test disturbing changes in present society against the actualities and possibilities of another time.

In the light of my observations on the speed of gathering and responding to news, it would be foolish to claim an influence of events across the Channel on the plays produced at the Haymarket during the summer of 1789, but, by interesting coincidence, Colman's new play for the season was an innovatory historical romance, *The Battle of Hexham* (11 August 1789). It was to become a model for many subsequent 'history plays', in which episodes of national history, in this instance the Wars of the Roses, provided a dramatic structure that could contain scenes not only of comedy, pathos and mystery but of political comment. Colman wisely acknowledged that, 'to aspire to a resemblance of [Shakespeare's] boundless powers would have been the labour of a coxcomb', but clearly Shakespeare's histories were his inspiration, not only in subject matter, but in characters – the melancholy Fool and the Viola-like heroine wandering the woods dressed as a boy; the archaic language – 'to copy. . . the general *tournure* of his phraseology is a mechanical task, which can be accomplished with a common share of industry and observation'[16] – and, most importantly, the mingling of comic and tragic elements, interspersed with songs. As an example of the increasingly popular 'mixed genre', it no doubt deserved the disapprobation that the English so resented French critics casting on Shakespeare himself. Yet, this kind of melange provided a range of emotional responses to traumatic contemporary events that could satisfy a variety of social and political attitudes without destroying the essential homogeneity of the Haymarket audience.

If *The Battle of Hexham* had any direct relevance to contemporary politics, it was to warn against civil rather than international hostilities. It was thus more informed by the Regency crisis than by developments in France. This is suggested by Paula Backscheider, who also argues that

It is now common to locate the gothic impetus in the French Revolution, but it seems to me that the great gothic impetus was born in an English crisis, and, from its inception to its demise, reflected British events and structures of feeling at least as much as it did any winds that blew across the channel to England.[17]

As yet few people were alarmed by events in France, so the Gothic elements of *The Battle of Hexham* cannot be attributed to anxiety over the Revolution. But the play as a whole does not fulfil the generic criteria of the Gothic as defined by Backscheider herself.[18] In particular it lacks the self-obsessed villain, whom she associates with the fear that 'What has gone berserk in this world is power' (*Spectacular Politics*, p. 163). Although the Yorkists win the battle of Hexham, we see nothing of them, and the plot centres on the victims of the historical conflict. This exclusion of any specifically villainous characters suggests an Enlightenment appreciation of a common humanity unaffected by the mechanistic process of history, rather than a Romantic anxiety about its arbitrariness. In her comments on the play, Mrs Inchbald raises an ironic question of Gondimar's eloquent declaration of loyalty to the crown: 'Did Gondimar know who his sovereign was? This question seems to be involved in that same degree of darkness, in which half the destructive battles which ever took place have been fought.'[19] That her remark was made in 1808 indicates her own awareness of how the political context for performing this play had changed since its debut in a time of pre-Revolutionary innocence.

The main thread of the drama concerns the escape from the battlefield of Henry VI's Queen Margaret and her young son Edward, Prince of Wales. She is aided by Cumbrian peasants and outlaws, who are the only specifically Gothic elements in this historical romance. The two main saviours of the royal fugitives are an old soldier, Barton, who, like the Governor of the Bahamas, declares his 'plainness is such that Nature gave me' (Act 3, scene 2), and Gondimar, chief of the bandits. He is in fact a disguised nobleman who will 'pluck you a hundred crowns from a rich fellow, with one hand, and throw his share of them into a hungry beggar's hat with the other' (Act 2, scene 1). The one demonstrates the instinctive benevolence of the common man, the other the repressed benevolence of a fugitive outlaw. That such benevolence brings all to rights, including Gondimar's reunion with the wife who has disguised herself as a young man to go in search of him, suggests something of the transcendent providence of a Shakespearean romance – but mainly the optimistic trust in rational common sense that typified Enlightenment sensibility. It would seem therefore that the particular fear of 'power going berserk', which Backscheider claims to be a defining quality of the Gothic, was less concerned with the sanity of George III than with the emergence of identifiably 'berserk' leaders in France – Danton, instigator of the September Massacres, Robespierre, demagogue of the Jacobin Terror, and the all-conquering Napoleon. They were to be the villains that inspired the *banditti* and malcontents of the truly Gothic dramas of the late 1790s.

As yet trust in the general benevolence of providence and the essential good sense of humanity encouraged most people to look with approval, or at least equanimity, at the developments in France. As viewed from England, the early months of the Revolution really did seem like the dawn of Wordsworth's apostrophe. The French king not only acquiesced to, but apparently welcomed reforms that gave France a liberal constitution and her citizens' equality before the law, rights that the English believed to be their own special inheritance. Indeed, despite the violence of July in Paris – which was far more controlled than the anarchy of London's own 1780 Gordon Riots – the tenor of the politics during 1789 was fraternity and reconciliation. Although 'Le Grand Peur' of peasants invading provincial chateaux to destroy evidence of their feudal servitude, and the lynching of Bertier, Intendant of Paris, and his stepfather Foulon on the suspicion of grain hoarding, indicated a potential for mob violence, the establishment of a National Guard of 'responsible citizens' and the voluntary abrogation of feudal privileges by the first two Estates on 4 August 1789, seemed to be the rational responses of benevolent enlightenment. The popular song proclaimed *Ça ira!* – all will come right – and on 26 August the Declaration of the Rights of Men and of Citizens seemed to open the way to an era of justice and responsibility.

However, France was not the American colonies, where mutual interest in the face of imperialist power encouraged pragmatic compromises as well as idealistic declarations. The enemies of French progress were internal and were perceived differently by each section of society – the king might reassert his prerogative with the aid of the army; the aristocratic officers of that army might act without royal authority; the provinces might demand independence; the anarchic mob might plunder the property of individuals and the state. Mutual suspicions were long-standing and deep seated, so it is no surprise that of the three slogans of the Revolution 'Fraternité' was the first casualty. Idealistic benevolence was soon transformed in the face of political actuality into class interest and ideological dogma. The new men, particularly the lawyers who took 210 of the 621 seats allocated to the Third Estate, were particularly adept at foreseeing conflicts of interest and protecting the property rights that had enfranchised their electors. In the early stages, when central authority and entrenched privilege seemed the main enemy, there were several acts of fraternal solidarity – the most crucial being the Tennis Court Oath of 20 June 1789. Alliances across the formal divisions between the Estates provided programmes of reform, and the support of the Parisian citizens empowered the Estates General to transform itself into an assembly that could claim to represent the nation. Indeed it can be argued that the main achievement of the Revolution, the dismantling of traditional feudal privilege, was essentially completed by July 1790 with the promulgation of the Civil Constitution of the Clergy.

Inevitably there was a fragmentation of this initial solidarity, but the desire for a united National Will continued to find cultural expression, particularly in theatrical production. Managers, driven by the pragmatics of business as well as their ideological sympathies, wanted to avoid splitting audiences into the sort of cliques that had threatened to demolish Drury Lane during the *fête chinoise* riots. So they found fraternal appeals to reconciliation and Fédération both practical and ideologically suited to the communality of theatrical performance. Thus the most spectacular theatrical events of the Revolutionary period were the public festivals, and the *Fête de la Fédération*, which started informally across provincial France and culminated in the grand Parisian *fête* of 14 July 1790, were specifically designed to celebrate national unity. However, the first stage drama to be produced in Paris as a deliberate contribution to the political debate was a historical narrative that, far from advocating reconciliation, warned against the malign influence of court and church over a weak, though well-intentioned, king. Marie-Joseph Chénier originally wrote *Charles IX* in 1787, and it was accepted for production by the Comédie in September 1788, but promptly banned by the royal censor Antoine Suard. Chénier started a campaign of private readings, similar to that for *The Marriage of Figaro*, not only in fashionable salons but also, during the autumn of 1789, in the new political clubs. On 6 October the March of the Women brought the royal family to Paris from Versailles, on 2 November the Assembly approved the sale of church lands, and on 4 November the bans against *Charles IX* were lifted by both the royal censor, Suard, and the mayor of Paris, Bailly.[20]

By dramatising how the Cardinal de Lorraine and the Duc de Guise used Marie de Medici to force Charles IX to authorise the St Bartholomew Massacre of 1572, Chénier was warning against the power that the counter-revolutionary church and aristocracy might wield through the agency of Louis' foreign wife Marie Antoinette. This use of national, rather than classical, history to comment on contemporary issues had been anticipated by Voltaire himself in 1764: 'Some day we shall introduce popes on the stage, as the Greeks represented their Atreus and Thyestes, to render them odious. The time will come when the massacre of Saint Bartholomew's Day will be made the subject for a tragedy.'[21] That such a dramatisation was now considered not only a comment on the politics of the day, but a weapon of ideological conflict is apparent from the vehement support given to it by deputy Danton, playwright Fabre d'Eglantine and journalist Collot d'Herbois. Danton claimed that 'If *Figaro* killed the aristocracy, *Charles IX* will kill the royalty', and Desmoulins suggested that 'This play will do more for our cause than all the events of October.'[22] However, although the parallels in Chénier's play, produced in a context of political turmoil, were far more pertinent and serious than those of Colman's drama of 'national history', *The Battle of Hexham*, the 'Shakespearean' form, which could contain comedy, pathos, spectacle and music, was potentially wider in its metaphorical resonance than the consistently serious tone of neoclassical tragedy. Like Mercier's *Déserteur*, Chénier's *Charles IX* was specific and didactic, and thus ideologically powerful in its original context but liable to become dated as circumstances changed. And circumstances in Paris changed drastically over the next few months. The very volatility of the situation meant that drama tended to be either occasional and celebratory or trivial and exotic – either specific in application, like the one-off festival performances, or so non-specific that Root-Bernstein has concluded:

Despite the political influences of the early Revolution, the boulevard's dramatic mainstream continued viable and strong. The most successful plays of the period were indistinguishable from those written before 1789 . . . Egalitarian expression on the boulevard stage in the first four years of the Revolution stopped short of radical social upheaval. As long as traditional dramatic structures were not abandoned, boulevard theatre did not move beyond the reaffirmation of rank and place and the sentimental sublimation that had characterised the pre-Revolutionary stage.[23]

Because the 'traditional dramatic structures' – the classical genres of French neoclassicism – remained so ingrained, even after the creation of a free theatrical market in January 1791, the distinctions between theatres, plays and entertainments coninued to be greater, both aesthetically and socially, than in England, where the Shakespearean tradition facilitated a swifter development of 'mixed' genres.

If Colman's *Battle of Hexham* owed much to Shakespeare, it is interesting that Kemble chose to open the Drury Lane 1789 season with two of Shakespeare's history plays. *Richard III* (12 September) had long been in the repertoire, so little can be read into its opening the season, but the revival on 1 October of *Henry V*, with the subtitle *The Conquest of France*, would seem to have been inspired by the topicality of events in France. After the humiliation of the American War it was gratifying to be able to reassert a tradition of British superiority over the arrogant nobility of France. Thus Jonathan Bate argues that

To have mounted a production of *Henry V* in, of all years, 1789 must have been a political act, especially since the play was adapted to favour English prowess and subtitled 'The Conquest of France'. An ardent monarchist and a defender of 'rank and station' (Boaden 1825, i. 119), Kemble launched his *Henry V* in October 1789: a year before Burke published his *Reflections*, the actor-adapter was sounding a warning-note, raising patriotic fervour and dampening the enthusiasm with which the fall of the Bastille had initially been greeted in England.[24]

However, the time between July and October 1789 was hardly enough for Kemble to adapt the text and, more importantly, make production plans for a major Shakespearean revival, unless he was even more percipient than Burke himself in realising that France's internal convulsions were a prelude to a further outbreak of war with Britain. As with Colman's play, a more probable application was to the recently concluded Regency Crisis and to the popular perception of the character of the Prince of Wales as irresponsible as

Prince Hal's. Indeed Bate himself cites several political cartoons of the 1780s in which Fox and Sheridan – the patentee of Drury Lane for whom Kemble was acting manager – were depicted as Falstaff and Bardolph. For instance Gillray caricatured Fox at the height of the crisis as Falstaff crying: 'The Laws of England are at my commandment. Happy are those who have been my friends; and woe to my Lord Chancr! [*sic*].'[25]

It is easy to perceive the pertinence of Shakespearean references in political cartoons, but it is more difficult to judge how such applications might have been read into live performances by auditors, or brought out by the actors. If such references were made explicit in the written text the Lord Chamberlain would strike them out, so parallels had to be suggested by inflexion, nuance and business.[26] Bate's evidence of the extensive use of Shakespeare in political cartoons strongly suggests audiences would be quick to read the plays metaphorically, and, although I question his reading of Kemble's 1789 *Henry V,* I fully accept his general argument:

That Richard II could be compared to Elizabeth I, not least by the Queen herself, demonstrates that a play about the past could be applied to the present. By the same principle, a play *from* the past could be applied to the present: Shakespeare's political influence thus extended beyond his death. The enduring popularity of the plays was both a cause and an effect of their being applied to the public affairs of later ages.[27]

He also suggests a significant synchronicity in the fashionable interest in both Shakespeare, as championed by Garrick and Kemble, and satirical cartoons, as perfected by Gillray and Cruikshank:

Caricature is invested with precisely the qualities which made Shakespeare so central to that taste for the irregular, the imaginative, and the profuse which became so characteristic in the second half of the eighteenth century. Shakespeare and caricature were twin weapons in the hands of the English readers and critics waging chauvinistic battle against the neoclassicism associated with Voltaire and the French.[28]

Although Kemble himself considered Henry V his most complete characterisation, and many admired his reflections before the Battle of Agincourt,[29] he became more closely associated with the role of Coriolanus, which he had revived the previous season, in his own adaptation. If it had not been produced in February 1789, when matters in France were not yet critical, it might have seemed Kemble's most anti-revolutionary production, in which the aristocratic General scorns the 'voices' of the Roman mob. Indeed this was its usual interpretation in the 1790s, but Kemble originally revived *Coriolanus* as a vehicle for his sister Sarah Siddons in the role of Volumnia, replacing the usual subtitle 'The Invader of his Country', which dated back to Dennis' 1720 version, with that of 'The Roman Matron'. In the event, however, his own playing of Coriolanus became the production's chief merit. Shakespeare's text is so open to interpretation, that, even the same production of the play could be read with a variety of applications in the light of new and unforeseen events, such as the emigration of aristocrats from France after the October Days of 1789, the raising of the émigré army in 1791, and the defection of Lafayette and Dumouriez in 1793. David Rostron argues that Kemble intentionally and 'discreetly retired from his new – and much-acclaimed – role' when parallels with France became too obvious in 1790 and 1792, but that in his 1796 revival he changed his interpretation to emphasise Coriolanus' 'nobility' and ridicule the fickleness of the 'mob'.[30] Again it is difficult to judge whether this was an intentional rethinking by the actor, or a new insight by the audience, but the *Times* of 12 April 1796 described the audience's

laugh of contempt which accompanied every appearance of the rabble, 'that would soar to clip the wings of eagle authority'; and Tullus Aufidius' description of the Romans, bore so strong a likeness to the savage barbarity of modern France, that it rushed through the House like lightening.

Inchbald's introduction to her 1808 edition suggests rather ironically a less reactionary explanation of the play's unpopularity with audiences – or the authorities – stating it was

withdrawn from the theatre of late years, for some reasons of state. When the lower order of people are in good plight, they will bear contempt with cheerfulness, and with even mirth; but poverty puts them out of humour at the least disrespect. Certain sentences in this play are therefore of dangerous tendency at certain times . . . the multitude at present are content in their various stations; and can therefore, in this little dramatic history, amuse themselves with beholding, free from anger and resentment, that vain-glory, which presumes to despise them.[31]

The timing of this comment was particularly unfortunate as in the following year, 1809, the O. P. Riots were to bring a group of very discontented 'plebeians' into conflict with the manager, their 'voices' undoubtedly pitched against his overweening arrogance.[32] The full implications of this 'Napoleonic' perception of Coriolanus/Kemble will be considered later, but this outline of how the character could be read differently in different circumstances confirms a crucial difference between the English Shakespearean tradition and the neoclassical precision of French dramatic forms.

Typical of the literalism that was a product of both neoclassical culture and new Revolutionary ideology was the rewriting of Molière by Fabre d'Eglantine. On 22 February 1790 his *Philinte de Molière* was presented by the Comédie. Although its Revolutionary sentiments were unambiguous, it was uncomfortably compromised in both its political implications and its dramatic form. Continuing the story of Molière's *Misanthrope* it depicted Alceste as principled and unbending as ever, and Philinte as detached and urbane. A poor but honest lawyer – like many of those elected to represent the Third Estate – reveals a plot to defraud an unknown gentleman. Alceste is filled with righteous anger and tries to persuade Philinte to ask his uncle, the minister, to intervene. Philinte, unmoved and blasé, refuses on the grounds that 'That's how things are . . . There are thousands of injustices every day', and that one should only be concerned on behalf of 'us and ours'.[33] He swiftly changes his tune, of course, when it emerges that he himself is the intended victim. All is brought to a happy conclusion by the combined skill of the honest advocate and the fiery rhetoric of Alceste. This alliance of the aristocratic Comte d'Alceste and the humble lawyer, on behalf of the property rights of Philinte, Comte de Valencés, was hardly democratic, and ultimately justice depended on the existing system. Fabre's politics were to be outdated within the year.

In comparison to the openness to interpretation of Shakespeare, Molière's original, despite its canonical status, could not carry the weight of a political interpretation, so Fabre had restructured it in his sequel. But the classical restrictions of place, time and language, which Fabre adopted more rigorously even than Molière, created a closed form of drama, which, despite Alceste's vehemence, demanded a literal response to its rational debate. This limited the play's application, and it enjoyed success only briefly whilst its relevance lasted. The clarity of explication demanded by the prescriptive form of French legitimate drama suited the intellectual ferment of Paris in 1789 and 1790, but the more elusive, suggestive, almost mythic, quality of Shakespeare's texts – as well as his status as national bard – made them more appropriate for advocating stability, conformity and reconciliation. Edmund Burke may well have appreciated this difference, for in his *Reflections on the French Revolution*

(November 1790) he argued that British liberty was the product of a process of reinterpretation: the slow organic development of Common Law precedents and the political negotiation of meanings appropriate to circumstances. The French were trying to create laws and rights by a process of intellectual definition, which, far from being open to adaptation and interpretation, would, whatever their good intentions, become tyrannical because inflexible:

> Our constitution preserves an unity in so great a diversity of its parts. We have an inheritable crown; and inheritable peerage; and an house of commons and a people inheriting privileges, franchises, and liberties, from a long line of ancestors. This policy appears to me to be the result of profound reflection; or rather the happy effect of following nature, which is wisdom without reflection, and above it. A spirit of innovation is generally the result of a selfish temper and confined views. People will not look forward to posterity, who never look backward to their ancestors.[34]

The British constitution was the product of benevolent providence, of 'wisdom without reflection', and was thus 'natural' – just as Shakespeare was 'natural'. In his analysis of eighteenth-century political rhetoric Paul Fussell asserts that 'so deeply permeated is Burke's imagination with material of *King Lear*, that at times he actually identifies himself with Lear'.[35] Burke was certainly aware of the symbolic interconnectedness of Shakespeare's 'Great Chain of Being'. In the *Reflections*, his sensational description of the 'mob' disrupting the family of Louis, Marie Antoinette and the young dauphin suggested that the Revolution was destroying the established order of nature, and several of his apocalyptic outbursts sound very like Lear on the heath: 'These miscreants had not only broken with their old government. They had made a schism with the whole universe!' Less cataclysmically he also described the National Assembly as 'comedians of a fair before a riotous audience . . . domineering over them with a strange mixture of servile petulance and proud presumptuous authority. As they have inverted order in all things, the gallery is in the place of the house.'[36]

When Thomas Paine tried to refute Burke in *The Rights of Man* (March 1791), he transposed the particular theatricality of this rhetoric:

> I cannot consider Mr Burke's book in any other light than a dramatic performance; and he must, I think, have considered it in the same light himself, by the poetical liberties he has taken of omitting some facts,

distorting others, and making the whole machinery bend to produce a stage effect . . . and accommodated to produce through the weakness of sympathy a weeping effect. But Mr Burke should recollect that he is writing history, and not *plays*; and that his readers will expect truth, and not the spouting rant of high-toned declamation.[37]

Paine precisely identified in Burke's generalised outrage against the 'unnatural' conspiracy of politicians, philosophers and Freemasons, the anti-intellectual prejudice that was to inform most theatrical responses to the later development of Revolutionary politics. Indeed Burke had even asserted that 'Prejudice renders a man's virtue his habit; . . . Through just prejudice, his duty becomes part of his nature.'[38] Paine on the other hand warned against letting principles conform unthinkingly to the stock plots, genre and rhetoric of the theatre. It was fair enough for Colman, Reynolds or Sheridan to find *metaphorical* expression for aspirations or anxiety, but Burke was purporting to write 'history and not *plays*'. Just because his emotive imagination seemed to have foreseen subsequent events, his political analysis was not necessarily validated. It does suggest, however, that his dramatic narrative of conspiracy, anarchy and ultimate tyranny was, as Paine acknowledged, theatrically effective of itself and provided a narrative structure and generic tone that was easily adopted by playwrights and performers. As with the excessive banalities of our own 'heritage industry', there is always a danger in theatricalising history: in the case of Colman's *Battle of Hexham* it may seem harmless fun, but when it infects the narratives and arguments of politicians it can valorise tradition at the expense of analysis. A politician as eloquent as Edmund Burke can create an establishment myth that bolsters hegemonic power for generations – not because he consciously fabricated evidence, but because he trusted his 'natural sympathies'. In his dedication to tradition, Burke also appreciated the unifying power of rituals and thus regarded the stability of Anglicanism as a cornerstone of the national cohesion. It did not surprise him that French ideas were championed by Dissenters like Priestley and Price, although his particular bugbear was the atheistic tendencies of the *philosophes* Voltaire, Holbach and D'Alembert, whom he categorised as a 'literary cabal [who] had some years ago formed something like a regular plan for the destruction of the Christian religion'.[39]

The French however, influenced in this instance more by Rousseau than Voltaire, also recognised the communal power of ritual, and in the public *fêtes* they tried to create – in Burke's view synthetically rather than organically – revolutionary festivals to encourage emotional identification beyond the power of argument. The first *Fête de la Fédération* of 1790 combined formal religion, military pageantry and celebratory entertainment, but had less of the scenic symbolism that was to become a feature of subsequent festivals. This was due to the organisers' belief that it was not to commemorate the start of the revolution, but its ending – a symbolic consummation of what had been achieved, whereby the whole nation was to be welcomed *and settled* into the new age. The Assembly drew up a formal Oath of Federation that bound the people to defend not only the reforms of the Revolution, but the rights of property and the rule of law. There had been several local festivals of solidarity throughout France, mostly of an improvised nature involving parades, speeches and oaths of 'Fédération', followed by informal eating, drinking and dancing round a symbolic Tree of Liberty. Some of these local festivals grew out of, or led up to, direct action against the persons or property of the aristocracy and the church. However, as Mona Ozouf, historian of the festivals, points out, 'In the minds of its organisers the "Great Federation" was a way of bringing the turbulent period to a close rather than setting men in motion. They had not foreseen that collective enthusiasm would spill beyond their joyless projects.'[40] There were several elements to the *Fête de la Fédération*: a musical *drame sacré* in Notre-Dame on the night of 13 July, composed by Désaugiers to lyrics by Marie-Joseph Chénier and choreographed by Maximilien Gardel of the Opéra; on the 14th a procession of National Guardsmen and deputies from all provinces, starting at the site of the Bastille and crossing a specially constructed bridge over the Seine into the huge stadium on the Chaps-de-Mars; speeches from the king and Lafayette leading to the communal Oath of Federation; and finally a mass celebrated on the Altar of the Fatherland by Tallyrand, bishop of Autun. These formal celebrations were complemented by sports, dancing and feasting throughout the city in specially designed booths and decorated squares, including a spectacular pavilion erected on the ruins of the Bastille. The very scale of the preparation, which involved Parisians in weeks of voluntary labour erecting the stadium and other decorations, and provincials in arduous and memorable journeys to and from the capital, gave the whole event a more than theatrical impact. Although it engendered a range of responses from exhilaration to fear to a cynical disinterest, Ozouf correctly points out 'that by 1790 no fatal gap had yet opened up between principles and reality: perhaps this is what makes the Federation still a happy time'.[41] Indeed Wordsworth's famous delight in the Revolution received personal confirmation by his arriving in France 'on the eve of that great federal day' and meeting shortly after a band of *fédérés* returning from the celebrations; 'Like bees they swarmed, gaudy and gay as bees.'[42]

That, as yet, England generally sympathised with the achievements being celebrated in Paris is confirmed by the Lord Chamberlain's raising no objection to Harris' plan to present *A Picture of Paris, Taken in the Year 1790* by Charles Bonner and Robert Merry, with music by Shield (Covent Garden, 20 December 1790) with scenic representations of:

View of the Champs de Mars, with the grand Pavilion preparatory to the Festival; a Grand Assembly; View of the Triumphal Arch, prepared for the Procession to the Champs de Mars; Perspective view of the Champs de Mars, with the Bridge of Boats. With an exact Representation of the Banners, Oriflammes, &c. &c. in the Grand Procession to the Champs de Mars. The whole to conclude with a Grand Representation of the Grand Illuminated Platform, as prepared by the City of Paris, on the Ruins of the Bastille for the Entertainment of the Provincial Deputies and the Public.[43]

The simple plot of this musical afterpiece concerns various British characters visiting the *fête*, and the Prologue, spoken by a 'Travelling Artist', sets a tone of curiosity rather than approval:

> He comes not to *consider*, but to *see*,
> A Painter, not a Satirist is *he*.
> . . . So we, in all our Wand'rings, seek to find
> New moral landscapes for the public mind
> Unbias'd by Design, or party Rage,
> We wish to please you, and adorn our Stage
> . . . But think not, we presumptuously intend
> To censure other Nations, or commend.
> . . . No, be it ours, those comforts to revere,
> Which Liberty and Justice settled *here*,
> Where the Free heart a genuine tribute brings,
> And hails with Gratitude the best of Kings.

Adding to this patriotic distancing from French politics was Captain

O'Leary's assertion that Ireland is freer than France because, 'there, if you don't like the cut of a Jontleman's face, you've always the liberty to fight him, and what can any loyal Subject wish for more,' and the discovery that it was no longer possible to pack rebellious daughters off to French convents, because now all the nuns were getting married.

The only exception to this patronising tone is the chorus sung at the *fête* itself:

> Hark to the general voice:
> Rejoice, rejoice, rejoice,
> A brighter day succeeds at last
> Oppression's heavy hour is past.

But even this is followed by:

> Then let us learn of Briton's favour'd land,
> To greet with loyal love a due command.
> From virtuous rule her bounteous blessings spring,
> Her laws are honour'd, and ador'd her King.

No doubt heedful of his previous experience of censorship, Harris insisted on emphasising his patriotic perspective on a spectacle so impressive that it demanded representation. As the scenes were advertised as 'taken from accurate Drawings made on the Spot', and were realised by the full complement of Covent Garden's crew of painters and machinists, led by Inigo Richards, the whole project must have been planned since before July, with the Licenser's authority cleared in advance. That the licence was actually granted suggests that the authorities in England shared the belief of French moderates that the *fête* marked the end of the French Revolution.

The magistrates who regulated performances in the minor houses must have taken an equally sanguine view, as the pantomime *The Paris Federation* at the Royalty Theatre was a far more engaged presentation. As was usual with pantomimes, the published version is 'a sketch of the entertainment', listing scenes and action without words other than for the songs.[44] The music however included the Revolutionary *Ça ira!* among the French melodies and the words to several expressed far more radical sentiments than the chauvinistic platitudes of Covent Garden:

> The cruel Aristocracy
> Ne'er shed a tear at misery;
>   'Twas that which caused our strife.

> But now's arriv'd the happy day
> When all our sorrows fly away
> 'Tis that which gives us life.

Reference is made to the main events and achievements of the Revolution:

> We now possess the rights of man,
> Our king no longer heads their plan . . .
> In dust are laid the proud Bastille's
> Horrific dens and tortu'ring wheels . . .
> The throne of Liberty we raise
> And loudly sing in Fayette's praise;
>   He gives the people life.

Clown is stripped of his motley by a crowd who consider it to be the livery of a servant:

> But doff it all,
>   For, great and small
> Are equal in this nation;
>   Arms, titles, liv'ries, they
>   Are for ever done away
> In total annihilation.

The action of the pantomimes consisted as usual of Harlequin and Columbine being chased from scene to scene by Pantaloon and Clown, but in each they meet different groups of people making their way towards Paris where citizens are busy erecting the amphitheatre on the Champs de Mars:

> In social bands united
> We work at the Champs de Mars
> We toil with cheer and glee,
> Enroll'd by Liberty
>   And fame's regard
>   Be their reward
> Who work at the Champs de Mars.

In the final scene the songs recreate in considerable detail the actual ceremony of dedication led by Bishop Tallyrand and joined by King Louis:

On the right, the king is seated on the throne, erected by the people; on the left are three triumphal arches, which form the entrance to the Champs de Mars; and, in the centre, is l'autel de la patrie, at which the flags were consecrated, and following ceremony performed.

BISHOP. Frenchmen attend; Assembled to receive

What honours men to take and kings to give:
Take liberty, by no harsh laws confin'd,
Great nature's charter to the free-born mind.
The flames of liberty, serene and pure,
Swear henceforth to preserve.
KING. – Je le jure, je le jure.
PEOPLE. Vive la loi, vive la nation, vive le roi;
The king's the guardian of the law.

In this East End version of the Federation, in the theatre which had seen Palmer's unsuccessful attempt to break theatrical privilege, the triumph of the French people and the citizens of Paris is given a genuine celebration, rather than the patronising tone adopted in the privileged theatres themselves.[45]

It is ironic that British theatrical depictions of French politics were virtually restricted to visual and musical representations, because the Festival itself was more symbolic spectacle than political achievement. The king only attended under *force majeure* and within a month of the *fête* attacks on church property sparked off riots in Nancy and Provence, while better organised resistance began in the Vendee and Brittany. In Paris itself extreme politicians refused to consider that the Revolution was over. In the Assembly, Robespierre and Danton denounced the hypocrisy of the aristocratic liberals Mirabeau and Lafayette, and at the Jacobins' club and in popular pamphlets Marat and Desmoulins demanded the 'heads of five or six hundred aristocrats' to forestall a counter-revolutionary coup.[46] During early 1791 the Assembly passed more 'liberations': convents were closed down, trade and tax barriers removed and slavery abolished. On 13 January 1791 theatrical privilege was dismantled, thus allowing the boulevard theatres the same rights as the Royal Theatres, now renamed Theatres of the Nation. In April the death of Mirabeau contributed to the despair of the king, who made his ill-fated flight from Paris on 20 June, ending in his ignominious recapture at Varennes. Although a second *Fête de la Fédération* was celebrated on 14 July 1791, three days later the Champs de Mars witnessed a massacre of fifteen citizens when Lafayette ordered the National Guard to fire on a crowd petitioning for a republic.

Given the speed with which the political landscape was changing, it is not surprising that theatres tried to disengage their productions from the specificity of contentious political argument.[47] The boulevard theatres could use the symbolism of spectacle, song and pantomime, as in the British entertainments, but the Comédie was bound to present articulate dramas in tune with the times. The technique they employed was the traditional one of the history play, as historical images helped distance writers, performers and audiences from the dangers of immediate controversy. Classical parallels with contemporary politics were already well established in the paintings of David, who was responsible for devising and designing the *Fête de la Fédération,* and who had exhibited his masterpiece of republic stoicism, *Brutus Receiving the Bodies of his Sons* at the salon in 1789. Voltaire's plays *Brutus* and *Le Mort de Caesar,* originally produced under Louis XV, when republicanism was certainly more academic than practical, were both revived by the Comédie to escape the stigma of being the 'King's Players'. But even historical plays were open to ideological criticism, as had been Chénier's *Charles IX,* and it proved safer to move beyond actual history into historical fantasy, or even scientific fiction.

The most popular play in Paris at the end of 1790 was *Nicodème dans la lune,* presented at the Théâtre Comique et Lyrique on 7 November. It was written by Louis-Abel Beffroy de Reigny under the reassuring *nom de plume* 'Cousin Jaques', who transported his hero to the moon by means of a balloon similar to the one launched by André Garnerin during the 14 July celebrations. Nicodème, a naïve peasant apprenticed to an old inventor, steals the balloon, in which his master was planning to escape the Revolution, and being unable to control it is carried to the moon. Here he finds a society very like the ancient regime. Despite the hostility of several courtiers, Nicodème advises the lunar monarch to benefit his subjects by following the example of France. His simple eloquence not only convinces the well-meaning king, but the whole court, including ministers and bishops. Thus the benefits of the Revolution reach the moon. It was a simple optimistic piece of propaganda avoiding the problematic issues of the real world, and it proved immensely popular, being performed 363 times by the time the theatre closed in 1793. Cousin Jaques' moderate support for constitutional monarchy was ideally pitched for the times, though by 1793 the Jacobins attacked him for the monarchist principles that many of them had shared in 1790. Nicodème's journey to the moon once again suggests that the popular sense of living through great and generally welcome changes could be reflected more vividly through the images of a science fiction, or at least artistic fantasy, than through heated debate in Philinte's salon or the chambers of Marie de Medici, as depicted by Fabre d'Eglantine and Chénier.

The persistent political turmoil in France began to undermine the initial popularity with which the events of 1789 and 1790 had been viewed in Britain. Outright calls for a republic, the persecution of aristocrats with attacks on their persons and property as well as their privileges, and the increasingly blood-thirsty tone of Parisian debate, alienated moderate opinion, particularly when the 'patriotic' press began to fall in behind Burke's interpretation of French politics as being out of control. In this period of uncertainty, when opinions were shifting and the government's attitude was becoming more hostile to radical ideas, theatre managers became even more wary of commenting on the situation in France. Indeed the one play of 1791 that was open to direct application to France seems so distant from the contemporary situation that it would seem that any similarity was entirely unintentional. And yet, whether deliberately or not, Colman's *Surrender of Calais* (Haymarket, 30 July 1791) gives some indication of an ambivalent attitude towards the French. It tells the well-known story of how Edward III, to save their city from pillage and destruction, demanded that six burghers of Calais deliver up the keys of the town and themselves to execution. Although the king is persuaded to spare them by his wife, and the melodramatic inter- vention of the governor's daughter offering to take the place of her lover, the main feature of the play is the heroism of the French citizens under siege, and in particular the defiance of the old merchant Eustache de St Pierre and his headstrong son La Gloire, played by Bannister in the style of Inkle's good-hearted servant Trudge. Although it is difficult to recognise a direct similarity between the famine of the besieged city and the turmoil of con- temporary Paris, Eustache's plain-spoken condemnation of hypoc- risy may well have echoed the complaints of the émigrés who were now reaching London in increasing numbers:

> I love my country, boy. Ungraced by fortune,
> I dare aspire to the proud name of patriot.
> If any bear that title to misuse it –
> Decking their devilships in angel seeming,
> To glut their own particular appetites –
> If any, 'midst a people's misery,

> Feed fat, by filching from the public good,
> Which they profess is nearest to their hearts –
> The curses of their country, or, what's sharper,
> The curse of guilty conscience, follow them!

And although the burghers delivering themselves as hostages were hardly the same as aristocrats fleeing from persecution, it was reassuring to those who wanted to believe that the politics of Paris were untypical of France as a whole, that they left their native Calais with a chorus of praise from fellow citizens:

> Peace to the heroes! peace! who yield their blood,
> And perish, nobly, for their country's good!

Finally of course it was to Britain's credit that these miserable victims eventually met with a merciful welcome from the more fortune British, who in the position of victors were able to deal magnanimously with their enemies. Reassuringly the play closes with both English victory and French thanksgiving. *The Siege of Calais* received twenty-eight performances in the summer of 1791, often alternating with *The Battle of Hexham*, and remained in the repertoire even after hostilities broke out between England and France in 1793.

CHAPTER 3

From the Federation to the Terror

Although during 1789 and 1790 there had been a widespread welcome in Britain for the Revolution, in 1791 attitudes began to polarise as France continued to drive out émigrés, bringing tales of persecution, and advocate revolution in neighbouring states, while failing to bring its own constitutional debates to a settled conclusion. In October 1791 the new constitution had been promulgated, but, although Louis XVI had been proclaimed chief executive, with the power to appoint ministers and a royal veto over the Legislative Assembly, after his flight to Varennes his support for it was very suspect. Separating the powers of the executive and legislature may have served the Americans well, but in France it led to a rivalry between the Assembly and the king's ministers – complicated by the power of the Paris Commune and the Revolutionary clubs to organise direct action within the capital – and out of this confusion came the declaration of war against Austria on 20 April 1792. Aristocrat émigrés, including the king's own bothers, had gathered in the Rhineland cities of Coblenz and Trier and were threatening to create a counter-revolutionary army with the support of Leopold II of Austria – Marie Antoinette's brother – and Frederick William II of Prussia. During the winter and spring of 1790–1 the question of war dominated French politics. Ministers and generals appointed by the king – Narbonne, Lafayette, Brissot and Dumouriez – secretly looked to a war as the best excuse for repressing the radicals, the Jacobins fearing such a policy clamoured against the ministers, while the idealistic central party, soon to be known as the Girondins, hoped that war would lead to liberal revolutions across the rest of Europe. This belief was strengthened not only by the struggle of Belgium against Austrian rule and the assassination of the King of Sweden, but also by messages of support from British radicals.

However, France declaring war with the central European powers did not mean that England would necessarily become involved on either side. The Tory government, although it had recognised the constitution of 1791 and rejected advances from the royalists in Coblenz, was quite content to see its continental rivals locked in armed conflict. Sympathetic Whigs and committed radicals on the other hand organised formal support for the endangered Revolution. The Whig Club had celebrated Bastille Day in 1790 with a banquet for 'the friends of liberty' and in April 1792 the Society of the Friends of the People was founded to argue for the moderate reform of parliament and the electoral system. John Cartwright, Richard Price, Christopher Wyvill and John Horne Tooke, who had been reformers since the days of John Wilkes in the 1760s, founded the Revolutionary Society of 1788 (to commemorate 1688), and revived their Society for Constitutional Information in 1789. These societies were primarily concerned with British reform, but corresponded with several French political clubs. However on 25 January 1792 the London Corresponding Society was formed with the express purpose of establishing mutual support between democratic radicals in London and Paris. The LCS was led by shoemaker Thomas Hardy, and among its nine founding members was Thomas Holcroft the dramatist. As well as corresponding with the French, the society established a network of branches to exchange letters and speakers supporting their programme of universal manhood suffrage, annual elections and the redistribution of parliamentary seats. Although ministers could regard developments in France with equanimity, they became more concerned by such organised activity in England, particularly as it was not restricted to London, but emerged in provincial centres such as Bristol, Birmingham, Manchester, Liverpool, Norwich and Portsmouth. They also became more sensitive to the expression of political sentiment in the theatre.

As indicated in the last chapter, it is not always easy to recognise in retrospect a politically sensitive performance, but it may have been more than coincidental that the first production at Covent Garden after the promulgation of the French constitution was *The Earl of Essex; or, The Unhappy Favourite*, with Reynolds' *Crusade* as afterpiece. We know *The Crusade* as a distant reworking of the fall of the Bastille but Henry Jones' *Earl of Essex*, not performed since 1784, told of the treason and downfall of Elizabeth's favourite and could have been read as a comment on the treacherous tendencies of Louis XVI's advisors. More clearly indicative of political sympathies was the interruption on 18 February 1792 of Kemble's first revival of *Macbeth* since April 1789: 'Between the first and second acts *Ça Ira* was loudly called for from the pit and gallery. The clamour, after preventing the first part of the second act from being heard, subsided as unaccountably as it arose.'[1] Perhaps the demonstration had something to do with the performance at Covent Garden which was the first night of Holcroft's *The Road to Ruin*. The event suggests, though hardly conclusively, that audiences were aware of the political sympathies of authors and theatre managers, and, on this occasion at least, preferred the radical Holcroft to Kemble, the establishment's favourite.

Holcroft's radical commitment had kept him from the theatre for some time. Through Mrs Inchbald and John Johnson, their mutual publisher, he had become closely involved with the intellectual circle of William Godwin, with whom he collaborated in 1791 to see Thomas Paine's *Rights of Man* through the press. In 1792 he met Mary Wollstonecraft, who was to become Godwin's wife in 1797, while she was writing her famous elaboration of Paine's radical thesis, *A Vindication of the Rights of Woman*, and in 1793 Godwin completed his own philosophical work, *An Enquiry Concerning Political Justice*. Both authors acknowledged the assistance of Holcroft in refining their ideas.[2] Holcroft himself had started writing a 'Jacobin' novel, *Anna St Ives*,[3] which exemplified many of Wollstonecraft's ideas, and in the midst of all this politically inspired composition he produced his most successful play, *The Road to Ruin*, at Covent Garden, 18 February 1792. The prologue satirised Holcroft's reputation as a radical political commentator. The conceit was that his original prologue was lost, which enabled the actor to describe how polemic it was going to have been:

> The Author had mounted on the Stilts of Oratory and elocution:
> Not but he had a smart touch or two about Poland, France, and the
>   – the Revolution.
> Telling us that Frenchmen, and Polishmen, and every man is our
>   Brother,
> And that all men, ay, even poor Negromen have a right to be free,
>   one as another![4]
> Freedom at length, said he, like a torrent is spreading and swelling,
> To sweep away pride, and reach the most miserable Dwelling! . .
> Thus he went on, not mentioning a word about the play.[5]

At first sight the play itself seemed innocuous enough, but it might well have inspired the criticism of the anonymous 'E', cited in my introduction: 'The sole interest now turns upon poverty and wealth . . . the distress arises from urgent creditors and sheriffs; and the happy catastrophe from the intervention of fortune . . . in the shape of an unexpected bequest.'[6] The gambling debts of Harry Dornton threaten to bring down the family banking house, while Dornton Senior is torn between redeeming and punishing his son. When Harry learns of the consequences of his extravagance he tries to marry the rich and repulsive Widow Warren. Although, as in Cumberland's *West Indian* and Colman's *Inkle and Yarico*, disaster is averted by the enlightened benevolence of Old Dornton and his banking partner Mr Sulky, the play is remarkable for making money a motivating force for virtually all the characters, except young Sophie, whose adolescent devotion to Harry is ingenuously innocent. The widow and her servant Jenny are as rapacious as Mr Silky the money-lender; the bankers Dornton and Sulky, although ultimately benevolent, argue whether young Dornton can be reformed by cutting his funds, and Harry's extravagance is encouraged by his friend Milford, who gets imprisoned for his own debts, and Gold-finch, who is cynically wooing the rich widow to finance his passion for horses.

Holcroft can hardly be credited with a proto-Marxist analysis of capitalism, but his demonstration of how cupidity determines not only behaviour but feelings, suggests a more perceptive awareness of hegemonic influences than can be explained by his own lowly origins. He certainly drew on his experience as a Newmarket stable lad to characterise Goldfinch, a type that was to be more famously caricatured by Cruikshank as Tom and Jerry the Regency bucks.[7] Goldfinch is a petty bourgeois who believes enough cash and a sense of style will make him a gentleman:

GOLDFINCH. Father a sugar-baker, grandfather a slop-seller – I'm a
    gentleman – That's your sort!
HARRY. Ha, ha, ha! And your father was only a man of worth.
GOLDFINCH. Kept a gig! [*With great Contempt*] – Knew nothing of life! –
    Never drove four!
HARRY. No, but a useful member of society.
GOLDFINCH. A usef- ! – What's that?
HARRY. Ha, ha, ha! A pertinent question.
GOLDFINCH. A gentleman like me a useful member of society? Bet the long
    odds, nobody ever heard of such a thing! (Act 2, scene 1)[8]

However, the characterisation of the Dorntons suggests more gra-
phically the psychological conflict between financial and moral
responsibility. Old Dornton determines to cut Harry off without a
penny, but cannot bring himself to hate the boy. Holcroft dramatises
each contradictory motive to the full in a dialectical technique rather
like that employed by Brecht in *Puntilla and his Man Matti*. Dornton
orders his clerk not to lend anything to the spendthrift son:

DORNTON. Be his distress what it will, not a guinea! Though you should
    hereafter see him begging, starving in the streets, not so much as the
    loan or gift of a single guinea! [*With great Passion*]
MR SMITH. I shall be careful to observe your orders, sir.
DORNTON. Sir! [*Terror*] Why, would you see him starve? – Would you see
    him starve and not lend him a guinea? – Would you, sir? Would you?
MR SMITH. Sir! – Certainly not, except in obedience to your orders!
DORNTON. [*Amazed and Compassion*] And could any orders justify your seeing
    a poor unfortunate youth, rejected by his father, abandoned by his
    friends, starving to death?
MR SMITH. There is no danger of that, sir.
DORNTON. I tell you the thing shall happen! He shall starve to death![9]

Although this swing of passions is intentionally amusing, especially
as Dornton was played by the low comedian Munden, the equally
violent extremes of Dornton Junior are more than mere sentiment:

HARRY. [*Wildly*] – My father! – Sir! [*Turning away*] Is it possible? –
    Disgraced? – Ruined? – In reality ruined? – By me? – Are these things
    so? – [*Momentary fury*] Tol de rol –
DORNTON. Harry! – How you look! – You frighten me!
HARRY. [*Starting*] It shall be done! . . . Don't despair! I'll find relief – [*Aside*]
    First to my friend – He cannot fail? But if he should! – Why, ay, then
    to Megæra! – I will marry her, in such a cause! were she fifty widows
    and fifty furies! (Act 3, scene 2)

Being a comedy, the stolen will is retrieved and all ends well, but
banker Dornton's final judicious sentiment is hardly an unequivocal
celebration of omnipotent benevolence: 'If you can, be honest with a
good grace. Everything will then be readily adjusted, and, I hope to
the satisfaction of all parties' (Act 5, scene 3). Because the play
conformed from scene to scene to the conventions of social comedy,
the Licenser expected little subversion, and, unlike in some of his
plays, Holcroft provided enough wit and intrigue to entertain while
propounding his moral position. The play achieved a very profitable
run of thirty-seven performances.

    Later in the same season Richard Cumberland submitted a

history play to Covent Garden which met with an outright ban from the censor. Harris sent Larpent the manuscript of Cumberland's *Richard the Second* on 8 December 1792 and it was returned with the note that 'It appears Extremely unfit for representation at a time when ye Country is full of Alarm, being the story of Wat Tyler, the killing of the Tax Gatherers & very ill Judged.' However all was not lost as Harris arranged a meeting between the playwright and Licenser, whose wife recorded in her diary for 12 December: 'Mr Larpent had Mr Cumberland abt his play – true Author's Agony. A curious tete à tete.'[10] The result was that all the explicit politics were removed and the rewritten play went forwards as *The Armourer*. The differences between the two versions are highly instructive as to what was considered subversive and what inoffensive.

In *Richard the Second* a blacksmith, Jerry Furnace, will not declare his daughter for the Poll Tax on the grounds that she was not born in England, but Ralph Rackum the tax gatherer threatens to drag her before the courts. In a fury Furnace kills the tax gather and then flees to join the outlaws, Wat Tyler and Jack Straw, who are leading the Peasants' Revolt against the Poll Tax:

> Is it not a capital grievance that we should pay for the privilege of wearing our own heads? . . . Did they, that tax our heads, make our heads? . . . 'Tis the luxuries and superfluities of life that should be tax'd – Are our Noddles of that number? . . . Should the tax imposed exceed the value of the thing taxed?[11]

This is followed by a chorus in praise of the rebel leaders:

> Our gallant Wat Tyler, and brave Captain Straw
> Set us free from our Taxes and Order and Law;
> And when war is awaken'd, destruction's the word,
> And our March shall be trac'd by fire, famine and Sword.

One of the group, the banished Earl FitzAllen disguised as a peasant, admonishes the rebels:

> Desperate, devoted wretches, who are blindly hurrying to your own destruction, ye know not what you do. Wretched Country, that must now be torn to pieces by thine own Children.

On their march towards London they are berated by a town clerk for destroying their own homes, whilst Diggory, the comedy constable, is berated by his wife for joining the protest. They all reach Blackheath in a festive rather than dangerous mood, but Jerry warns against confronting the king with violence:

JERRY. I don't like your dealings, therefore I am silent. When it comes to
     fighting I know what to do:
          'Gainst the Leeches that suck out the blood of the land
               My weapon with vengeance I wield,
          To haughty Court Minions opposing I stand,
               But to Richard of England I yield . . .
STRAW. And who but we are the Protectors of the People?
JERRY. If you plunder the people, if you murder the people, can you be said
     to protect the people?

In the third act Straw, who just wants to plunder, falls out with Tyler
and then flees at the arrival of the king's army. After a scene between
Diggory and his wife, Jerry returns with news of Tyler's death.
Young King Richard then arrives and doles out justice and mercy.
FitzAllen is pardoned, as is Jerry Furnace for helping the disguised
aristocrat and his betrothed Rosamunda. The play ends with a song
in praise of civil peace.

Clearly Cumberland was not advocating rebellion, nor even
protest against taxation: his hero had attacked a tax collector, but he
proves a loyal subject in the end. Nevertheless, whatever gloss the
writer put upon it, the story itself was about a rebellion and could
not be allowed. In 1792 *Helvetic Liberty*, a version of the William Tell
story, was published anonymously by 'A Kentish Bowman', who
claimed the play had been refused by an unnamed theatre manager
for being too political.[12] Many of its speeches were far more pointed
than Cumberland's and would certainly have been cut by the
Licenser:

> Deprived of our natural rights, and over burthen'd with immense
> Taxation, and forced by an alien despot's power to bend our bodies
> low to objects vile . . . [we should swear] to oppose these evils we
> endure by every means we know, till we have broken the chains of
> despotism, and given the mortal wound to ruthless tyranny; so we
> shall renovate our natural rights.[13]

The political debate that was being waged in newspapers and
pamphlets with far greater freedom than in the theatres was much
concerned with feudal rights. Edmund Burke cited the obligations of
feudal privilege as the basis of British liberty, while radicals harked
back to examples of pre-Norman self-government, and this argument made any reference to ancient events like the Peasant's Revolt
as politically sensitive as to the freedom of the Swiss Cantons.
William Tell could be addressing Burke directly:

What bears expensive royalty upon its crimson throne? – the prodigious labour of the people – proud Aristocracy and the Priesthood proud are all supported by the people . . . [for the people] to bear such insult is to lose their majesty and become that '*swinish multitude*' the courtly hireling writes [Burke's description of the Paris mob] – away – we will renounce all Gothick darkness – all musty records and the conqueror's sword, and look upright to Heaven as free born men.[14]

Although Cumberland had included no such radical rhetoric as this, it is not surprising that his play nearly suffered the same fate as *Helvetic Liberty.* In the event however, he was able to rewrite it with Larpent's assistance. In the revised version, *The Armourer,* Harry Furnace kills an inn-keeper, Ben Bluster, when he tries to abduct his daughter to feed the lustful desire of the Earl of Suffolk. Thus the villain is a rapist, rather than the government, and his henchman a 'publican' in the sense of innkeeper, rather than in the older sense of tax collector. The protest of the townspeople is no longer against an unjust tax, but against the arrest of a father justly provoked by a rapacious landlord. But their protest stops short of rebellion and Harry is released from prison when Ben Bluster turns up not dead but injured. Although the whole story is thus reduced to coincidence and misperception, an element of class consciousness remains when the hen-pecked Diggory (now a tailor rather than a constable) makes a comically sentimental declaration:

Neighbours, tho' I be but an ordinary work-man, or more modestly speaking, a member of other men's work, as you all do know; and one, withal, who rarely speaketh for himself, seeing there is one at home who commonly speaketh enough for us both; yet I have a heart for my friend, and when it is overfull it will out. There is my Cabin and within is my wife Kate; never trust me for a true man, but I would give up House, Chattels and Kate into the bargain to save this honest armourer from prison.

Instead of scenes of revolt we see Harry languishing in a dungeon, and instead of the king dispensing justice, good old Sir Theodore sorts everything out in the castle hall. The final song, too, is changed into a wedding masque with fairies, elves and sylphs, though it still ends with the same verse as in *Richard the Second*:

> Happy nation, such your bliss,
>   May no feuds destroy it,
> And your only strife be this,
>   Who shall best enjoy it.

Thus it would seem that the new version had been completely stripped of its political relevance, but I believe the subversion is still there if read metaphorically, particularly as the rapacious landlord, his flinty dungeon and the solidarity of the working classes, reappear in play after play. The political injustice had been transformed into an individual one, taxation into abduction, the overt rebellion into a dungeon scene – the images, though personal, still represented oppression, and the action was still an overthowal of that oppression.

Even more than the suppression of *Helvetic Liberty*, this particular example of censorship, forcing the author to recast *Richard the Second* into acceptable form, demonstrates the various levels at which drama could respond to political stress. As history plays all three dramas were distanced from contemporary affairs, but only *The Armourer* was allowed performance, as its distance from specific issues was apparently considered safe. But it was still open to a metaphorical reading as one of Sinfield's 'ghostly narratives' that shadow apparently innocuous stories. Frederick Jameson describes this process as 'the symbolic enactment of a social narrative', which might not be openly didactic but does touch what he defines as the 'Political Unconscious'.[15] Such patterns of oppression and resistance might indeed be unconsciously adopted by any writer, but in a period of censorship metaphorical distancing may well have been a deliberate decision. This does not mean that Cumberland, unlike the 'Kentish Bowman', intended either form of his play to incite political action, but the humanitarian sympathy and the perception of political power that had led him to dramatise the Peasants' Revolt in the first place remained unchanged in *The Armourer*. The authorities were determined that theatre should not be used as a weapon, but they were unable to stop it addressing the feelings of anxiety, injustice and resentment felt by many of its audience.

Many in the French Assembly and in the Commune wanted to use theatre as a political weapon, but Parisian theatre managers, though for different reasons than their English counterparts, preferred the clichés of popular entertainment to didactic propaganda that might inspire Revolutionary fervour one month and attract ideological condemnation the next. After the declaration of theatrical free trade in January 1791, a flush of new theatres opened, but few survived competition with the established expertise of the once privileged Comédie-Française and Opéra-Comique, the still fashionable

Opéra, the commercial acumen of Nicolet and Audinot on the Boulevard du Temple, and the star appeal of Talma and La Montansier in the Theatres of the Palais-Royal. As Michèle Root-Bernstein records:

the liberation of the theatre had not eradicated the hierarchies of the past; more precisely, it had not eradicated the popular stage. It did eliminate the legal sanction of theatre-types and repertory control. Aesthetic distinctions between theatres broke down when economic and social ones did not. All theatres could perform any genre of play indiscriminately, whether appropriate or not to their theatrical means or public.[16]

However the mixing of the repertoire was mainly one way. The boulevard theatres, including the established Gaité and Ambigu-Comique, the newly founded Variétés-Dramatiques, Lycée-Comique and Elèves de Thalie, and even the politically committed Délassements-Comiques and Théâtre-Patriotique, proudly presented the classical plays denied them under the old regime. Molière in particular appealed to all.[17] My earlier discussion of the power of narrative in periods of ideological reassessment suggests why the popular theatres seized on the regular drama, particularly plays of class conflict. It is equally understandable why the classical theatres did not appropriate much from the boulevards, not only was such material considered vulgar by even radical intellectuals, but it depended on specialist performers – acrobats, children or animals. In this respect the Comédies remained different from the London Patent Houses, which employed variety artists as readily as legitimate actors. The influence on them of popularisation, or, rather, anti-aristocratic opinion, was more complex than borrowing directly from the boulevards. Newly written plays increasingly abandoned the classic genres of comedy and tragedy for the kind of 'mixed genre' of comic opera and historical romance that was proving successful in London. In 1791 the *Almanac de tous les spectacles* deplored the corruption of classical forms after theatre deregulation, and attributed it to the degrading influence of commercial competition. Actually the shift in theatrical taste had already begun in 1789 when the Comédie-Française employed singers from the Comédie-Italienne to insert choruses into Racine's *Athalie*.[18]

However, the main competition for the Comédie-Française, or Théâtre de la Nation as it was now called, came from within. Ever since his success in Chénier's *Charles IX*, Talma had made professional and political enemies among the older generation of classical actors. After many internal disputes, he left the Comédie in June 1791 to set up a rival Théâtre Français in the Palais-Royal, a building originally designed by the Duc d'Orleans as a rival to the Comédie. This company, known as the Richelieu, after the street where it stood, became the main venue for new classic dramas, many of which were histories paralleling the past with present-day politics. Chénier's *Henry VIII* had been banned in 1789 but its anticlericism was highly popular in 1791. Similarly his *Caius Gracchus* appealed to the Girondins of 1792, with Talma as the incorruptible republican who dies to uphold the rule of law. The style and rhetoric of this play precisely echoed the classicism of David's painting of Brutus and his dead sons. Jean François Ducis' *Jean Sans-Terre ou La Mort d'Arthur* (Richelieu, 1791) used Shakespeare's *King John* to discredit the monarchy, and in November 1792, after Louis' deposition, he adapted *Othello* for Talma. These performances of Shakespeare not only suggest a radical change in theatrical taste, but, according to a contemporary critic, reflected radical politics:

Louis XIV enslaved the taste of artists, as he enslaved the liberty of his subjects. I have no doubt that the men of the court would have mocked Héldemone [Desdemona] who, young and beautiful, loves a moor; but the men of the Tenth of August will not employ the aristocracy of colour at the theatre, and they will find it quite acceptable that a white woman loves a man of colour somewhat different from her own if that man is young, handsome and passionate. They will not be scandalised to see a bed upon the stage; for republicans, who have more manners than the subjects of a monarchy, are not, as the latter, slaves to false delicacy, which is the hypocritical affectation of decency.[19]

In the event however, Othello murdering his bride was too much for audiences accustomed to the poetic justice of French classicism – and perhaps already longing for the wish-fulfilment of melodrama. The final scene was greeted with outrage and Ducis swiftly agreed to provide a happy ending. That theatre audiences were so susceptible a month after the September massacres, led Ducis to remark 'Why talk to me of composing tragedies? Tragedy walks the streets. If I put my foot out of doors, I have blood up to my ankle.'[20] He wrote no more plays.

The king's deposition, after the invasion of the Tuileries by the Paris sansculottes on 10 August 1792, left power in dispute between the Assembly and the Commune. Faced by invasion by Austria and Prussia, desertion by the royalist general Lafayette, distrust of his replacement Dumouriez, and counter-revolution in the western provinces, the Commune, urged on by Robespierre, demanded that tribunals be set up to try the potential traitors already imprisoned in Paris. Danton, having organised the coup of 10 August, was the Minister of Justice, and, unable to persuade the Assembly to appoint tribunals, he connived in the infamous September massacre of prisoners. The combination of a power vacuum, ideological extremism and panic in the face of invasion led to a violence far beyond the destruction of the Bastille three years before. Fear that the Revolution itself was in imminent danger propelled events from the Republic of 22 September to the king's trial of 3 December. These developments may have seemed logical in Paris, but they alienated moderate support across Europe.

The course of the Revolution now entered uncharted territory. The optimistic principles of Enlightenment rationality could no longer guide France through the unprecedented events of 1792–4. The Republic of 1792 may have been the inevitable outcome of the failure of constitutional monarchy in the face of foreign invasion and internal strife, but its baptism was one of blood. The Girondins inspired by the ideal of the Rights of Man, but materially wedded to the Rights of Property, found ideological refuge in a patriotic defence of Revolutionary ideas rather than in its actuality. The Montagnards of the left, deserting the benevolent principles of Liberty and Fraternity, demanded, in the name of Equality, a dictatorship of the people. Drawing support from the sansculottes, whose chief objectives were food, work and self-respect, the Jacobin leadership was itself divided between the pragmatic Dantonists, whose power base was the Paris Commune, the anticlerical Hérbertists, strong in the metropolitan Sections, and the circle of Robespierre, whose strength was the ruthless intellectual clarity with which he debated at the Jacobin Club and was to dominate the Committee for Public Safety. Driving these factions on were radical journalists, including Marat, Roux and Babeuf, who, beyond calling for the blood of 'traitors', were groping towards alternative principles of communal ownership and a proletarian society.

Not all these factions had emerged by January 1793 when the king was executed, an event shortly followed by the declaration of war against England and Holland. In March, General Dumouriez, who had successfully halted the Austrians and Prussians, planned to advance on Paris to suppress the Jacobin extremists, but ended up deserting to the Royalists. Each of these crises led to greater radicalisation in Paris, establishing on 10 March 1793 the Revolutionary Tribunal, on 4 April Representatives on Mission to prosecuted counter-revolution in the provinces, and on 6 April the Committee of Public Safety. These were the instruments of the Terror, which, from 1793 to 1794, saw wave after wave of aristocrats, speculators, political rivals and innocent spectators trundled off to the guillotine. The ideological climax came when Robespierre crowned his ruthless Rule of Virtue with the re-establishment of religion in his Festival of the Supreme Being, 8 June 1794. Two days later the Law of Prairial confirmed the dictatorship of the Committee of Public Safety, and in forty-seven days of the 'Great Terror', between Prairial and Thermidor (11 June – 27 July 1794), 1,376 people were executed – 125 more than in the previous fourteen months.[21]

These violent developments shook the theatres of Paris. During 1791 presenting plays with Revolutionary themes and sentiments became politically and commercially prudent, although most followed traditional formulas – just as the British plays dramatising the Feast of Federation had tacked spectacular finales onto conventional comedies. Typical was *Le Retour des fédérés; ou, Ça ira* at Nicolet's Gaité (April 1791) in which a local *seigneur* is converted to the Revolution and his repudiation of feudal rights facilitates the betrothal of the young lovers. Though the rhetoric is radical, the plot line is traditionally sentimental, with the aristocratic patriarch merely adopting a different kind of benevolence. But at least the titles became acceptably Revolutionary: the Théâtre-Patriotique presented *Le Tripot des emigrans*, *Le 14 juillet* and in 1792 *Le 10 août*, while other popular theatres produced *Les Citoyens français; ou, le Triomphe de la révolution*, *La Constitution villageoise* and *La Journée de Varennes* .[22] Even the Opéra introduced a swathe of radical entertainments, some in the form of classical operas – *Fabius*, *Horatius Coclès* and *Miltiades à Marathon* – but most of 'mixed genre' including rhetorical arias, patriotic choruses and symbolic spectacles – *Le Camp de Grandpré; ou le Triomphe de la République*, *L'Apothéose de Beaupaire*, *Toulon soumis*, *La Journée du dix août* and *Le Siège de Thionville* – while *La Montagne; ou, la Fondation du temple de la liberté* employed the allegorical method of the public *fêtes*.[23] Particularly popular were plays on the closure of monasteries and convents, like *Le Couvent; ou, les Fruits de l'éducation*, *Les victimes cloîtrées*, *Les Capucins* and *Le Déménagement du curé*, which presented either the sins of the clergy or the rescue of young women incarcerated by their families. Although intended to dramatise recent scandals and the forcible closure of monasteries by the National Guard, they were closely related to the Gothic horror stories already available in the novels of de Sade and soon to be dramatised in the melodramas of Pixérécourt. Indeed *Les victimes cloîtrées* was adapted into English by the radical Samuel Birch and presented at Covent Garden, 18 December 1798, as *Albert and Adelaide*, and was adapted again by Matthew Lewis in 1808 as *Venoni*. In the English context these plays could be read as traditionally anti-Catholic, but they also indicate how the Revolutionary culture of France influenced the British taste for Gothic allegory.

Highly influential in developing French audiences' ability to read theatrical metaphors, were, of course, the Revolutionary *fêtes* themselves. On 15 April 1792 David, Chénier and d'Herbois co-operated on a Jacobin *fête* to celebrate the release of the Swiss guards sentenced for mutiny in 1790, and in response to this radical demonstration moderate Girondins mounted a *fête* to honour the Rule of Law on 3 June 1792.[24] In July, at the third *Fête de la Fédération*, a tree was burnt hung with emblems of feudalism. The Federation was not celebrated the following 14 July – Paris was in mourning for Marat, murdered the day before – but on the anniversary of 10 August the promulgation of the 1792 republican constitution (which remain in abeyance throughout the Jacobin Terror) was celebrated on the site of the Bastille with a symbolic statue of an Egyptian goddess as the Fontaine de la Régénération spouting milk from her breasts. On 10 November 1793, most scandalously to the rest of Europe, a singer of the Opéra, Mlle Maillard, representing the Goddess of Reason, presided over a bacchanalian celebration in Notre-Dame.

This act of de-Christianisation was organised by Hérbertists and deplored by Robespierre, who mounted his own quasi-religious *Fête de l'Etre supreme* on 8 June 1794. This was to be celebrated across France, and to avoid the discredited ceremonial of the Catholic Church, citizens were encouraged to create their own allegorical symbols for the creator who had mysteriously led France into the paths of freedom. Robespierre's theology, described by Mona Ozouf as a 'Return to the Enlightenment',[25] was a combination of the rational deism of Voltaire and the mystic pantheism of Rousseau. Provincial celebrations were encouraged to stress themes of restoration, renewal and rebirth. According to Ozouf,

compared with the festivals that preceded it, it was the least improvised . . .
In Paris endless instructions were issued, appointing the organisers who
would place the groups, hand out ears of corn and baskets of flowers, and
order the movements . . . the Institute National de Musique was given the
task of supervising the feverish rehearsals of the singers of the Sections in
the anthems chosen for the occasion . . . lists of those who were to pay for
the festival were drawn up, and punishment specified for those who
sabotaged it; a whole coercive apparatus was in place.[26]

The allegorical symbols dominating the Paris festival were a triumphal column, an actress with wheat sheaves and a fruit tree on a
chariot drawn by bullocks representing Bountiful Nature, and a
mountain, crowned by a tree of liberty, up which marched surviving
members of the Convention. Across the country the keynote was
pastoral abundance and the birth of infant republicans. The metaphors of this festival were intentionally peaceful and restorative, as if
the depiction of a utopia might reconcile the people to the cruel
necessities of the Jacobin Terror.

Indeed these symbolic celebrations were overshadowed by the
theatricality of real politics in the public trials and execution of
counter-revolutionaries, and the funerals of Revolutionary heroes –
though in the case of Voltaire and Rousseau these too were
essentially symbolic. The theme running throughout these dramatic
manifestations, whether allegorical performances or irretrievable
acts of judicial terror, was, according to Emmet Kennedy, one of
humanisation:

The key homology is popular sovereignty – an inversion of divine right
absolutism. Not only had the living king to be eliminated as altogether
incompatible with the notion of popular sovereignty . . . but the authority
and mystical qualities formerly vested in the king as an image of God
Himself were transferred to the collective people . . . This religion of
humanity . . . found ultimate expression in the desanctification of the
church of Saint-Geneviève in 1791, the scattering of the ashes of this sixth-
century patron of Paris, and the rededication of this temple 'To Great Men,
the Patrie, in Recognition.' It was here that Voltaire, Mirabeau, Marat, and
Rousseau came to rest, at least temporarily . . . In the same line of self-
apotheosis is Napoleon's act of crowning himself in 1804 in the presence of
the Pope . . . Hegel summed up the meaning of the Incarnation of Christ
as a high point in history, but one in which man became God rather than
one in which God became man. Human apotheosis substitutes for divine
incarnation. What better expression is there of the ascending principle of
authority, of popular or human sovereignty.[27]

During the Reign of Terror, September 1793 to July 94, theatres had to ensure they conformed to the ideological culture of the Jacobin dictatorship. Although the Catholic Inquisition, the Puritans of Geneva and the English Commonwealth had imposed similar cultural dictats, they had appealed to the authority of tradition or a fundamentalist reading of the Bible. The Jacobins were the first to *invent* a cultural code based on a political ideology in the process of definition. Theirs was an improvised model of political correctness that was going to be exploited with greater sophistication by Fascist and Stalinist Ministries of Culture. One simple adjustment made by theatre managers to satisfy sansculotte taste during the height of the Terror, when Hérbert preached Atheism, Danton Equality and Robespierre Virtue, was to replace the titles Monsieur and Madame by Citoyen and Citoyenne – even in historical and classic plays.[28] Nevertheless, institutions associated with the ancient regime were under close surveillance, the Théâtre de la Nation (the old Comédie) was closed in September 1793 to reopen as the Théâtre de l'Egalité in June 1794 with its socially divisive interior redesigned as a single democratic amphitheatre. When members of the Opéra refused to perform Fabre d'Eglantine's blasphemous *La Passion du Christ* they were imprisoned – as were several actors from the older theatres.[29] Although the boulevard theatres maintained a predominantly apolitical – though democratic – repertoire of Harlequinades and acrobatics, the Variétés-Amusantes restaged Marat's murder and funeral with a scenic apotheosis surpassing the real ceremony in Saint-Geneviève. The newly founded dramatic theatres of the Palais-Royal, in particular La Montansier, tried to distance themselves from their original patron the Duc d'Orleans, who, despite taking the name Philippe Egalité, was heading for the guillotine, and they adopted an increasingly melodramatic political repertoire. In April 1792 the police had reported that

The small theatres frequented by the less well-to-do citizens, show . . . a patriotic spirit pleasant indeed to the true republican; while the more elegant houses, excluding all but the rich by their high prices, receive only the enemies of liberty and those indifferent to it. But . . . there are exceptions, such as the Theatre of the Republic [ex Richelieu]. This theatre truly deserves its name; the most ardent patriots gather there to applaud the smallest action, the least reference to patriotism. Last night this theatre gave *Robert, the Brigand Chief*, and one might say that no play is more in tune than this one with our present spirit. It exhales virtue, true republican virtue worthy of the founders of Rome.[30]

This play by La Martelière, possibly following Schiller's *The Robbers*, was a Gothic romance of noble *banditti*, whose hero was a cross between William Tell, Robin Hood and Chénier's Caius Gracchus. Its genre was that of Colman's histories and the play could well have found its way onto the British stage if it were bowdlerised of its politics like Cumberland's *Richard the Second*.

One play that could not cross the Channel was Sylvian Maréchal's *Le jugement dernier des rois* presented in the same Théâtre de la République on 17 October 1793, the day after the execution of Marie Antoinette. During the nineteenth century this play was often cited as the depths to which Revolutionary drama could sink.[31] But to the twentieth century, with its long experience of propagandist theatre, it resembles nothing so much as Mayakovsky's *Mystery Bouffe*, which depicted the events of Russia in 1917 as the Deluge during which the Unclean workers threw their Clean oppressors overboard from the ark. In Maréchal's play the kings of Europe, including the Pope, are left stranded on a volcanic island, the spectacular eruption of which brings down the curtain. Like Mayakovsky, Maréchal was using an apocalyptic metaphor to both commemorate and predict the death of monarchy. The play enjoyed great success through 1793 and 1794, and possibly inspired Gillray, the Tory cartoonist, to depict in July 1794 the few remaining parliamentary champions of the Revolution, led by Sheridan, as the Archbishop of Scoundrels, offering the head of Charles James Fox, as that of St Januarius, to an erupting volcano spewing lava over Vienna, Rome and The Netherlands.[32] Cartoons such as this, as well as plays like *Le jugement dernier des rois*, suggest the reading of political metaphors was well established on both sides of the Channel. However, whereas Gillray was free to make his metaphors transparent, with recognisable characters, identifying emblems and even explicit speeches, the censorship of the British stage meant that dramatic metaphors had to remain opaque, relying on audiences being more perceptive than the Examiner of Plays.

The death of Marie Antoinette, which may have inspired the metaphorical celebration of *Le dernier jugement des rois*, was the subject of a more realistic drama in England, which was of course banned from the Theatres Royal, but may possibly have been performed in an illegitimate theatre.[33] *The Death of the Queen of France* by Edwin Eyre was submitted to Larpent in 1794 and immediately rejected. Mrs Larpent was as unimpressed by its style as her husband was by its political sensitivity:

A Strange Absurd Jumble of C. Corde killing Marat. The prison of ye French Royal family introduced, their Sufferings, ridiculous attempt at simplicity in the young Kings conversation. One part perfectly ridiculous. His mother tells him God is his father, he Alas has no Other. The Boy asks if God will take him on his knee & fondle him. In short it is as devoid of poetry and judgement as it can be & highly improper just now were it otherwise.[34]

Refused a place on stage, Eyre published it under the title *The Maid of Normandy* in 1794. A shortened version under the title *The Death of the Queen of France* was resubmitted in 1804 by the manager of the Theatre Royal, Norwich.[35] Perhaps he hoped that by this time hatred of the French under Napoleon was such that he could present a condemnatory account of the events as history, but the style was too unambiguous and liable to create a precedent for more subversive dramatisations of contemporary events. Nevertheless it is enlightening to see how events might have been presented had the censorship allowed, and this in turn illuminates the indirect methods adopted by uncensored writers.[36]

Unlike history plays, which presented contemporaries under the mask of historical figures, or the patriotic masques, which presented them as abstract allegories, this play featured Robespierre, Marat, Charlotte Corday (Cordé in the manuscript) and Marie Antoinette in their own persons. The author's sympathies are strongly anti-Jacobin, but his rhetorical technique is that of the established dramaturgy: the historical characters are given individual motives and emotions so that the historical story is 'melodramatised' into a stereotypical plot of personal oppression. Robespierre and Marat are denied any political principles and are presented as personifications of malevolent ambition and lust. The model is part Shakespearean, but more Gothic Romance. Robespierre opens the play with a soliloquy worthy of Richard III:

> Ambition. Child of honour!
> Thou golden danger of aspiring thoughts,
> How few have courage to pursue thy course
> Or climb, with cautious step, the steep ascent
> Of tow'ring Eminence! – by subtle craft,
> That secret engine of destructive harm,
> I have remov'd each barrier, that oppos'd
> My bold admittance to the seat of Kings.

In an echo of Macbeth he plans the destruction of the late King Louis' dependants and descendants:

> – tho Capet has Expir'd,
> Yet must another sacrifice be made
> Ere we can sleep secure within our gates.

But unlike the assassins of Dunsinane, the henchman that Robespierre charges with persecuting the queen spurns the villainous plan, because he is not the simple peasant Theodore but Alberto, a disguised Girondin beloved of Charlotte Corday. Corday meanwhile, believing her lover executed, has come to Paris with a wild plan of revenge against Marat the most bloodthirsty of the regicides. While Robespierre is allowed some memories of earlier virtue:

> This Theodore, 'tho in a peasant's garb
> Is happier far than I –
> The worm of conscience feeds upon my life . . .
> Oh conscience, conscience, – would I could recall.
> But since that hope is vain I'll steel my breast
> Against compunction.

Marat, like the hypocritical Angelo in *Measure for Measure*, is sexually stimulated by Corday's righteous indignation:

> Yet there was something in her awed my Rage,
> Nay more, her charms engrossed my Amorous thoughts –
> Ha – a happy project like the dawn of light
> Bursting through Chaos, strikes upon my mind.
> Guards shall attend to seize upon her person.
> I'll have her apprehended as a Rebel –
> Then may I glut at once my love and vengeance.
> 'Twill be a feast, the luxury of Revenge.

However, these two Gothic villains are opposed by two models of Romantic feminine heroism. The queen, like Gillray's portraits of Britannia swooning under the assault of French barbarism, is a heroic victim, spurning the crafty approaches of Robespierre, but reduced to madness by the severity of her incarceration, the threat of being severed from her children and the bitterness of her memories:

> For when I think on what I've been – a Queen!
> And think on what I am, forlorn, Abandon'd
> Bereft of everything but conscience Virtue,
> My frantic feverish brain runs mad – See
> Ah sacred form, dear semblance of my love.
> Oh Ecstasy! my King – my lord, my Louis.   [*Faints*

Although the archetype can be traced back to Shakespeare's Queen Margaret and even Euripides' Hecuba, this speech is typical of a number of female protagonists, such as in Matthew Lewis' *The Captive* (1803), which is discussed in the next chapter. As victims of male oppression they are driven to such distress that they lose their reason and whole sense of identity:

> Thus mad, distracted, raging with my wrongs
> My screaming agonies shall haunt thy Soul,
> My Echoing groans shall hunt thee like a fury
> And halloo to thy hardened guilty Ear:
> Revenge for Murder, for a Monarch's Murder!

The setting of Marie Antoinette's incarceration, although of course historically justified, also resembles the countless dungeons that featured in Gothic dramas and escape operas. Charlotte Corday too conforms to a theatrical stereotype, but one of more recent origin than the fulminating widow. She is a rational heroine, driven as much by political principal as by personal vengeance, who confronts Marat in argument before his assault on her person goads her to stab him to the heart. She first speaks of those forced into exile:

> MARAT. There let them starve, and all who would combine
>   To overturn the freedom we have rais'd –
> CORDÉ. Your boasted freedom is the savage law
>   To sanction murder and applaud Rebellion.
>   If reason, Justice, and the generous instinct
>   Which makes us feel for Virtue in distress
>   Be not absorb'd by blood-fed cruelty,
>   Relax the rigor of Rebellious hate,
>   Restore the ancient government of Kings,
>   Release the Royal Captives,
>   And by one Act of mercy show the World
>   Thou hast not lost the feelings of a Man.
> MARAT. This Woman's War of Railing I despise,
>   For from this hour, I swear to sacrifice
>   Each foolish pity to Vindictive Ire,
>   And above all, the Queen shall feel my power –
> CORDÉ. Hear it ye nations and record the deed!
>   This mighty Champion of a peoples' right
>   This wise interpreter of Nature's laws
>   This great retailer of deflected freedom
>   This Valiant Hero, this Exalted Man
>   Bravely resolves, and then as bravely dares
>   To wreak his vengeance on an helpless Woman
>   But mark me Monster –
>   The day of Retribution is at hand –

And it is she, a not so helpless woman, who exacts the retribution, rather than Theodore/Alberto, who remains an inconsequential character in comparison with the villainous Jacobins and the valiant heroines. Perhaps, as a fictitious character he could not intrude into recorded history, but his dramatic impotence is typical of many heroes of Gothic romance. As a disinherited aristocrat he seems less capable of action than Corday's faithful servant Dumenil, or even 'Theodore' the peasant persona he has been forced to adopt.

Although the play is strenuously anti-revolutionary it does include a number of democratic sentiments in which the safety and innocence of poverty are envied by the noble and royal characters who are now persecuted and alienated from society:

> DAUPHIN. I wish I had been some shepherd boy
>   Rather than what I am –
> QUEEN. Had fate allotted thee an humbler Birth
>   Then balmy slumbers might have bless'd thy Nights –
>   And Roseate Health, the smiling Child
>   Of jocund labour, crown'd our waking hours.

Such sentiments are hardly radical, but would have been well received by the more popular audience of a minor theatre, for whom scorn of pampered aristocracy was quite compatible with a detestation of extreme radicalism. The democratic credentials of John Bull were emotional not ideological.

But if John Bull, by whom I mean the unthinking populous, had a pragmatic disregard for the abstractions of liberty, equality and fraternity, his cherished Roast Beef and his myths of British Liberty were as much ideological constructs as the political philosophy and the radical programmes of Paine, Godwin and the London Corresponding Society. The difference was one of acknowledgement. While apparently relying on established laws to condemn radicals of sedition or treason, the government had discreetly appropriated Burke's philosophical reflections and adopted the abusive rhetoric of the anti-Jacobin journals. Tarring British reformers with the same brush as the French extremists, the loyal press had labelled them as English Jacobins, though, being mostly non-violent constitutional monarchists, their true French equivalents were the Girondins. Many of the more literate reformers were solidly middle class and

expected the lower orders to follow the lead of enlightened men in the middle and upper ranks of society . . . Furthermore, in the struggle for the rights of man, most radicals were concerned quite literally with the liberty of adult males . . . They regarded the position of women as analogous to that of children – they were dependant creatures, incapable of exercising independent political judgement.[37]

In chapter 1 I argued that cultured intellectuals, including theatre administrators and artists, were considerably more cosmopolitan than the mass of the population, who had since the wars of William III been confirmed in their chauvinistic attitude towards the French. Thus it was not difficult for pro-government journalists to discredit radical attitudes as un-British, particularly as many radical intellectuals were disenfranchised Dissenters, who had long been advocating the repeal of the Test and Corporation Acts. This formula inspired the Church and King mob that violently disrupted the 1791 Bastille Day celebration in Birmingham led by the veteran reformer, scientist and Dissenter Joseph Priestley.

Distrust of reform as unpatriotic was intensified as soon as the country went to war with France, and a royal proclamation was issued against seditious writing and meetings early in 1792. When Scottish radicals called for a national convention in Edinburgh, 30 April 1793, the authorities prosecuted Thomas Muir (who had read out a message from the United Irishmen) for sedition and he was transported to Australia. A further meeting in November 1793 led to the transportation of several Scottish and English delegates. But the Home Office was particularly keen to prosecute members of what seemed to be the most dangerous organisation, the London Corresponding Society, and in November 1794 they arrested, amongst others, John Thewell, Thomas Hardy, John Horne Took and the playwright Thomas Holcroft and accused them not only of sedition but treason. However, their skilful defence by Thomas Erskine, and their own obvious respectability, led to the charges against Thewell, Hardy and Hook being thrown out by the Grand Jury, and the cases against the others being dropped. The failure of these cases prompted the government to draft more specific repressive legislation. That no one was actually punished under the Treasonable Practices and the Seditious Meetings Acts of 1795 discredits the description of the repression as 'Pitt's Reign of Terror', but they clearly warned radicals not to pursue their arguments into direct action. With the pro-reform Whig opposition in parliament dwindled to a much derided handful, the government, despite its network of internal spies, was generally content to rely on journalistic propaganda and the brilliantly vicious cartoons of Gillray,

Cruikshank and Richardson to counteract the subversive strategies of 'Jacobin' novelists and philosophers.

That a leading playwright had spent some weeks in prison under threat of execution and remained stigmatised as an 'unacquitted felon' hardly encouraged London theatres to countenance radical productions, even if they were to escape censorship by the Lord Chamberlain's office, a branch of the repressive government. If such a blatantly anti-Jacobin play as *The Death of the Queen of France* was banned, there was little hope for other plays depicting contemporary politics. No doubt Larpent was instructed to refuse anything that might provoke a public reaction from either reformers or reactionaries. Even a light-hearted fantasy *The Whim* received heavy cutting. It was submitted in 1795 by the Ramsgate Theatre Royal on behalf of the eccentric Lady Eglantine Wallace, whom the *National Dictionary of Biography* describes disapprovingly as, 'a boisterous hoyden in her youth and a woman of violent temper in her maturer years'.[38] Her farce *The Ton*, satirising excessive fashions, had been produced at Covent Garden in 1788 with a little success, but *The Whim*, her second play, ran into considerable trouble with the censor, as she explained at length when it was published.[39] Originally written to 'relieve the distress of the poor of the Isle of Thanet', it was specifically Kentish in its references, and in her preface Lady Wallace speculates that the local nobility had urged its suppression. Although its anti-aristocratic sentiments were cause enough for Larpent to censor it, its complete suppression caused the author to cast care aside and declare in the printed preface her radical sympathies:

> If to feel contempt for profligacy, injustice, or deceit, even if detected in a palace; or, if to respect virtue, and integrity, even in the humble obscurity of the cottage, be deemed exceptionable, I plead guilty; for I exult in such opinions . . . Happy! thrice happy, had the French Nation been! had the press, or drama, permitted those who were disinterested in the cause of honour and humanity, to raise their voice, to reprobate or ridicule their [aristocrat's] vices . . . This reflection might have rescued them in time from vices, immoralities, and cruelties, which have finally hurled them from their fancied greatness, and deprived them of even the *Rights of Men!*

With reference to the powers of the Examiner himself, she compares the rigour applied to the stage with the licence allowed to political cartoons, and declares that 'the Stage is the only school which overgrown boys and girls can go to, and did the Licenser permit more satire, more sentiment, and less ribaldry, *outré* pantomime, it would be doing the State more service'.

The play itself is a carnivalesque comedy in which antiquarian Lord Crotchet is so enamoured of Roman nobility that he revives the Feast of Saturnalia and insists that his servants take control for the day.[40] When the servants hear of his whim to celebrate what they call 'Satin-Ally' they speculate on what they might do:

NELL. Lord how I should change the face of affairs! You know, we females make the best of kings . . .

FAG. I trust you'd make peace?

NELL. Oh that I would; I should have a fine glorious crop next year, for I'd convert all their swords into plough-shares.

FAG. Then the French would come and gather it; and I suppose, you'd surely untax us?

NELL. No:- taxes are necessary evils. But I'd tax all luxuries, gaming, men-milliners, men-servants, dogs and dollies, so completely, that every one should be able to pay for bread, even if twice as dear. I'd like to do like Queen Anne – I'd give all the money I could muster to relieve my people.

In the event the servants use their power for a day to make Crotchet agree to the marriage of his daughter to her beloved, and when the status quo is restored master and servants reflect on what they have learnt:

CROTCHET: Now I find what a judicious ceremony this was of the ancients. I am sure I shall be a better master for it, all my life, having learned, how painful it is for a British mind, however humble in fortune, to bend to any yoke, but that of reason

FAG. . . . I have found how apt one is, when in power, to abuse authority, and, amidst indulgences, to forget the hardships we impose.

NELL. Remember, as well as I do, a maxim which I learnt at Mrs Reform's school – Never to let a flaw be long of mending, least it get incurable – *a stitch in time saves nine.*

Presented at a time when England was at war with France, these Figaro-like reflections were quite unacceptable to the Licenser and had Lady Wallace been more conversant with Larpent's normal practice she would have realised it was not enough to conclude her play with a speech in praise of the British constitution, particularly when phrased with ironical reference to the French Estates:

I call your attention to the last speech in the Comedy. I leave you to judge, if it is not expressive of such respect for the British Constitution, as should prove acceptable to all mankind: . . .

CROTCHET. I for my part never again shall give up, even for a day, the duties of my situation; but ever endeavour to act worthily as a member of one of the three parts of our glorious constitution; who, I hope, will each for ages yet to come, discharge uncorruptibly, and distinctly, their several duties; without encroaching on each others prerogative; so that the name of Briton, may prove to the latest ages, an example to nations, and the Admiration of Mankind.

In the event Lady Wallace was so outraged by what she considered an unwarrantable infringement of liberty that she left for France, where she narrowly escaped arrest as an English spy, and ended up in Brussels befriended by the turncoat General Dumouriez.[41]

Before examining the strategies adopted by more level-headed radical sympathisers than Lady Wallace, James Borden's *The Secret Tribunal* provides an example of how direct condemnation of the French extremists could legitimately be made when Edwin Eyre's *Death of the Queen of France* was considered too specific. Presented at Covent Garden, 3 June 1795, Boaden's adaptation of a historical romance by the Swedish Count Skjödebrand set in the fifteenth century was a thinly disguised attack on the Revolutionary Tribunals, which were providing the guillotine its victims. As usual the prologue suggested the metaphorical application:

> When SUPERSTITION held her sanguine state
> And dealt at will the rapid blow of fate;
> The world beheld all pledge of *safety* gone,
>   [a possible reference to the Committee of Public Safety]
> And even MONARCHS TREMBLED ON THEIR THRONE.
> JUDGES, with functions unconfin'd and *free*,
> At midnight issued many a dark decree –
> The culprit ONCE CONDEMN'D – a numerous Band
> Of secret Agents, hunt him through the land.
>
> Britain rejoice! . . . Open as day our Courts judicial move,
> And RICH and POOR their equal influence prove.[42]

As a history play it was described by the *Morning Herald* as 'elucidating an Institution, which, by Secrecy and Certainty of its Judgements produced many alarming Events in the fifteenth Century, throughout the Germanic Empire'.[43] Herman is a member of the secret religious knighthood, which is sworn to uphold the feudal rights of the Holy Roman Empire, and discovers that Ratisbon is scheming to replace his brother as Duke of Wurtemberg. Ratisbon, aware of his danger, persuades the Knights to prosecute both

Herman and his beloved Ida. Ida's father describes what happens to those accused by the Tribunal, a fate uncommonly like that of those accused by the Jacobins:

> All accus'd
> When the first quarter after midnight tolls,
> Go to the centre of the market-place –
> Thence they are led before the Secret Judges.
> If guilty, they are never heard of more.

Ratisbon commands Ulrich, an agent of the tribunal, to seek out and kill Herman. The reluctant agent is much relieved when Herman, who is a close friend, reveals Ratisbon's treachery to him:

> 'Tis virtue now to disobey the mandate,
> Given by a murd'rer, who usurps the judge.

Ulrich teaches Herman the passwords to enter the Tribunal, disguised in his armour, so he can save Ida and confront the treacherous Ratisbon. Act 5 is set in a typical Gothic dungeon, but the decorations combine authentic medieval symbols with images associated with Freemasonry, which many believed had inspired the French Revolution.[44] Certainly the all-seeing eye was an emblem much used by the Jacobins and featured in the *Fêtes de l'Etre suprème*:

> Act 5: *The Scene represents a spacious Crypt, or vaulted Court of Justice, under ground, of Gothic Architecture – At the upper end is a luminous Cross of a deep red, and over this, surrounded by Clouds, an Eye, radiated with points of Fire. A Throne adorned with trophies in gold upon a ground of black velvet – the benches of the Judges the same.*

Having listened to the deliberations of the judges, masked by his visored helmet, Herman reveals himself, denounces Ratisbon and inspires the rightful Duke of Wurtemberg to disband the Tribunal.

We have already seen how Gothic tales and scenery were used to symbolise tyranny, and some of the persecuted radicals might well have compared the secret oppression to the Home Office's own use of spies and *agents provocateurs*, but, as if the Masonic symbols had not been enough, Boaden drives home his anti-Jacobin intentions in the epilogue:

> But are these institutions quite destroy'd?
> SECRET TRIBUNALS, are none employ'd?
> THOUSANDS. Yes, while we sink in soft repose,
> Our Judges eyes no gentle slumbers close:

> The HEART is the tribunal which we fear,
> For ever hid, and yet for ever near;
> Its AGENTS are the SENSES, and they gain
> Intelligence for that shrewd JUDGE the Brain.
> The mighty censure, carefully conceal'd
> Until that DOOM is fix'd lies unreveal'd.
> Lo! the PATRIOT, that, with ceaseless din,
> Clamours against his rival, who is IN;
> Who loads the land with ruin and disgrace,
> And paints the charms of REVOLUTION's face –
> What says the HEART to this? – He wants a PLACE.

Thus Boaden, well known to the radical circles, especially those working in the theatre, not only adopts the Enlightenment sentiment of trusting to the benevolence of fate and the innate generosity of the heart, but damns all politicians, including the radical Whigs along with the French Jacobins, with the traditional accusation that they are less motivated by principle than desire for office. This play is no less political than *The Death of the Queen of France*, but the strategy adopted got it past the Licenser. By using a metaphorical method there was little chance that large sections of the audience would take immediate offence at its disguised sentiments, but when experienced as a whole it efficiently instilled distrust of secret societies and inspired confidence in the impartiality of British justice.

If a fully scripted history play had to rely on such a metaphorical strategy to present political attitudes, it is not surprising that more conventionalised dramatic forms employed less precise imagery to address and appeal to audience anxiety. It has long been recognised that operas across Europe made particular use of the theme of liberation from incarceration in the years after the French Revolution. Although the earliest example of an 'escape opera', Grétry's *Richard Cœur de Lion*, libretto by Sedaine, dates from 1784 – reaching the London stage in two versions in 1786 – which shows that escaping was not an invention of post-Bastille writers. Indeed, as will be discussed in the next chapter, the dungeon was already a common feature of Gothic literature. However, plots centring on rescue and escape became particularly popular in the 1790s.[45] The major operas of Stephen Storace, the most talented English composer of the period, were all examples of the genre: *The Haunted Tower* (1789), *The Siege of Belgrade* (1791), *The Pirates* (1792) and *Lodoiska* (1794).[46] This last was particularly successful with a text by John Philip Kemble after Dejaure's libretto for Kreutzer's *opéra comique*, which had opened shortly after another version by Cherubini in Paris 1791. Both French *Lodoiskas* had been seen by Michael Kelly, who suggested the subject to his friend Storace. The action was set in Poland at an unspecified time of Tartar invasion. The villainous Baron Lovinski has imprisoned the beautiful Lodoiska in his castle. Her true love Count Floreski and his servant Varbel get lost in the woods but are found and befriended by the invading Tartars. The two men trick their way into the castle and confront Lovinski, who promptly imprisons them with Lodoiska and her father. Typically the villain, the personification of feudal tyranny, is driven by a confusion of passions: 'Love, Hatred, Jealousy, Ambition, Scorn and Fury, rack my distracted Brain and rend my Heart to Pieces – Wou'd I were dead myself.'[47] Only music can calm his ravings. Eventually, the Tartars attack and seize the tower, and, believing his prisoners dead, Lovinski throws himself into a hopeless battle. However, the generous Tartar leader Kora Khan has ordered that all prisoners should be spared. Brought before him, he expresses his own desire for Lodoiska, but when Floreski challenges Khan's 'Right of Conquest', the noble general gives them both their liberty. The opera finishes with a grand battle set in the burning castle.

This plot has no references as specific as in Boaden's *Secret Tribunal*, never mind Eyre's *Death of the Queen of France*, but, as might have been expected from the original 1791 Parisian versions, its metaphorical implications tend towards the radical. The tyrant lives in a feudal castle and the rescuers include a servant, who is rather more resourceful than his master, and a romantic troupe of 'noble savages'. However, although a radical reading is possible, the conventionality and generalising tendency of its popular form as entertainment suggests the audience response would have been one of equally generalised emotional pleasure, rather than the consciously political response demanded by the anti-revolutionary dramas of Eyre and Boaden.

But was it only the Licenser's censorship that prevented politically committed dramatists adopting a similar metaphorical strategy of presenting their radical principles in the guise of popular entertainment? Not really – the English Jacobins were too imbued with the spirit of rational Enlightenment to rely on irony and innuendo, and their ambitions were too serious to use popularist forms of non-literary entertainment, which was itself becoming increasingly reactionary as it became more blatantly patriotic.[48] They wanted to speak directly to their audience, and, as they were banned from publicly *advocating* radical politics, they use the traditional forms of social comedy to *demonstrate* how the principles of liberty, equality and fraternity might inform social behaviour.

CHAPTER 4

Dramatising (the) Terror

Politically motivated playwrights wish to influence the lives of their spectators – their understanding of material circumstances and their determination to change them – and therefore audiences must recognise their own lives in the life on stage. The historical plays that were the predominant new form of the 1790s tended to suggest that if the present resembles the past, then it is essentially unchangeable. The similarity was one of types rather than individuals – archetypes, to which present circumstances conformed, or stereotypes which transposed modern circumstance and character anachronistically into the past. In either case the result confirmed continuity and conformity. The playwrights who most sympathised with the radical objectives of the French – though massacres and judicial murders might shake their resolve – tried to depict their own society both accurately and critically. And the form best suited to this task was already to hand – the social comedy or comedy of manners. However, an examination of the plays performed at the established theatres, as listed in *The London Stage*, reveals that the production and success of new five-act comedies was rapidly declining,[1] Sheridan, having written two of the finest comedies of manners in the 1770s wrote no more. O'Keefe had written none since *Wild Oats* in 1790 and Hannah Cowley's *The Town Before You* barely lasted the 1794/5 season.

Richard Cumberland attempted nine comedies between 1794 and 1800, but seven closed after only a few performances. One of his successful plays, *The Wheel of Fortune* (Drury Lane, 28 February 1795), resembled Colman's only five-act comedy of the 1790s, *The Heir at Law* (Haymarket, 15 July 1796). Both revolved around unexpected inheritances, which thrust lower-class characters into positions of power. Colman's play was more of a farce of cross purposes than a satire of manners, and Cumberland's Penruddock, as played by

Kemble with 'studious and important preciseness',[2] was closer to a repentant villain than a classic comedy character. Both plays concluded with a thankful repudiation of the undeserved wealth, thus locating them in the movement towards 'the modern comedy of poverty and wealth'.[3] Penruddock declared: 'I have escaped the perils of prosperity . . . temperate recollection . . . has taught me to know that the true use of riches is to share them with the worthy'. (Act 5, scene 1). Although Thomas Morton and Frederick Reynolds each produced three or four comedies, they, like Cumberland's and Colman's, tended towards the domestic or rural melodrama of *John Bull* (Covent Garden, 5 March 1803). Morton's *Speed the Plough* (Covent Garden, 8 February 1800) was a splendidly successful example of 'mixed genre' comedy with Farmer Ashfield anticipating the Job Thornberry role, Sir Philip Blandford behaving like a Gothic villain and Able Handy fulfilling the only traditional comic role of an amiable scrape-grace. Reynolds never repeated the success of *The Dramatist* of 1788, and his *How to Grow Rich* (1793), *The Rage!* (1794), *Speculation* (1795) and *The Will* (1797), although fairly popular, also relied on mistaken identities and concern over the corrupting power of money. Most of these comedies 'realistically' depicted the concerns of their bourgeois audiences, but hardly in a critical or radical way. Their techniques were either farcical or sentimental, and, with the possible exception of Cumberland's *Wheel of Fortune*, tended to confirm rather than disturb social attitudes.

Radical intentions had always informed the work of the so-called English Jacobins, but they were silenced in the later 1790s by official censorship or public disapproval. Both Elizabeth Inchbald and Thomas Holcroft withdrew from writing drama and turned instead to novels, which escaped censorship by addressing the individual reader rather than publicly running the gauntlet of a patriotic audience. Inchbald's first loosely autobiographical novel, *A Simple Story*, was published in 1791, though written over several years, and has been described by Gary Kelly as 'pre-Jacobin' in that it centred on education. This is a theme that was developed in later novels by the 'Jacobins' Godwin and Holcroft, and was to dominate the writing of the 'feminists' Wollstonecraft, Edgeworth and Reeves.[4] In 1792 she started another more deliberately political novel, *Nature and Art*, which was completed in 1794, but, because of the persecution of radicals, not published until 1796. Both novels could be described as sentimental in that, after identifying moral and psychological issues related to social inequality and oppressive systems of education – especially of women – Inchbald tried to resolve them by the benevolence traditionally attributed to human nature by Enlightenment thinking. Here the English Jacobins differed from the French, who had learnt from bitter experience that progressive attitudes had to be imposed and defended by violent means. British intellectuals still believed in 'the system of rational optimism which had been seized on so zealously in the early 1790s, and which the English Jacobins hoped would advance humanity to the last age of moral, physical and social perfection'.[5]

But if there was an element of Pangloss in the optimism of English radical writers, the power of censorship meant they had to relinquish the theatre as a means of rational instruction. Inchbald submitted no plays for performance between November 1794, the month of Holcroft's treason trial, and March 1797. In 1791 she had adapted Mercier's *Jean Hennuyer, Evêque de Lizieux* (1772), set during the Bartholomew's Day Massacres, but now she updated it to the present. Entitled *The Massacre* and submitted to Harris and Colman during 1792, when the threat of greater massacres was looming in Paris, both managers prudently declined to send it to the Examiner.[6] As adapting French texts was becoming suspect for one of her sympathies, her next two plays were both original. *Every One Has His Fault* (Covent Garden, 29 January 1793), a five-act comedy, was produced in the week Louis XVI was executed. It was more psychological drama than social satire, although it contained sentiments reflecting on the heartlessness of the rich – 'We are savages to each other; nay worse – The savage makes his fellow savage welcome; divides with him his homely fare' (Act 2, scene 1) – and a reflection that crime was caused 'because Provisions are so scarce' (Act 1, scene 2). Most of the characters behave completely contrary to their own interests, and indeed their own deepest feelings. The devoted husband seeks a divorce, the divorcee tries to remarry, the father disowns his daughter but tries to keep his grandson, and each encourages the others in their perversity. That is except Mr Harmony, who, like a comic version of the benevolent Haswell in Inchbald's *Such Things Are* of 1787, tries to contrive a happy resolution by telling white lies. Although many of the situations are not new to social comedy, there is more than misunderstanding and cross purposes. Inchbald seems to imply the institution of marriage is itself absurd – 'Now Sir Robert, you have had the good nature to teach this husband how to get rid of his wife, will you have the goodness to teach me how to procure one?' – and that her characters are utterly confused by their own emotions – 'I cannot bear what I feel, and yet I am ashamed to own I feel anything.' There was little here to upset nationalist sensibilities, but there were serious echoes of the personal politics of her more critical novels.

Inchbald's last play before withdrawing from drama, *The Wedding Day* (Drury Lane, 1 November 1794), seems an innocuous farce, written to provide Dorothy Jordan with another of the ingenue roles that were her speciality. However, when considered alongside the criticism of education in her novels, the ingenues who appear in several Inchbald plays, may not have been quite as innocent as each might seem in isolation. Since her translation of *Zelie, ou l'Ingenue* by Madame de Genlis as *The Child of Nature* (Covent Garden, 28 November 1788), Inchbald had specialised in writing apparently innocent and ignorant young women whose lack of conventional education lets them make devastating comments on the hypocrisy of their supposed betters. According to Patricia Sigl, their naïveté reflected Inchbald's own lack of affectation, and she quotes Frances Ann Kemble's description: 'Mrs Inchbald had a singular uprightness and unworldliness, and a childlike directness and simplicity of manner.'[7] Directness and simplicity were not the conventional qualities expected of fashionable ladies in the 1780s, but they were becoming more prevalent and more acceptable female attributes during the turbulent 1790s. During the decade when France explored the full range of political conflict, England saw a no less radical exploration of personal identity, especially by women. Marjean Purinton claims the 'the revolution in women's manners . . . parallels the political upheavals of the French Revolution and its aftermath. Gender issues are conflated with the historical events of the period and so too become politicized.'[8] Perceptive and eloquent women were questioning established sexual attitudes, the most famous of which was Mary Wollstonecraft, whose conduct, conversation and philosophy all challenged traditional patterns of female behaviour.[9] Mary Hays' *Appeal to the Men of Great Britain on Behalf of Women* (1798) attacked the stereotypical characterisation, in both literature and life, of women as helpless and over emotional, and both Clara Reeve's *Plans for Education* (1792) and Maria Edgeworth's *Letters to Literary Ladies* (1795) argued for a reform of the way girls were brought up. Even conservative or politically uncommitted women novelists like Fanny Burney, Hannah More and Jane Austen gave their female characters such psychological depth and ironic intelligence that women readers were encouraged to develop their own independence of feeling and thought, leading them to rebel against the commodification of the female role in courtship, marriage and motherhood. Such issues may not have been openly debated in stage plays, or indeed in all novels, but the female presence was changing and becoming more confrontational. This will be discussed further in chapter 5 below, with reference to the stage presence of Sarah Siddons as the vengeful victim and Dorothy Jordan as the flirtatious ingenue, but for the moment the English Jacobin writers, Wollstonecraft, Inchbald, Godwin and Holcroft can be identified as arguing that education was the key to this personal emancipation. As political action, and even aspirations, became seemingly impossible in the face of anti-French patriotism, radical intellectuals turned their attention to the politics of personal liberty rather than the reform of national government.

Thomas Holcroft had, however, identified himself so closely with the movement for political reform that he was indicted with other members of the London Corresponding Society in 1793 for the sedition of undermining the constitution and the treason of assisting the enemy. As soon as he knew of the indictment, Holcroft presented himself before the Lord Chief Justice demanding an opportunity to prove his innocence. Part of his evidence was that his particular contribution to the discussions on reform held by the Society for Constitutional Information had been on 'The Powers of the Human Mind'. He had advocated, with Godwinian optimism, 'the more powerful operation of Philosophy and Reason to convince man of his errors; that he would disarm his greatest enemy by those means, and oppose his fury. – Spoke also about Truth being powerful.'[10] Even when imprisoned for his views, Holcroft stoutly maintained his belief in 'the power of Truth', and both his radicalism and his art were inspired by the ingenuous principle of enlightenment, that 'man is happy, in proportion as he is truly informed; that his ignorance, which is the parent of misery and vices, is not a fault, but a misfortune, which can only be remedied by infusing juster principles and more enlightened notions into his mind.'[11] Fear that a popular jury would not condemn the radicals, among whom Holcroft had been arrested,[12] led the authorities to drop the arraignment for treason. But being officially registered as an 'acquitted felon' caused a man of Holcroft's principle and probity as much distress as an unwarranted conviction. The irrationality of an incomplete prosecution disturbed his sense of logical causality as much as the extremes to which the French revolutionaries were forced. Although Holcroft never repudiated his belief in rational goodness, it would seem that neither France nor England had a place for such enlightenment in 1794. Certainly the theatre was closed to the ironic commentary and social sensibility that had typified Holcroft's *Road to Ruin* of 1792. However, he still hoped to make a living from the stage.

In 1794, *Love's Frailties* (translated from Otto von Gemmingen's *Der Deutsche Hausvater*, Covent Garden, 5 February 1794) received only six performances after some of the audience objected to the political sentiment: 'he was bred to the most useless, and often most worthless, of all professions, that of a gentleman'. Holcroft protested it was 'a sentence in itself so true as to have been repeated under a thousand different modes; and under a variety of forms and phraseology, to have been proverbial in all countries'.[13] It was not so much the sentiment that caused offence as the author who had presumed to write it so soon after being tried for treason. Like Inchbald, Holcroft turned to dramatising personal relationships rather than risk the damning of his criticism of the aristocratic class system, and the success of *The Deserted Daughter* (Covent Garden, 2 May 1795) marked a recovery in his reputation. Hazlitt considered it 'perhaps the best of Mr Holcroft's serious comedies,'[14] and it is indeed very serious. Mr Mordent's ignorance of his own best interests is potentially funny, but he is so impassioned against himself and the world for his mistake of not acknowledging an illegitimate daughter, a mistake that distresses his wife, his friends and his faithful servants, that the comedy is very dark indeed. Although intended as comically exaggerated, Mordent's principles are utterly bleak:

> None but fools condescend to live. Men exert their whole faculties to torture one another. Animals are the prey of animals. Flowers bloom to be plucked and perish. The very grass grows to be torn and eaten: trees to be mangled, sawed, rooted up, and burned. The whole is a system of exquisite misery, and I have my full proportion.
> (Act 1, scene 2)

Added to this domestic near-tragedy is the financial double-dealing that typified many of Holcroft's plays, so the whole play goes beyond the distresses of misunderstanding that motivated most 'sentimental comedies' into the realm of domestic melodrama. Gone is the benevolent rationalist of Holcroft's earlier plays, to be replaced as an agent of salvation by the incomprehensible bluster of a Scottish footman and the artless good humour of two young lads, the poor one of which is naïve, the rich one a clown. The happy outcome was no longer caused by beneficial providence or enlightened good sense, but by fortunate accidents of coincidence.

In her introduction to the 1808 *British Theatre* edition of the play Inchbald commented:

But when, by degrees, the fashionable world shall have become so philosophic in love, and concerning the rights of wedlock, that scarce any event in gallantry shall cause embarrassment on the score of refined sentiments, the resources of an author, in his profession, will then be nearly destroyed; for scrupulous purity of character, and refinement of sensations, are the delightful origin of all those passions, those powerful impulses of the mind, on which works of imagination are chiefly founded.[15]

Leading characters like Penruddock, Mordant and her own Sir Robert Ramble in *Every One Has His Fault* were not so much distressed by refined embarrassment as *alienated* in their circumstances and relationships by a lack of self-knowledge. Certainly, by 1795 the destructive passions of loveless marriages, social envy and material greed were becoming too prevalent to be satisfactorily addressed by fashionable refinement and witty repartee, and new dramatic forms were replacing traditional comedy – of both manners and sentiment. Most, like farce, musical comedy and spectacular pantomime, were of a less demanding, less disturbing, genre, but others, like history plays, the Gothic romance and ultimately melodrama, gave greater scope for extravagant passion and aberrant behaviour.

We have seen how political concerns had encouraged the composition of historical dramas, loosely based on the 'mixed genre' of Shakespeare's histories, and in the last chapter Boaden's *Secret Tribunal* was cited as having to adopt the distancing technique of a historical parallel to dramatise the terrorist tactics of the Revolutionary Tribunal. But it was perhaps just as important for the theatre to address the emotion of terror itself as to depict the political machinery that was being invented in France. A social comedy like *The Deserted Daughter* could evoke anxiety and personal feelings of guilt, but its conventions were inappropriate for exploring, or exploiting, the panic induced by the ruthless seizure and speedy public execution of apparently innocent citizens in the names of Security and Virtue. Boaden's *Secret Tribunal* and Inchbald's *Massacre* had identified historical examples of institutionalised murder, but their very specificity failed to evoke the emotional identification that was the particular concern of the 'Gothic'. Although set in the past, Gothic romances did not dramatise specific historical events. They used antiquarian settings to provide a mysterious context for supernatural visitations and 'unnatural' behaviour. Although Gothic novels predate the Revolutionary era,[16] their popularity boomed with Ann Radcliffe's best-selling *The Mysteries of Udolpho* (1794) and Matthew Lewis' scandalous *The Monk* (1796).

The earlier works originated in dissatisfaction with both the realism of Fielding and the sentimentality of Richardson; as Walpole put it, 'I was so tired of sets of people getting together, and saying "Pray, Miss, with whom are you in love?"'[17] They turned instead to the Romance tradition of the Middle Ages, which was currently being researched by antiquarian scholars, as in Bishop Hurd's *Letters on Chivalry and Romance* (1762), and theorised in Burke's *Enquiry into the Origin of Our Ideas of the Sublime and the Beautiful* (1756). Burke argued that sublimity differed from harmonious beauty by inspiring a passionate response, and that, as pain is a stronger passion than pleasure, the most sublime emotions are astonishment and terror. These emotions were seldom found in the social drama of earlier novels or in comedies of manners, but Gothic novels could inspire terror with lowering landscapes, ghostly apparitions, mysterious ruins and the unnatural perversions of their villains. These were usually representative of feudal power: the *seigneur* of an ancient castle or abbot of a secluded monastery. In either case their strongholds contained vaults and dungeons in which innocent victims were incarcerated, tortured and raped. The symbolism of the dungeon in history plays has already been associated with the feudal fortress of the Bastille, but in Gothic romances the oppression was more psychological than political, threatening individual victims – young women or aged parents. But although authors explored the extravagant emotions of victims and the aberrant psychology of villains primarily as individuals, the narrative pattern of oppression and escape was also open to a political reading.[18] Thus the extraordinary burst of popularity for the Gothic in the 1790s suggests a correlation between individual artistic angst and the social stresses of Revolutionary politics.[19] Robert Miles describes how even the semiological significance of the Gothic dungeon changed over a few years:

The Bastille was typically figured as an instrument of Gothic live burial – it was a 'cemetery of the living'. In Gothic romances representations of institutional oppression, such as the Inquisition, resonate with the Bastille imagery generated by the prison literature . . . By 1792 such representation would have acquired a seditious edge: it could be read as implicit support for the Revolution, for it was, after all, the Jacobin's own reading of the Bastille. By 1797 it would be idiosyncratic. The prisons of the Terror had by this time erased the image of the Bastille in the European mind, replacing it with the image of another kind of nightmarish enclosure. In Germany, in particular, the claustrophobic spaces of torture and confusion were now the Jacobinical cells of the Illuminati, often figured as crypts or caves.[20]

By the 1790s Gothic romances drew on more than the English models of Walpole and Burke. Beckford's *Vathek* of 1786 was originally written in French and was informed both by his own study of the Orient and knowledge of French literature.[21] Matthew Lewis too was a fluent linguist and began *The Monk* while on diplomatic duty in Weimar in 1792, where he met Goethe and discovered *Sturm und Drang* literature, with its evocation of mythology and self-destructive passions. He probably started translating Schiller's *Kabale und Liebe* at this time, though it was not published until 1797.[22]

Although Walpole had created a rapacious villain in the *Castle of Otranto* and an incestuous one in his unperformable play *The Mysterious Mother* (1768), the English tradition of the Gothic novel, particularly as developed by the female writers Clara Reeve, Charlotte Smith and Ann Radcliffe, was characterised by complicated plots contrived to produce situations of terror for the victims rather than the exploration of the villains' psychological perversities. Keily's disparaging description of *The Castle of Otranto* could be applied to most of them: 'Apart from the exhausting rate at which the characters are made to dash about the castle, there is a disturbing lack of focus on any single person or event. The plot is part obstacle course, part free-for-all, and part relay race in which the participants run through a cluttered labyrinth passing the baton to whomever they meet.'[23] Miles defines the difference between Radcliffe's novels written in the late 1780s and Lewis' German-inspired *Monk* of 1796 more precisely, separating

Radcliffe's 'female Gothic' from the German *Schauerroman* (literally shudder-novel). In the first, extreme violence is only threatened. In the second, it is delivered in spades (as good an example as any is the scene in

Lewis' *The Monk*, where Agnes awakes in the convent crypt with the putrefying body of her dead baby, whilst in earshot of the monk Ambrosio raping and murdering his sister) . . . [Thus] it is wrong to imagine Radcliffe writing in coy opposition to the infamous but popular 'shudder-novels', for the simple reason that such novels did not appear in English (if anywhere) until 1794 at the earliest.[24]

This emergence of a more desperate and disturbing form of the Gothic occurred after the initial years of the French Revolution. No longer was the effect one of titillating terror of what might be round the corner, but of horror at actual torture, rape and murder, a horror verging on the pornographic and blasphemous. No wonder the Marquis de Sade declared *The Monk* was his favourite contemporary novel, or, indeed that he claimed that the novels of both Radcliffe and Lewis were 'the necessary fruit of the revolutionary tremors felt by the whole of Europe'.[25] De Sade's own work was not yet published in England but Lewis may possibly have read him in French – though not before embarking on *The Monk*. Both de Sade and the Gothic employed a symbolic individualisation and internalisation of fear, oppression and constriction associated with the obscurantic tyranny of the past.

Ronald Paulson identifies another ideological shift between Walpole's novel and Lewis', which he attributes directly to the influence of the Revolution: '*The Monk* is about the act of liberation [Ambrosio's insane, uncontrolled rush into freedom], whereas *The Castle of Otranto* was about a man's attempt to hold together his crumbling estate and cheat others of their rightful inheritance. One is a fable of revolution, the other of the *ancien régime*.'[26] Jeffrey Cox also argues that the attraction of the Gothic villain reflected ideological as well as psychological ambiguities:

We are drawn to the villain, his mysterious milieu, and the power granted him by his position and his heroic hauteur. We are invited to admire these oppressors, for they embody the possibility of an individual revolt counter to the communal liberation celebrated in hymeneal union and uncovered social identities. Shadowing the ideology of liberation is the ideology of the isolated rebel, the suggestion that true liberty lies not in the social rejuvenation captured by comedy and romance but in the isolated pursuit of the individual's fears and desires tracked by tragedy.[27]

However, while novels were capable of dissecting psychology and expounding moral implications, the plays developed in the same mode tended to display situations of terror and embody images of depravity in a more unmediated form, contrasting them violently with joyful scenes of last-minute escape and rhetorical denunciations from paragons of virtue.

Not only was the Gothic drama a 'mixed genre', but the mixture was so extreme and extraordinary that it is difficult to interpret from the texts alone the overall effect or meaning of its performance. As Robert Miles comments,

Gothic texts of the 1790s in a certain respect resemble those visual puzzles where, for instance, a picture looked at in one manner produces a vase, in another, two faces in profile. Representations of profligate European aristocrats or Inquisitional dungeons could be seen as patriotic British attacks on the lamentable state of manners and society across the channel; or they could be seen as coded assaults on aristocracy and institutional despotism everywhere.[28]

As I have argued from the start, the ideological implications of a performance cannot be identified solely by considering the intentions of the author. In the case of Matthew Lewis, the contradictions of liberal sentiment, perverse indulgence and fervid imagination could be attributed solely to his youth and sexual confusion – all his Gothic works were written between the ages of fourteen and twenty-one[29] – but, by elaborating on fashionable models and pushing them to logical extremes, he concretised in fantastic form a wide range of popular anxieties. Perhaps Cox's judicious conclusion, after considering how different critics have read spiritual, psychological and political meanings into the Gothic iconography, that the form embodied 'the rhythms of the Revolution',[30] is the safest, in that, unlike the novels with their mediating authorial voice, the plays enacted the escape from enclosure to open air, from darkness to light, and from the past into the future as a *ritual* of liberation. This ritualistic journey demands interpretation because the actualities of castle, dungeon, long-lost relatives and supernatural visitations are so obviously fantastical that metaphorical readings are the only satisfying ones.

Lewis' quintessential Gothic drama, *The Castle Spectre*, was performed at Drury Lane on 14 December 1797.[31] It was one of the most popular productions of the 1790s, receiving forty-seven performances in its first season and remaining in the repertoire well into the nineteenth century. Although the theatre management warned Lewis against staging a ghost, he – and the theatre technicians – succeeded in creating an apparition so effective that James Boaden, whose *Fontainville Forest* had brought a ghost on stage in 1794,[32] could recall years later 'the waving form of Mrs Powell, advancing from the suddenly illuminated chapel, and bending over Angela (Mrs Jordan) in maternal benediction; during which slow and solemn action, the band played a few bars [of] unearthly music'.[33] The plot is a classic of the genre; Reginald and his wife Evelina have been murdered by his malevolent brother Osmond, who is now seeking to win the affection of their daughter, Angela, imprisoned in the castle. Angela's true love, Percy, Earl of Northumberland, disguised as a peasant, gains access to the castle with the aid of his foolish servant Motley, the gluttonous Friar Philip and Angela's old nurse Alice. Hidden in a suit of armour, he overhears the villain's threats but is overpowered by Osmond's agent Kendric and his black servants. He escapes by leaping from a window into a boat below. Meanwhile Angela has learnt of the survival of her father Reginald, who has been kept alive by Kendric, ashamed of his involvement in Osmond's usurpation. By means of secret passages within the walls of the castle, Angela is reunited with her father, and when Osmond enters the secret dungeon, she stabs him to the heart, just as Percy arrives with a band of soldiers.

Actually this plot needed no assistance from the ghost of Evelina, who first appeared to bless her daughter, except that her second appearance halted Osmond in his tracks with his sword raised, thus giving Angela time to thrust her dagger home. That a innocent maiden, rather than her lover, avenged her own oppression is the more significant stroke of originality, suggesting the influence of Wollstonecraft as well as the model of Charlotte Corday.[34] For the rest, Lewis acknowledged his debt to existing stereotypes: 'To originality of character I make no pretence. Persecuted heroines and conscience-stricken villains certainly have made their courtsies and bows to a British public long before . . . And Percy is a mighty pretty-behaved young gentleman with nearly no character at all.'[35] That the nominal hero was apparently so innocuous, indeed incompetent, as to fail in all his attempts to defeat the villain (despite an athletic piece of business when Kemble leapt from the castle window), may reflect either Lewis' personal sense of adolescent impotence, or the nation's sense of frustration in failing to make peace with France at Lille (September 1797), when Bonaparte's Italian victories had forced the withdrawal of Austria from the alliance at Campo-Formio in October. Such a precise metaphorical application is probably absurd, but Larpent recognised several political references to strike out, though he left a surprising number of controversial passages unexpunged.[36] One that was left in was seized on by the critics and led Lewis to comment on the readiness of people to read politics into every line. Motley remarks (Act 3, scene 2): 'The Courtier [fishes] for titles which are absurd', and Lewis noted that 'On the strength of this single sentence, it was boldly asserted . . . that the whole Play was written to support the Cause of Equality.'[37] It was not just this line that provoked the accusation, but the widespread assumption that the whole Gothic fashion owed too much to German and French models, assumed to be advocating democracy, atheism and sexual immorality. Certainly Coleridge later described such Gothic plays as 'the modern jacobinical drama' which intended 'a subversion of the natural order of things'.[38]

The most intentional political element in the play is also the most incongruous: the characterisation of Osmond's servants as Negro slaves. We have already noted how anti-slave trade polemics avoided the censor's pencil, and Lewis, the son of a wealthy West Indian planter, deliberately inserted a sympathetic explanation for the brutal behaviour of the black henchmen:

HASSAN. European gratitude? – Seek constancy in the winds – fire in ice – darkness in the blaze of sun-shine! – but seek not gratitude in the breast of an European!
SAID. Then, why so attached to Osmond? For what do you value him?
HASSAN. Not for his virtues, but for his vices, Saib: Can there for me be a great cause to love him? – Am not I branded with scorn? – Am I not marked out for dishonour? – Was I not free, and am I not a slave? – Was I not once beloved, and am I not now despised? – What man, did I tender my service, would accept the negro's friendship? – What woman, did I talk of affection, would not turn from the negro with disgust? – Yet in my own dear land, my friendship was courted, my love was returned. – I had parents, children, wife! . . . Attached to Osmond, say you? Saib, I hate him! Yet viewing him as an avenging Fiend sent here to torment his fellows, it glads me that he fills his office so well! (Act 4, scene 1)

This perversion of emotion into hatred when love is given no scope for expression, is in itself typical of the greater Gothic villains, who, according to Cox's analysis of Mortimer in Francis North's *The Kentish Barons* (Haymarket, 25 June 1791), having 'no outlet for his love or his hate . . . finds his emotions "more deeply rooted by reflection," by the dangerous inward turn to self-consciousness that is found throughout the gothic and romantic drama.'[39]

We have already noticed a tendency for introspection in the later comedies of Inchbald and Holcroft, a sense of identity being lost as dynamic political imperatives were disappointed or thwarted. In Gothic drama such introspection is a sign of evil, a suggestion that those who nurture alternatives to straightforward common sense are dangerous and subversive. But Hassan's anguished reaction to oppression suggested that 'deep rooted reflexivity' could destroy even the innocent, and in his monodrama *The Captive* (Covent Garden, 22 March 1802), Lewis demonstrated that while frustrated affection did not inevitably engender dreams of vengeance, it could lead to the insanity of complete alienation. Paulson describes *The Captive* as radical in contrast to the Burkean paranoia implicit in *The Castle Spectre*, as it concentrates on the oppression of an incarcerated wife, rather than on any Faustian ambitions of her oppressive husband.[40] However the ritual dynamic of liberation is similar to Lewis' other plays, only intensified by focusing on a single protagonist.

The scene is a typical dungeon, but located in a modern 'private madhouse', where the Captive has been incarcerated by her husband. In six eight-line verses that comprise the text we are told little of why she is here:

> A tyrant husband forged the tale,
>   Which chains me in this dreary cell . . .
>   What? I, the child of rank and wealth,
> Am I the wretch who clanks this chain,
>   Bereft of freedom, friends and health?[41]

These hints prompted spectators to associate the scene with the stories regularly found in feminist literature of wives whom husbands had registered insane in order to gain legal access to the jointures bestowed on them by their parents as a resource for their widowhood. The classic example was Mary Wollstonecraft's *Maria; or, The Wrongs of Woman*, published posthumously in 1798, which was the probable inspiration of Lewis' play, although Maria, far from going mad, escapes from her wrongful incarceration and achieves an ideological liberation. The political motive for writing the novel was, according to its author, 'the desire of exhibiting the misery and oppression, peculiar to women, that arise out of the partial laws and customs of society'.[42] Such an example validated *The Captive*'s bringing Gothic fantasy into a contemporary context, though, rather than a social drama, the monodrama was conceived as a miniature tragedy. It was written in verse and contained the typical Gothic elements of a cruel gaoler, an escaped lunatic who rattles at the bars of the Captive's cell, and a supernatural vision, though this is seen only by the Captive as she finally goes mad:

> I *am* not mad . . . but soon *shall* be!
> Yes! Soon! – For Lo you! . . . while I speak . . .
> Mark how yon Daemon's eye-balls glare! –
> He sees me! – Now with dreadful shriek
> He whirls a scorpion high in air! –
> Horror! – the Reptile strikes his tooth
> Deep in my heart so crush'd and sad! –
> Aye, laugh, ye Fiends! – I feel the truth!
> Your task is done! – [*With a loud shriek*] I'm mad! I'm mad!

This unprecedented intrusion of Gothic horror into a modern setting had an equally unprecedented effect on its audience, especially the women for whom the performance seemed a concrete realisation of their own worst nightmares, for many 'normal' marriages of the time could well be described as dungeons for the wives entrapped by their arranged betrothal to loveless partners, who completely controlled their property and their conduct:

Mrs Litchfield recited the monodrama in the most perfect manner; and gave to the performance all the effect of fine acting. Her character was that of a maniac, and her embodiment of the author's horrible imaginings, combined with the scenic effect, and other startling appearances, which with his usual skill he introduced into the piece, threw a portion of the audience, whose nerves were unable to withstand the dreadful truth and horror of the scene, into hysterics, and the whole theatre into confusion and horror. To judge from the appearance of the house, it might have been imagined that instead of the representation of a maniac, one of Lewis' 'gibbering ghosts' had favoured the stage with a visit *in propria persona*. Never did Covent Garden present such a picture of agitation and dismay. Ladies bathed in tears – others fainting – and some shrieking with terror – while such of the audience as were able to avoid demonstrations like these sat aghast with pale horror painted on their countenances. It is said, that the very box keepers took fright, less perhaps at the occurrences on the stage than at the state of the theatre; and such was the general confusion that a few were ignorant that the piece had really been performed throughout.[43]

It was never performed again, except as a solo recitation, but the remarkable power of this brief monodrama demonstrates how closely the Gothic approached sensitive pressure points, and how necessary were the distancing devices of historicisation and the alienation effects (to adopt Brecht's use of the term) of 'comic relief' and 'musical interludes' that were normally included in full length dramas.

A major contribution to the sensational power of *The Captive* was contained in the stage directions, which specified in more detail than any earlier text the lighting effects, musical accompaniment and 'naturalistic' sounds of chains, creaking hinges, shot bolts and echoing footsteps. These noises would have been made backstage as scenery was still constructed from wood and canvas and generally relied for its effectiveness on illusionistic painting. Just how naturalistic the lighting could have been is problematic, as the front of house could only be partially dimmed by raising the chandeliers into the roof-space, but Lewis suggests an intriguing effect as the gaoler leaves the cell:

> *The bars are heard replacing –*
> CAPTIVE. He smiles in scorn! – He turns the key!
>   He quits the grate! – I knelt in vain!
>   Still – still, his glimmering lamp I see.
> *Music expressing the light growing fainter, as the* GAOLER *retires through the gallery.*

Such a combination of visual and aural effects were more often employed in such spectacular moments as the supernatural apparition of Elvira's ghost in *The Castle Spectre*:

> *The folding-doors unclose, and the Oratory is seen illuminated. In its centre stands a tall female figure, her white and flowing garments spotted with blood; her veil is thrown back, and discovers a pale and melancholy countenance; her eyes are lifted upwards, her arms extended towards heaven, and a large wound appears on her bosom.* ANGELA *sinks upon her knees, with her eyes riveted upon the figure, which for some moments remains motionless. At length the* SPECTRE *advances* ANGELA, *seems to invoke a blessing upon her, points to the picture and retires to the Oratory. The music ceases.* ANGELA *rises with a wild look, and follows the Vision, extending her arms towards it.*
> ANGELA. Stop, stay, lovely spirit! – Oh! stay yet one moment!
> *The* SPECTRE *waves her hand, as bidding farewell. Instantly the organ's swell is heard; a full chorus of female voices chaunt 'Jubilate', a blaze of light flashes through the Oratory, and the folding doors close with a loud noise.*
> ANGELA. Oh! God of Heaven protect me!
> *She falls motionless on the floor.*

With such spectacular scenes combining the attractions of atmospheric scenery and supernatural magic, hitherto restricted to the artificial conventions of pantomime, with the emotional intensity of a terror-inducing narrative, it is not surprising that two theatrical masters, playwright George Colman and singer-composer Michael Kelly, joined forces for yet another hybrid genre – the 'Gothic opera'. Their *Blue Beard* of 1798 turned to the Orient of Beckford rather than the Middle Ages of Walpole and Lewis. Although the story came from Perrault's collection of fairytales published a hundred years before, the immediate source was the opera *Barbe bleu* by Gréty produced in 1789 and seen by Kelly in Paris. Colman and Kelly relied not only on the supernatural effects popularised by Lewis, but on the interest stirred up by Bonaparte's military expedition to Egypt, and on the continuing potency of the escape metaphor – in this case from the harem of a wife murderer – which, like *The Captive*, combined resonances of sexual oppression and political terror. It could even be argued that the megalomania of the oriental despot anticipated the apparent omnipotence of General Bonaparte, for although in 1798 his victories were as yet restricted to Italy, the Egyptian adventure suggested an extraordinary personal ambition. Certainly when the opera was revived in 1811, in an even more spectacular hippodramatic version, the parallel between the evil Abomelique and the French emperor was increasingly appropriate.

Colman claimed he wrote the piece as a substitute for a Christmas pantomime,[44] but its phenomenal success did not depend upon the comedy, charm and scenic display of the traditional harlequinade. According to Barry Sutcliffe, 'Colman had written something totally alien, a gothic fantasy, using scenery to heighten its blood-chilling horror.'[45] Early in the drama the despotism of the Turkish bashaw, Abomelique, is challenged by Selim, played and sung by Kelly, when his beloved Fatima is dragged away: 'When power is respected its basis must be justice. 'Tis an edifice that gives the humble shelter, and they reverence it. But 'tis a hated, shallow fabric that rears itself upon oppression. The breath of the discontented swells into a gale around it, till it totters' (Act 1 scene 1). Had this speech been written in 1790 it would have been related to the *ancien régime*, but by 1798 it is contrasting British justice, deemed to have a solid basis, with the 'shallow fabric' of French legislation based on the oppression of terror. Indeed Abomelique justifies his practice of beheading his wives just as the Jacobins had argued that the Terror was necessary for self-protection: 'Such punishment might outrun even Turkish justice. But in me 'tis prudence, self-preservation' (Act I scene 3). Soon it appears that Abomelique is not just a tyrant to his subjects, but has contrived a horrendous Blue Chamber which, once the 'forbidden door' is unlocked, is transformed from a voluptuary's boudoir into a combination of torture chamber and charnel house:

> SHACABAC *puts the key into the lock. The door instantly sinks, with a tremendous crash, and the Blue Chamber appears, streaked with vivid streams of blood. The figures in the picture over the door change their position, and* ABOMELIQUE *is represented in the action of beheading the beauty he was before supplicating. The pictures and devices of love change to subjects of horror and death. The interior apartment – which the sinking of the door discovers – exhibits various tombs in a sepulchral building, in the midst of which ghastly and supernatural forms are seen, some in motion, some fixed. In the centre is a large skeleton seated on a tomb, with a dart in his hand, smiling, and over his head, in characters of blood, is written*: 'THE PUNISHMENT OF CURIOSITY'. (Act I, scene 2)

No doubt it was an unintentional irony that the tyrant was played by John Palmer, who had been prosecuted for speaking in prose at the Royal Circus in 1789, when he delivered Henry Dubois' oration on the fall of the Bastille.[46] In that play the dungeon had been occupied by the skeleton of a victim entrapped in an iron mask, but now the skeleton is Blue Beard's demonic servant/master:

> Demon of blood, death's courier, whose sport it is to sound war's clarion, to whet the knife of the suicide, to lead the hired murderer to the sleeping babe, and, with a ghastly smile of triumph, to register the slaughtered who prematurely drop in Nature's charnel-house, here, here I have pent thee, a prisoner to my art, here to circumscribe thy general purposes for my particular good. (Act I scene 4)

That the once theatrical 'revolutionary' John Palmer had been thus transformed into a sadistic monster is itself a suggestive metaphor for the transformation that had taken place in theatrical representations of unorthodox and alien ideologies. Similarly, the noble Tartars who had overthrown the oppressor's castle in Storace's *Lodoiska* were now transformed, as an image of oriental Otherness, into barbaric Turks, whose Islamic marriage customs were depicted as cruel imprisonment with death the 'punishment for curiosity'.

Blue Beard was, of course, like *Lodoiska*, a 'popular entertainment' and as such made no claim to an ideological stance, but like many 'innocuous' cultural productions it revealed a deep distrust of foreigners and tyrants – and women, whose curiosity violated the forbidden Blue Chamber of male ascendancy. Unlike *The Captive*, which had terrified women by its realistic images of oppression, the pantomime conventions of the fairytale defused some of its immediate relevance as drama. So too did the jokes of Abomelique's terrified henchman Shacabac, but, as they were mostly about gossiping wives and feminine perversity, they conform to the reactionary perspective of the play as a whole. Compared to the conservative Kemble and Storace, whose *Lodoiska* contained potential Revolutionary metaphors, neither Colman nor Kelly were particularly reactionary – Colman had attempted on many occasions to subvert repressive theatre regulations and Kelly continued to visit Paris after the Revolution.[47] But, to make *Blue Beard* appeal to popular taste they used Gothic conventions to depict the politically and culturally Other as dangerously attractive, and for this they employed images, if not arguments, that were chauvinist and reactionary.

However not all playwrights were as ideologically myopic as the professional showmen, and the conventions of Gothic drama could occasionally be used with a consciously subversive intent. But, because managers believed they best understood the taste of the town, such plays had little chance of actually being staged. Towards the end of 1797 William Wordsworth's *The Borderers* was rejected by Thomas Harris of Covent Garden. Later the poet declared he was not disappointed when 'the piece was *judiciously* returned as not calculated for the Stage. In this judgement I entirely concurred.'[48] He did not publish the play until 1842, so it can have had little influence on plays that were actually performed. But, because of Wordsworth's literary reputation, it has been the subject of considerable critical interpretation, and much that has been written of *The Borderers* is relevant to other Gothic plays, particularly as the French Revolution was a major subtext of the play. For many years after its publication opinion tended to follow manager Harris' view that it was unstageworthy. Indeed, it is clumsy when compared with other theatrically successful historical dramas. The plot line gets lost in philosophical reflections, the motivation is based on implausible credulity, and, worst of all for performance, the narration of past history destroys the pace of present action. The Romantic poets tended to scorn such criticism, arguing that the same could be said of Shakespeare's plays which, in a nicely ironical comment, Charles Lamb described as 'less calculated for performance on a stage, than those of almost any other dramatist'.[49] Until the 1960s critics argued that the Romantic poets' plays shared the self-reflectivity of their lyrical verse, and were thus correctly described by Byron as 'mental theatre' whose only effective stage is the reader's imagination.[50]

However, if Wordsworth did not adopt the existing stage practice of ghostly visions, comic relief and happy endings, his play borrowed several images from popular historical romance: ruins, dungeons and wild mountains with the freebooting Borderers as a kind of *banditti*. However, one feature of the play not found in the theatrical repertoire is the complexity of the hero's behaviour and motivation, which has led to the play's being described as a introverted 'mono-drama'.[51] Set in the reign of Henry III, Mortimer (renamed Marmaduke in the published edition of 1842) is persuaded by Rivers (Oswald[52]) that his beloved Matilda (Idonea) has been 'sold' by her father, Baron Herbert, to the lecherous Lord Clifford, despite her having been Herbert's sole companion and guide since he lost his sight during the Crusades. Although Mortimer's gullibility resembles Othello's, Rivers' malignity is not as motiveless as Iago's. Alan Richardson argues that Rivers leads the young naïve Mortimer to commit a crime similar to the one that poisoned his own conscience years before – he deserted the captain of the ship taking him to the Holy Land – from a combination of psychological compulsion, Satanic temptation and misguided philosophy. Wordsworth himself described how guilt and remorse had corrupted Rivers:

A young man of great intellectual powers, yet without any solid principles of genuine benevolence, has deeply imbibed a spirit of enterprise in an tumultuous age. He goes into the world and is betrayed into a great crime . . . his reason is almost exclusively employed in justifying his past enormities and enabling him to commit new ones . . . [imagining] possible forms of society where his crimes would no longer be crimes . . . every fresh step appears a justification of the one which preceded it, it seems to bring again the moment of liberty and choice; it banishes the idea of repentance, and seems to set remorse at defiance.[53]

Richardson expounds how this sense of fallacious 'liberty' actually enslaves Rivers to despair, compelling him to seduce the morally superior Mortimer, in whom he recognises his earlier innocent self, into the same destructive self-knowledge by committing the same crime: 'He cannot imagine their separation. His youthful crime, rather than liberating him, began by determining his character and actions. Now he binds himself in turn to a living mirror image, one that ultimately reflects only his incompleteness.'[54] A similar analysis could be applied to many Gothic villains, from Lewis' Osmond to Baillie's de Monfort, Godwin's Mortimer and Shelley's Cenci. But, unlike the typical Gothic hero, Wordsworth's Mortimer succumbs to the villain's plot and is himself infected with the canker of remorse after deserting the innocent, old and blind Herbert to the mercy of the moorlands. As he becomes aware of his own crime, it is like Adam's fall into self-knowledge:

> in plumbing the abyss for judgement,
> Something I strike upon which turns my mind
> Back on herself, I think, again – my breast
> Concentrates all the terror of the Universe.   (Act 2, scene 3)

Crime leads to self-analysis, self-analysis leads to crime, and both open up an abyss of existential void. Unlike the popular historical romances, which end in reconciliation and forgiveness, Mortimer repeats the destructive pattern of Rivers' behaviour. He tricks Matilda into cursing her father's murderer before revealing that he himself left the old man to die. He thus forces her to condemn him to the life of an outcast, like the Ancient Mariner or Wandering Jew:

Critical opinion divides at this point, some readers impressed by the hero's remorse and endurance, others by his anguish and isolation. Though Marmaduke [Mortimer]'s prospects are undeniably bleak, I would argue that the ending is left intentionally open, and reflects the unresolved conflicts underlying the composition of the drama.[55]

Richardson's suggestion of a bleak disillusionment being the result of Mortimer's misguided attempt to take justice into his own hands and to overthrow the supposed tyranny of Baron Herbert, certainly coincides with my own cultural analysis of the dismay and bewilderment that beset British intellectuals at the Revolution's descent from Enlightenment into Terror.

Most commentators have identified Wordsworth's disappointment in the 'dawn' of 1789 as the impetus behind *The Borderers*, and he himself wrote that it echoed 'reflections I had been led to make during the time I was witness to the changes through which the French Revolution passed'.[56] More precisely the evil sophistry of

Rivers can be identified with that of Robespierre in France and William Godwin in England. A similar perception of Robespierre as a flawed saviour can be seen in a play written a couple of years before *The Borderers* by Wordsworth's younger companions, Southey and Coleridge, who in 1794, while still at Cambridge, wrote *The Fall of Robespierre*, which was no more likely to have been performed than Eyre's *Death of the Queen of France* (discussed in the last chapter). In the dedication Coleridge described it as

A Dramatic poem, in which I have endeavoured to detail, in an interesting form, the fall of a man, whose great bad actions have cast a disastrous lustre on his name . . . it has been my sole aim to imitate the empassioned and highly figurative language of the French orators, and to develop the characters of the chief actors on a vast stage of horrors.[57]

At this time the two authors had not yet abandoned republicanism, and were exploring the concept of a 'Pantisocracy', which would avoid both the deadly traditions of Burke's Briton and the cruel abstractions of Jacobin France. Their Robespierre was an ascetic hypocrite:

> ROBESPIERRE JUNIOR. If all forsake thee – what remains?
> ROBESPIERRE. Myself! the steel-strong Rectitude of soul
>   The giant Victories my counsel form'd
>   Shall stalk around me with sun-glittering plumes,
>   Bidding the darts of calumny fall pointless.
>   [*Exeunt caeteri. Manet* COUTHON
> COUTHON (*solus*). So we deceive ourselves! What goodly virtues
>   Bloom in the poisonous branches of ambition!
>   Still, Robespierre! thou'll guard thy country's freedom
>   To despotise in all the patriot's pomp.

The play ends with a peroration from Barrère in support of the coup of Thermidor, rallying France against the 'leagued despots' that still threatened her, despite the fact that:

> In the goodly soil
> Of Freedom, the foul tree of treason struck
> Its deep-fix'd roots, and dropt the dews of death
> On all who slumber'd in its specious shade.[58]

Later in the same year Southey's *Wat Tyler* addressed the Peasants' Revolt which had caused Cumberland such trouble with the Licenser, but, as a twenty-year-old undergraduate, Southey expected nothing more ambitious than a private reading in his rooms. Coleridge, however, redrew their portrait of Robespierre along the

lines of Wordsworth's Rivers in *Osorio*, which he submitted unsuc-
cessfully to Sheridan in 1797. This villain cultivates a moral image
but is inwardly rotten. He arranges for the assassination of his
brother, after poisoning his mind against the wife whom Osorio now
hopes to win for himself. Coleridge's description of Osorio could
equally be applied to his earlier Robespierre: 'a man, who, from his
childhood had mistaken constitutional abstinancy from vice for
strength of character – through his pride duped into guilt, and then
endeavouring to shield himself from the reproaches of his own mind
by misanthropy'.[59] And just as this echoes Wordsworth's notes on
The Borderers, so we can conclude that Rivers too could be read as the
incorruptible Jacobin: 'Having indulged a habit, dangerous in a man
who has fallen, of dallying with moral calculations, he becomes an
empiric, and a daring and unfeeling empiric.'[60] Both villains, like
Robespierre – and metaphorically like the whole Revolutionary
process – have been corrupted by early crimes into a path of
destruction. Their behaviour may have been rationalised by false
empirical logic, but could not be justified to any benevolent morality.

Such an ideological reading of these early Romantic dramas has
become more prevalent in recent years. As Marjean Purinton puts it,
The Borderers 'explores the conceptual paradigm of revolutionary
ideology . . . The historicism of the play replaces a specific history,
and ideological criticism is transposed or allegorised in different
forms.'[61] This perception of writers transposing ideology into cultural forms by allegorising social experiences into drama – even the
subjective dramas contained in lyric poetry – has been elaborated by
many critics of the Romantic movement. Indeed several suggest that
the dialectic between communal and individual experience that is
explored in much Romantic art can be read as a metaphorical
expression of specific ideological debates. Marilyn Butler, Jeffrey
Cox and Joseph McGann each write about 'formal discontinuities',
'displacing' and 'refiguring', and perceive in the originality of their
poetic processes a radical subversion of the reactionary political
stance that was publicly adopted by Wordsworth, Coleridge and
Southey in their post-Revolutionary disillusionment.[62]

Daniel P. Watkins' *Materialist Critique of English Romantic Drama*
presents the most consistent case for reading the Romantic drama in
the context of political change, and identifies a 'conflict between the
content of surface structure and a deeper political unconscious
[which] registers one of the key features of the Romantic historical

moment: namely the difficult struggle that marked the transition from an aristocratic to bourgeois worldview.'[63] Although his reading of the complex changes of the period almost exclusively in terms of class conflict detracts somewhat from the subtlety of his analysis of the plays themselves, he does identify the essential cause of *The Boderers'* lack of dramatic effect. By relying on a string of true or false 'tales' rather than the confrontational conflict of characters in a recognisable social context,

> *The Borderers* focuses on what is probably the single major difficulty that Romantic drama faced: the issues, and the values underlying those issues, that the drama wishes to explore concern the corruption and loss of social life, and its replacement with personal or subjective life; this shift of imaginative emphasis from public to personal life paralyses dramatic representation, which depends upon dynamic social exchange for its content. *The Borderers* . . . attempts to negotiate this overwhelming challenge by displacing social exchange into tales of social exchange, thereby preserving the core subjectivity that is the drama's real concern.[64]

To pursue the story of these essentially literary artists, who, despite their early forays into drama, later adopted a hostile anti-theatrical attitude, is outside the scope of the present work. However, it is hardly surprising that detailed analyses of the finer poetical minds of the age confirm my own reading of the general theatrical culture, in which 'political pressures exert both conscious and unconscious influences and can be expressed in intentional and unintentional forms.'[65]

However, before leaving the Romantic poets and their 'mental theatre', mention should be made of another fashionable critical discourse. This places the Romantics on the 'margins' and cultural 'borderlands' beloved of postmodernist artists and commentators, who tend to be more concerned with the performativity of identities than with politically ideological readings. They see art as an essentially personal expression rather than the communal experience or social ritual in terms of which earlier commentators described the Romantic's plays as unsuitable for theatrical performance. For critics such as Alan Liu, Julie Carlson and Anthony Kubiak, the 'mental theatre' of the Romantics is far from 'unstageable'. They suggest that it anticipated the conceptual performances of Robert Wilson, or – in a more Gothic spirit – the self-reflexivity of Artaud or Tadeusz Kantor. For them the concept of the mind as the creator of meaning – a concept more appropriate, I would suggest, to Kant than to the

English poets – provides a *new* stageability in what Kubiak defines not as 'mental theatre' but as the 'Theatre of Mind':

This mind . . . is not a real 'mind' or minds that exist somewhere as actual or essential 'spaces of thought'. Rather the very topographical metaphor of mind as a space of individuation is a result of romanticism's assumption of an imaginative interiority of thought, which was and is, in its structuring of experience as alien difference, primarily and distressingly theatrical. This alienating mind turned back on itself is the terrorising aspect of the Sublime in perhaps its clearest manifestation. The full political grandeur of this psychological, self-inflicted sublime terror is revealed when Kant elevates it to the level of the social, and reveals how even 'war itself . . . has something sublime about it' because it effects a kind of purification and discipline of the social fabric, which in times of peace becomes commercial, debased, cowardly and effeminate.[66]

Such a reading of the Romantics tends to suggest an almost fascistic political stance – an individualism to which all social considerations must give way – a radicalism of repression and reaction rather than of liberation and transformation. It is a reading that may have some relevance to the aggression and despair of Heinrich von Kleist, but seems too extreme when applied to the English theatre – to either the Gothic drama, which was most obviously concerned with the evocation of terror, or the closet drama dealing with psychological alienation.

Nevertheless several critics of the period – few of whom, save Coleridge, had any real knowledge of Kantian philosophy – did attribute to German drama a baleful moral influence more dangerous even than the political rhetoric of the French Revolutionary stage.[67] This German influence was chiefly transmitted through the popular dramatist August von Kotzebue, several of whose plays were translated and published by Benjamin Thompson as *The German Theatre* (1797–1801).[68] Most of his plays conformed to the Europewide desire for historical dramas, but what made them both popular and controversial in England, as in Germany, was their sympathetic portrayal of characters of dubious virtue. German critics accused him of a 'glorification of licentiousness, draped in the cloak of virtue'[69] and several English critics took the same line when Kemble performed Thompson's translation of *Menschenhass und Reue* (Berlin, 1789) as *The Stranger* (Drury Lane, 24 March 1798). Once again it could be argued that the personal drama of betrayal, guilt, forgiveness and reconciliation reflected a sense of political impotence among the fragmented states of Germany when challenged by the inspiration and by the aggression of the French Revolution, but the issues of marital duty were quite challenging enough to excite audiences across Europe. Kotzebue did not have the perception of Goethe or Schiller into either politics or psychology, but his story of 'Misanthropy and Regret', about adultery and its forgiveness, chimed well with the gender politics that paralleled the challenge to constitutional traditions.

In June 1798, three months after the performance of *The Stranger*, a definitive indication of the radical reputation of the German drama was provided by the publication of *The Rovers*, a dramatic satire, in George Canning's pro-government journal *The Anti-Jacobin; or The Weekly Examiner*. This parody, as well as referring to the 'Several children; Fathers and Mothers unknown' of *The Stranger*, was based mainly on Schiller's *The Robbers*, which had been translated by Francis Tytler in 1792, and elements of which had been incorporated into several Gothic dramas, including Lewis' *Castle Spectre*. In the spoof introduction the supposed author claims:

I have turned my thoughts more particularly to the GERMAN STAGE, and have composed, in imitation of the most popular pieces of that Country, which have already met with so general reception and admiration in this, a play; which, if it has a proper run, will, I think, do much to unhinge the present notions of men with regard to the obligations of Civil Society; and to substitute in lieu of a sober contentment, and regular discharge of the duties incident to each man's particular situation, a wild desire of undefinable latitude and extravagance; an aspiration after shapeless some-things, that can neither be described nor understood, a contemptuous disgust at all that *is*, and a persuasion that nothing is as it ought to be – to operate, in short, a general discharge of every man (in his own estimation), from every thing that laws divine or human; that local customs, immemorial habits, and multiplied examples impose upon him; and set them about doing what they like, where they like, and how they like – without reference to any law but their own Will, or to any consideration of how others may be affected by their conduct.[70]

Clearly the authors were not unversed in the philosophy of the *Sturm und Drang* writers, and were making an intelligent association between the moral liberty explored in Schiller's drama and the political liberty advocated by the French and English radicals. The stage directions of the play itself suggest an equal familiarity with – and contempt for – the recurrent stage image of the dungeon:

A Subterranean Vault in the Abbey of QUEDLINBURGH; *with Coffins,
'Scutcheons, Death's Heads and Cross-bones. – Toads, and other loathsome
Reptiles are seen traversing the obscurer parts of the Stage. –* ROGERO *appears, in
chains, in a Suit of rusty Armour, with his beard grown, and a Cap of a grotesque
form upon his head. – Beside him a Crock, or Pitcher, supposed to contain his
daily allowance of sustenance. – A long silence, during which the wind is heard to
whistle through the Caverns.*[71]

Ironically the *Anti-Jacobin*'s parody, rather than driving German
drama from the stage, predated the rash of translations for Kotzebue
that were produced in the season of 1798–9. These included
Inchbald's *Lover's Vows* (Covent Garden, 11 October 1798), which
received forty-two performances that season, and her *Wise Man of the
East* (30 November 1799); Monk Lewis' *East Indian* (Drury Lane, 22
April 1799); Henry Neumann's *Family Distress* (Haymarket, 15 June
1799); Prince Hoare's *Sighs* (Haymarket, 30 July 1799); Richard
Cumberland's *Joanna of Montfaucon* (Covent Garden, January 1800);
and Thomas Dibdin's three musical comedies at Covent Garden,
The Birth-Day (8 April 1799), *The Horse and the Widow* (4 May 1799)
and *Of Age Tomorrow* (1 February 1800). Also in the 1799 Haymarket
season (21 August) Schiller's *Robbers* was finally staged as *The Red
Cross Knights* by Joseph Holman, though it had to be considerably
rewritten and retitled by order of the Examiner.[72] That a whole raft
of plays could provoke vehement criticism and yet prove popular in
the theatres suggests that they were more than innocuous entertainment, even after the censor's scrutiny. The year 1800 saw two highly
significant German translations: Coleridge's of Schiller's *Wallenstein
Trilogy*, which failed, like his earlier plays, to find a theatre, and
Sheridan's *Pizarro*, a highly patriotic and popular success based on
Kotzebue's *Die Spanier in Peru*. However, as both translations, like
their originals, were deeply informed by the emergence of Bonaparte, their discussion is delayed to chapter 6 below.

My final example in this chapter is of a 'chamber play' that did
reach the stage, and which also presents an alienated personality
driven to crime by misapprehension hardened into obsession. In
1798 Joanna Baillie, a well-respected member of the literary scene in
Edinburgh, published *A Series of Plays: in which it is attempted to delineate
the stronger passions of the mind: Each passion being the subject of a tragedy and
a comedy*. Of these *De Monfort, a tragedy* was selected for performance
by Siddons and Kemble (Drury Lane, 20 April 1800) as it provided

them with a remarkable opportunity to play brother and sister, in roles probably inspired by the author's observation of their acting styles. The performance text was much corrected and reduced by Kemble.[73] Although it is unlikely that Baillie's conception of De Monfort owed anything directly to thoughts about the French Revolution, like Wordsworth's Mortimer and Rivers, the character, intended as a study in unjustified hatred, is another example of a noble mind overthrown – not just by a single rash act of violence but by deepseated alienation.[74] De Monfort has hated Rezenvelt ever since childhood, when he felt denigrated by his playmate's casual manner. The animosity led him to pick a fight in which Rezenvelt defeated and then spared him. This act of generosity rankled even deeper and De Monfort has fled his home to escape the memory of this humiliation. His sister Jane pursues him and, having drawn out his secret obsession, she tries to arrange a reconciliation. Rezenvelt treats the matter so lightly that De Monfort is incensed and determines to murder his enemy as he journeys through the forest. Monks from a nearby monastery discover the body and arrest the criminal, who is so full of remorse and self-loathing that he will not face his sister Jane when she is summoned by the Abbot:

> It must not be. – Run and prevent her coming.
> Say, he who is detain'd a pris'ner here
> Is one to her unknown. I am now nothing.
> I am a man, of holy claim bereft;
> Out from the pale of social kindred cast;
> Nameless and horrible. –
> Tell her De Monfort far from hence is gone
> Into a desolate, and distant land,
> Ne'er to return again. Fly tell her this;
> For we must meet no more.[75]

Like Wordsworth's Mortimer, De Montfort believes he is beyond forgiveness, human or divine, and the fulfilment of his destiny has branded him an outcast. Indeed when left alone in the same cell as the body of his victim, his anguish is so great it kills him: 'From violent agitation of the mind, / Some stream of life within his breast has burst.' Although his noble sister Jane refuses to condemn him, and Baillie, in the preface, claims 'it is the passion not the man which is held up to our execration', the dramaturgical implications of this 'Play of Passion' is spelt out by Joseph Donohue comparing it with earlier Gothic dramas:

De Monfort internalises the convention [of a secret crime] by redefining it as a psychological process in which an evil passion inexplicably takes root in the fallow soul of man and slowly chokes away his life force. Since the operation of fate has now been relegated to the human soul, the dramatist has no reason to base her play on a series of impassioned encounters with forces in the outside world . . . She has informed the reader in her introductory treatise that she eschews the sensationalism of performed drama . . . she has single-handedly (and perhaps unwittingly as well) effected on the stage a transformation in the nature of dramatic character . . . 'Some sprite accurst within thy bosom mates / To work thy ruin,' Jane De Monfort laments to her brother early in the play (I, ii). This force, and not that of exterior happenings, brings about his unspeakable death by a kind of spiritual internal bleeding.[76]

Of course the creation is not 'single-handed', as our examination of *The Borderers* shows, though that play was not yet in the public domain, and there were other less subtly delineated villains whose crimes and remorse were to be as equally self-destructive. De Monfort might be the precursor of Byron's Manfred, but he is also closely related to Osmond in the *Castle Spectre* and even Blue Beard, who are destroyed by supernatural personifications of the obsessions which drive them to threaten the innocent. Arguably, Baillie's real originality lay not in De Monfort's passion, but in the delineation of Jane De Monfort, who recognises the nobility behind his crime.

Significantly it is her moral ambiguity that so offended, amongst others, Kemble's biographer James Boaden, who in *The Secret Tribunal* had portrayed the Jacobins as the ruthless Illuminati, and he attributed the betrayal of traditional morality to the influence of the German drama:

that any *single* enormity, long indulged, from the natural operation of self-love, begot a specious sanction that satisfied the conscience . . . The *German* secret of interest tended to strengthen the self-delusion in actual life; it laid the 'flattering unction to the soul,' that any one vice might maintain its power in the most amiable minds; and exhibit the *adulteress*, and the *seducer*, and the *robber*, and even the *murderer*, as the most generous of the species . . . Thus sympathy usurped the place of censure, and a door was opened to that fatal fallacy, of making a *compromise* with morals.[77]

A play like *De Monfort* and those taken from the German – Thompson's *The Stranger*, Sheridan's *Pizarro*, Inchbald's *Lover's Vows* and Holman's *Red Cross Knights* – inspired condemnation from so many critics that once again it suggests a cultural crisis. The plays shared a moral ambiguity, however didactic they may seem on the page, and this was chiefly due to a shift of emphasis from social interaction – cultural and moral proprieties – to the personal identity of the protagonist, whose crimes are less important than the passion that inspired them and the emotions they excite in the audience during their commission. Donohue identifies this with the internalisation of psychic motivation, while more recent feminist critics identify it as a subversion of gender roles. Purinton argues that Baillie's play, by contrasting the traditionally 'feminine' Lady Freberg as frivolous and the 'masculine' Jane De Monfort as empowered and empowering (though ultimately suppressed), implied that 'a mental revolution must occur before political oppression, including gender relations, can be reformed' and that 'Baillie vigorously and actively participates in a political revolution that seeks to unveil the customs, habits and prejudices that enslave women.'[78] Ellen Donkin argues that Baillie suffered from an anti-feminist backlash in the late 1790s, after a brief period when women playwrights, like Cowley and Inchbald, had established a professional independence from the containing patronage of theatre managers.[79] In 1801 she certainly received a rebuff from manager Kemble – Donkin believes at the instigation of Sheridan – and so failed to produce the role specially requested of her by Sarah Siddons, who had asked the previous year: 'Make me some more Jane De Monforts.'[80]

Recent cultural criticism, especially that concerned with gendered social roles, has emphasised the performative nature of identity, and in our period probably more people were excited into reassessing their attitudes by the direct experience of actresses embodying 'new women' on stage, than by the didactic treatises of Wollstonecraft or Hays, which, although they clearly articulated emerging attitudes, could be dismissed as both unfeminine and Jacobinical. So, in order to examine more closely the shift into 'identity politics' that seems to have replaced the radical enthusiasm of the immediate post-Revolutionary period, I intend to turn from play scripts to their realisation on stage, and in particular to the embodiment of the psychological insights that the collapse of Enlightenment rationalism had engendered.

CHAPTER 5

Performance and performing

In the last quarter of our own century, much has been made of issues of personal identity. Concern for the individual rights of racial and sexual identities seems to have replaced for many people a consciousness of class and a sense of social solidarity. This is partly the cause, and partly the result, of changing political agendas on the national and international scene. One of the main cultural expressions of this desire for personal respect and visibility is how people dress to present themselves to the world – their appearance declares a 'self image'. So if we cannot argue with reality, we can at least manipulate appearances. The fashion statement is supposed to create a new personality, and clothes are marketed as a means of transforming the self by changing the image. Thus in our own time dress has become political. During the period of the French Revolution too, dressing was used to define and to proclaim personal identity in the face of social upheaval. Street fashions could assert, or disguise, political positions, while theatrical costumes were used to manipulate ideological opinion. Of course, the values and anxieties of any culture can be analysed by how it dresses, but the 1780s saw the emergence, not only of an organised fashion industry, but of a new self-consciousness of how dress can declare political alignment as well as social status – and this awareness was inevitably reflected in that living mirror of fashion, the stage.

During the mid-eighteenth century fashion was the exclusive concern of the rich, ostentatiously displaying their wealth and leisure. Coats and waistcoats, skirts and petticoats were constructed with the maximum of material, layered and embellished with lace and bullion. But in the 1780s the ideal image changed from the idle courtier to the useful merchant or worthy squire. Clothes became simpler with worsteds, cotton and muslin replacing silk, satin and brocade. Men dressed in tailored jackets and short waistcoats over riding breeches and boots; women discarded their towering wigs for natural hair, their voluminous hoops for comfortable skirts and their embroidered trimmings for a simple scarf or fishu. The style was designed more for the park than the salon, and its inspiration came from the English gentry rather than the French aristocracy.[1] Of course the image seldom reflected actuality – Marie Antoinette, playing at milkmaids in the gardens of Versailles, lacked George III's practical interest in the agriculture of the Windsor home-farm – but as political conflict became more real, so fashion became more acutely linked to status and opinion. From the beginning, French Revolutionary activity found expression in dress: representatives of the Third Estate were instructed to wear black suits, and soon all radicals wore black with pride. As Parisian artisans mobilised to support reform, the utilitarian clothes of the sansculottes became an ideological image particularly when crowned by the red cap of liberty. Although few middle-class revolutionaries discarded their bourgeois breeches, gradually a new trouser became fashionable, but it was the tight buckskin of the dandy rather than the worker's overall.

As the Revolution progressed, members of the Assembly adopted sashes and cockades self-consciously creating new symbols like the banners and tableaux of the Revolutionary *fêtes*.[2] In 1793 David designed a special costume for republican representatives. Artificially combining elements of Russian peasant, Spanish brigand and Roman citizen, it remained on the drawing board, though its relationship to theatrical costume is clear.[3] After Thermidor, political identification became less dangerous and 'fashion statements' took up where real politics left off, as flaunting an image was safer than fighting for a principle. Aristocrats and their sympathisers could now wear red ribbons round their necks to commemorate the victims of the guillotine, and celebrate their own escape. Women developed David's Grecian style into the statuesque 'nude' look, with damp muslin clinging to their enfranchised limbs, or affected the more elaborate trains and fishus of the *merveilleuses* – the prostitutes of the Palais-Royal. The male *incroyables* of the Directoire exaggerated the boots, trousers and neck cloth of the sansculottes into an elaborately impractical costume with a stock that virtually covered their mouths – symbolically protecting their necks now they were no longer really threatened. Eventually, still following the inspiration of David's paintings, the style became that of the Empire. The line of women's dresses reflected the historical inspiration of

Rome, but the emphasis given to men's legs owed more to the cavalry uniform of Napoleon's triumphant army.

In England, to adopt a Revolutionary dress would have been too provocative for safety, but the general trend towards the utilitarian was much the same. Once the militia was on standby and camps were established to the south of London, civilian fashion tended to develop elements of military uniform. Boots and buckskin typified the hunting–racing–boxing dandy, and women rejected padding and corsets for simple cotton frocks with a muslin neckerchief. Writing in 1817, Hazlitt recognised the impact of this change of fashion on the possibilities of sexual intrigue in comedy:

The extreme simplicity and uniformity of modern dress, however favourable to the arts, has certainly stript Comedy of one of its richest ornaments and most expressive symbols . . . The enormous hoops and stiff stays . . . assisted wonderfully in heightening the mysteries of the passion, and adding to the intricacy of the plot . . . The greedy eye and bold hand of indiscretion were repressed, which gave a greater licence to the tongue . . . Love was entangled in the folds of the swelling handkerchief, and the desires might wander for ever round the circumference of a quilted petticoat . . . What an undertaking to penetrate through the disguise! What an impulse must it give to the blood, what a keenness to the invention, what a volubility to the tongue![4]

According to Linda Colley, the British aristocracy had to shed its excessive leisure and its useless ornament in order to redefine its political function, at the same time as, according to E. P. Thompson, the working class was recognising its proletarian identity. These changes in social reality were inevitably confusing and individuals used dress to explore their aspirations and express their fears. More imaginatively, theatrical costume could not only exploit radical social images, but could express the sense of vulnerability and absurdity that permeated Gothic and Romantic drama – as Hazlitt concluded in his reflections on the costume of comedy: 'But now-a-days – a woman can be *but undressed!*'[5]

In France, Talma's republican toga in Voltaire's *Brutus* caused a shock that was both aesthetic and ideological, and it challenged propriety. On seeing his costume, Mme Vestris exclaimed:

> But Talma, your arms are bare!
> Roman arms were bare.
> But Talma, you have no breeches!
> The Romans wore none.
> Swine![6]

Later, at the end of his career Talma commented to Victor Hugo that he had never been asked to play 'a real part [with] variety of life . . . I asked for Shakespeare and they gave me Ducis. Truth in the plays was unobtainable; I had to be content with putting it into costumes. I played Marius with bare legs!'[7] Probably Talma was not so cynical about his roles when he first played them, as he created images on stage that were as powerfully ideological as David's on canvas. And it was the ability of both men to create powerful images, rather than their republican persuasion, which recommended them to Napoleon in the creation and dissemination of his own imperial image.

In England, Sarah Siddons too helped change both theatrical and fashionable costume. She believed her new simpler style of dressing would assist her physical expression of emotion, but it also anticipated the ideological classicism of France, a fact that disturbed her conservative biographer, James Boaden:

She now saw that tragedy was debased by the flutter of light materials, and that the head, and all its powerful action from the shoulder, should never be encumbered by the monstrous inventions of the hair-dresser and the milliner . . . What, however, began in good sense . . . was, by political mania in the rival nation, carried into the excess of shameless indecency. France soon sent us over her amazons to burlesque all classical costume, and her models were received among us with unaffected disgust.

He concluded with the comment that 'what Mrs Siddons had chosen remains in a great degree the standard of female costume to the present hour [1827]'.[8] Theatrical costume was designed to conform to a fashionable ideal, and, at the same time, an approximate historical accuracy – just as the new historical plays themselves adopted the guise of the past to comment on the present. Chapter two above discussed the symbolic and ideological significance of history plays, and theatrical production made similar compromises between antiquarian accuracy and contemporary relevance. Some artists, like Kemble and his scenic designer William Capon, delighted in research and the validation scholarship gave their art, but others, like George Frederick Cooke or Mrs Jordan, cared little for such pedantry, as long as a rapport was achieved in performance and audiences were touched or amused. Theatres not only provide a space to observe and to display behaviour; the actual techniques of performance and characterisation reflected the way in which people understood their own behaviour and personal identity.

Because creating a role is an artistic exercise of choosing characteristics and selecting means to embody and communicate them, processes of acting provide a kind of blueprint for the psychological perception of both performers and audience. In the British theatre today there is an emphasis on *physical expression* that probably mirrors the concern for personal identity mentioned earlier, while in the more 'naturalistic' medium of screen drama we still expect a psychological coherence based on *justified motivation* as expounded by Stanislavsky and developed in the American Method. Both these styles give a priority to individuality, of either character or performer, quite different from the exemplary class-based characterisation that Brecht and other socialist playwrights propounded, and also from the ritualistic archetypes of Expressionism, Artaud and Grotowski. The differences between the actors of these strands of twentieth century theatre are not just technical but philosophical and psychological. So too in the Revolutionary period, when the socially conceived characters of the comedy of manners gave way to the psychotics of Gothic drama, the melancholics of the Romantic closet, the eccentrics of farce, the stock types of pantomime, and the idealisations of ballet. As in our own time, the multiplicity of dramatic forms and performance styles suggests a variety of philosophical perspectives, a confusion of cultural values and, probably, a lack of conviction in peoples' self-perception.

To list the creative options available to the actors of the time tends to create a reified taxonomy of choices that were usually exercised instinctively. However, the different modes of dramatic personification can be interpreted as being suggestive of the different philosophical perspective of the age. During the Enlightenment both *philosophes* and performers had tried to balance reason and sentiment; the Revolution demanded a rhetorical declaration of conviction and commitment; Romanticism emphasised emotional responses and introspection; and the fervent style of Methodist and Evangelical preaching was validated by mystical inspiration. Thus, all these different ideological tendencies were reflected in the performance values of major theatres, opera houses and concert halls, and as the ideologies shifted towards individualism and identification, so performance styles became more emotional and personalised. Eventually the reactionary forces of Nationalism and Capitalism that triumphed in the postwar period were cynically to exploit the personality appeal of star performers and the sensational thrills of popular melodrama.

These rather generalised assertions can be given more substance by a closer examination of how performers themselves viewed their creative processes. In the mid-eighteenth century the drama of Voltaire, in the tradition of Cartesian idealism, suggested that an intellectual understanding of motive and interest should be expounded with eloquence and clarity, whilst the Sentimentalist Rousseau, distrustful of all artifice, looked to the instinctive impulses of sympathy and benevolence. For Voltaire passion was destructive, for Rousseau it was a source of inspiration and sublimity. Denis Diderot tried to resolve this philosophic dialectic in terms of the art of acting, not only in his famous *Paradoxe sur le comedién* (written in 1773), but also in *Eléments de psychology* (1765), *Le neveu de Rameau* (1765) and *Le rêve de d'Alembert* (1769).[9] The psychological analysis in the earlier works emphasised the creative force of inspiration and emotion, termed *sensibilité*, and endorsed the primal, though dangerous, agency of the sensory nervous system:

Sensibility is more powerful than will . . . The nerves are the slaves, frequently the ministers, and sometimes the despots of the mind . . . Everything goes well when the mind commands the nerves, everything goes wrong when the rebellious nerves command the mind . . . Whenever a sensation is violent . . . we feel, we scarcely think at all, and still less are we able to reason . . . It is thus when we are in awe, in sympathy, in anger, in fear, in pain, or in bliss.[10]

Thus the argument developed in the *Paradoxe* – that the actor's art should be controlled by intellect rather than by *sensibilité* – derives not from an underestimation of the power of passion, but from a distrust of its destructive tendencies. In *Le neveu de Rameau* he imagines an impromptu performance of a 'spontaneous pantomime, including a sound-and-action rendition of an entire opera' created by the *sensibilité* of the moment:

As his improvisation gathers itself into a crescendo, LUI waves his arms, runs about the room, dances all the solo parts as well as the corps de ballet, and then, foaming at the mouth, he utterly abandons himself in a pantomimic ecstasy . . . What did he not attempt to show me? He wept, laughed, sighed, looked placid or melting or enraged. He was a woman in a spasm of grief, a wretched man sunk in despair, a temple being erected, birds growing silent at sunset, waters murmuring through cool and solitary places or else cascading from a mountain top, a storm, a hurricane, the anguish of those about to die, mingled with the whistling of the wind and the noise of thunder. He was night and its gloom, shade and silence – for silence itself is depictable in sound. He had completely lost his senses.[11]

Writing in the 1770s from the moral perspective of his preferred form of theatre, the bourgeois *drame*, Diderot distrusted such a display, which in the 1790s could well have been greeted as sublime. In the *Paradoxe* he strongly advocated the controlled intentionality of imitation over the chaotic indulgence of emotional identification, mainly because he was fully aware of the irresistible power of surrendering rational control to the physiological stimulus of imaginative embodiment. As Joseph Roach concludes:

> This phase of Diderot's aesthetic based on scientific materialism, his mechanised ideal of the actor's impersonal craft, persists in theatrical theory down the present day – through Bertold Brecht, Futurism, Biomechanics, and the *übermarionetten*. At the same time, however, the more vitalistic strain in Diderot's materialism yielded an equally rich harvest for the modern acting theories on the other side of the vineyard. His allowance for the role of the unconscious in the creative process, his emphasis on the organism's capacity to remember and imagine sensation and emotion, his prophetic insistence that mind and body are inexorably interwoven in the same web of nervous fibres, which can be shaped into patterns of response by repetition, recur in some of the most influential writings of modern theorists and in the acting textbooks that dominate formal study in the field.[12]

His full analysis was not published in France for almost fifty years – and for one hundred in England – but he readily expounded the thesis in salon discussions, and his arguments informed the memoirs of the two actresses that he had cited as examples in the essay.[13] Mlle Clairon, Diderot's model of meticulous technique, had resigned from the Comédie in 1765, but continued to teach actors, and in 1799 she published her *Mémoires et réflexions sur l'art dramatique*. It provoked Mlle Dumesnil, Diderot's example of undisciplined sensibility, to attack her rival's pretentious artificiality in her own *Mémoires* of 1800. However, the difference between their methods was most succinctly expressed in an exchange that reputedly took place in 1787 in conversation with Talma, at the start of his illustrious career:

MLLE DUMESNIL. [*to Talma*] You must not *represent* Montagu [Romeo], you must *be* him . . .

MLLE CLAIRON. In theatrical art all is conventional, all is fiction . . . I wear the dress in order to delude the senses, and I have the figure and face of a woman, which completes the illusion. But what you must remember is that what I produce is an illusion . . .

MLLE DUMESNIL. I was full of my part, I felt it, I yielded myself up to it . . .

MLLE CLAIRON. Fiction.

MLLE DUMESNIL. Reality![14]

In the more considered opinions of their memoirs, Clairon argued for meticulous rehearsal:

What infinite pains and study must it not require to make an actor forget his own character; to identify himself with every personage he represents . . . [repeating] a hundred and a hundred times the same thing, in order to surmount the difficulties he meets at every step[15]

whereas Dumesnil advocated deep emotional identification:

Great emotions are the same from pole to pole . . . To imbue oneself with great emotions, to feel them immediately and at will, to forget oneself in the twinkling of an eye in order to put oneself in the place of the character one wishes to represent – that is exclusively a gift of nature and beyond all the efforts of art.[16]

Although Talma seems to have respected both actresses and their separate techniques, this famous 'actor of the Revolution' ultimately prioritised the power of *sensibilité* over that of craft:

that faculty of exaltation which agitates an actor, takes possession of his senses, shakes even his very soul, and enables him to enter into the most tragic situations, and the most terrible of passions, as if they were his own. The intelligence, which accompanies sensibility, judges the impressions which the latter has made us feel; it selects, arranges them, and subjects them to calculation. If sensibility furnishes the objects, the intelligence brings them into play.[17]

Throughout these actors' reflections, which were all framed in the terms that Diderot had expounded, runs the assumption that 'sensibility furnishes the object' of the dramatic experience. Whether emotions are recreated or imitated, intensity of passion is the chief purpose of the actor's art. Actors express passion in their own performances, and evoke passionate responses from their audiences. Arguably because of political censorship, formal or indirect, the dramatic debate of specific issues and principles in both France and England was restrained, and the intellectual pleasures of irony, argument and moral judgement, were lost to the emotional pleasures of intensity, rhetoric and moral conviction. As Brecht was to memorably complain, audiences were expected to leave their brains in the cloakroom.

That many performers were highly adept at stirring emotions, in themselves and in the audience, and at impressing spectators with the power of their personalities, confirms the impression that in the Revolutionary theatre performativity was at least as important as dramaturgy. The rational argument of political principle that began in 1789 and informed the debates on the republicanism of 1792, became swamped by the survival politics of 1793–4, with the persecution of 'evil traitors' by ruthlessly 'virtuous patriots', and eventually by the heroic cult of personality erected around Napoleon Bonaparte. The theatre's exploitation of star performers paralleled this conviction politics of heroic identity – not only the identity of heroic individuals, but the patriotic identity of the warring nations. The discussion of specific plays that embodied the themes of war and nationalism will be reserved for the next chapter, whilst this one will explore how the personalities and the artistic techniques of a range of individual British performers seemed to reflect the concerns of their society.

Although the psychological insights of Diderot and the French tragedians were formulated more articulately, the actual presence of French dancers and singers was probably more directly influential on the style of British performance. For example on the lyric stage, as discussed in chapter 1, the character-based concept of Noverre's *ballet d'action*, as well as the virtuosity of its dancers, Lepicq, Vestris, Rossi and Parisot, tended towards physical and emotional embodiment rather than the mechanical skill of earlier baroque ballet. In opera the introduction of British stars, such as Michael Kelly and Nancy Storace, as well as the development of English opera itself, also suggests a humanisation of the forms of musical theatre – most tellingly confirmed by the passing of the 'artificial' voice of the castrati in 1791. In that year, although the Pantheon employed the great Pacchierotti for his last season in London, Gallini at the Kings Theatre hired the tenor Giacomo Davide to replace Rubinelli as *primo uomo* of the company.[18]

Turning to changes in acting on the legitimate stage, it is difficult to identify any direct influence from France. Traditionally, theatregoers believed that the organisational hierarchy of the Comédie and its practice of passing roles on from *doyen* to *pensionnaire* made French acting more formal and rigid than the 'natural' style developed in London under the inspiration of David Garrick. However, Diderot, the most advanced critic of acting in France, had developed much of his own theory under the influence of English practice. He had observed Garrick during his visit to Paris in 1765, and the *Paradoxe* itself was written in response to Antonio Sticotti's *Garrick ou les acteurs*

Anglais (1769), an adaptation of John Hill's essay *The Actor; a Treatise on the Art of Playing* (1750), much of which itself had been translated from *Le Comédien* by Pierre Rémond de Sainte-Albine (1747). Thus at least the terms of sensibility and control were well understood on each side of the Channel, even if the greater subtlety of perception must be awarded to Diderot. It was even the case that Talma's first performances were on an amateur stage in London. His father was a dentist in the West End with a society clientele, and Talma *fils* was apprenticed to the trade. However, he preferred performing short after-dinner sketches or *'proverbes'* for the French community in London, and visiting the Theatres Royal.[19] He missed Garrick's final appearances, but saw many performers who had acted with him, such as Henderson, Smith and the Palmer brothers. Siddons made her second London debut in 1782 and Kemble joined her in 1783, so their careers can be seen as paralleling that of the French tragedian who returned to France in 1784 and joined the Comédie in 1787.

John Philip Kemble, the dominant tragedian throughout the period of this study, favoured the rational side of Diderot's dialectic rather than trusting to emotional sensibility. His technique was tightly controlled in order to master a permanent threat of asthma. However, although Kemble was in some ways 'classical' in his approach, just as he was scholarly in his editorial and directorial approach to play texts, like Talma – whose concern for accuracy in costume he shared[20] – he believed classicism should not exclude passion. He advised, as well as admired, his sister Sarah Siddons, and both her more infectious emotionalism and his structured approach are identified in Joseph Donohue's analysis as 'Romantic', because their

emphasis on interpreting characters was oriented towards the presentation of subjective response. The aesthetic impression derived from such an emphasis is that the character is by nature individual and so his response to a given situation is necessarily unique. Consequently the audience identifies sympathetically with the character, sees the world through his eyes, and ultimately finds the meaning of the play inseparable from, and in fact the same as, the meaning of that character's responses.[21]

David Garrick's 'naturalism' had been based on a process of passionate responses to the stimuli of the moment. His most typical effect was 'the start', an apparently spontaneous reaction of astonishment, terror or delight to an immediate perception.[22] The Kembles preferred to present an unfolding narrative of character development under the determining influence of a single 'Ruling Passion' – hence their attraction to Joanna Baillie's 'Plays of Passion'. At the end of Kemble's career, Hazlitt reflected on his technique:

> It has always appeared to us, that the range of characters in which Mr Kemble more particularly shone, and was superior to every other actor, were those which consisted in the development of one solitary sentiment or exclusive passion . . . his success depended on the increasing intensity with which he dwelt on a given feeling, or enforced a passion that resisted all interference or control . . . In Hamlet [he failed] from a want of flexibility, of that quick sensibility which yields to every motive, and is borne away with every breath of fancy . . . he played it like a man in armour, with a determined inveteracy of purpose, in one undeviating straight line.[23]

The characters in which Hazlitt most admired Kemble were his classical Cato and Coriolanus, which once again suggests an affinity with Talma, whose 'intense concentrated playing' the Goncourt Brothers described as the result of 'his work, his care, his sense of continuity in the part'.[24] However, Kemble was quite prepared to perform more romantic roles, in which his persona as 'Black Jack Kemble' provided intensity rather than dignity. He even brought a 'pantomimic' agility to the roles of Percy in *The Castle Spectre* and Rolla in *Pizarro*, but he was perhaps best suited to the gloomy introspection of Penruddock in Cumberland's *Wheel of Fortune*, Mortimer in Colman's *The Iron Chest*[25] and Baillie's *De Monfort*.

In his study of Gothic drama Paul Ranger makes a detailed study of how Baillie's stage directions in *De Monfort* indicate how she thought Kemble might perform the role. She wanted 'to show the effects of a mastering passion on a key character', and Ranger describes how the emotion of hatred was to be embodied, from the obsessional brooding of '*De Monfort with his Arms crossed, with a thoughtful frowning Aspect*', through the agitation of '*walks up and down impatiently and irresolute*', to the horror of the realisation that passion has driven him to murder, '*fix'd and motionless with horror*', and, when he is shown the body of his victim, '*a sudden shivering seems to pass over him*'.[26] Such gestures and variations of physical energy were typical of the style of the period, but when distraction turned to madness, the echo of Macbeth confronted by Banquo's ghost required a demonstration that in any other period might have provoked laughter rather than horror:

DE MONFORT. [*Runs to the corpse and tears off the cloth in despair*]
        All still beneath.
    Nought is there here but fix'd and grisly death.
    How sternly fixed! Oh! those glazed eyes!
    They look me still. [*Shrinks back with horror*]
    Come, madness! Come unto me senseless death!
    I cannot suffer this! Here, rocky wall,
    Scatter these brains, or dull them.
    Runs furiously, and, dashing his head against the wall, falls upon the floor.[27]

Such a sudden violent piece of physical business was typical of Kemble, and commentators, far from ridiculing their extravagance, suggested that the actor was sparing in 'those bursts of passion to which he gave such sublime effect',[28] because he had to harbour his strength and protect his asthmatic chest. Macready recalled Kemble's farewell performance of Macbeth:

The first four acts . . . moved heavily on: Kemble correct, tame and effective: but the fifth . . . he seemed struck to the heart . . . Then, as if with inspiration of despair, he hurried out, distinctly and pathetically the lines 'Tomorrow and tomorrow and tomorrow' . . . rising to a climax of desperation that brought down the enthusiastic cheers of the closely packed theatre.[29]

Perhaps making a virtue of necessity, Kemble combined the rational insights of a scholarly reading of the text, which provided him with a through-line of development, with a single emotional outburst at the climactic moment. The structure and purpose of his technique was thus centred in the individual character he was playing – his subjective responses, his psychological propensities and a consistency of moral conviction. His audiences read this as 'nobility'; today we might describe it as 'the construction of a coherent identity'.

In 1800 a similar coherence of conception was displayed in George Frederick Cooke's performance of Richard III, but this was from an actor who specialised not in noble introspection but in lip-smacking villainy. One reviewer commented:

We have seen *Richard* rendered more awful and terrific, but never more thoroughly detestable . . . sensible of his personal deformities, and the barrier which separated him from the rest of his brethren, *hugging himself up*, and enjoying a horrible satisfaction in the possession of a faculty by which he hoped to overreach the rest of mankind.[30]

That audiences preferred Cooke's dangerous criminal of a tyrant to the nobility with which Kemble played Richard III, reveals, I suggest, a change in attitude toward the nation's chief enemy,

Bonaparte. In the early years there was respect for his military genius and his achievement of Brumaire (November 1799) in over-throwing the corrupt Directory that had replaced Robespierre's Jacobins, but by 1800 the first consul himself seemed to be 'over-reaching the rest of mankind'. The dangerous egotism of such ambition was revealed by Cooke in an image worthy of a Gillray cartoon of Bonaparte accepting the Consulate for Life, when, after hypocritically accepting the reluctant support of the mayor and citizens, Richard made a 'transition from pious humility . . . to the exultation and hellish transport that swelled his bosom when they had gone. His whole frame seemed to swell as if to bursting; his utterance seemed to be smothered with joy; his face was a picture of damned ambition wild with gratification.'[31] However Cooke's Richard had its own sublimity, and the performance of his death scene inspired the same fascinated admiration that Napoleon drew from his enemies:

Cooke may truly say in the words of Richard 'I am myself alone' . . . But that which gives the finishing stroke to the picture is the look which, raising himself on his elbow, he darts at Richmond. It was terrible, it had soul in it; it looked a testamentary curse, and made the death exactly correspond to the life and living character of the monster Richard.[32]

Donohue suggests that these transforming elements of terror and sublimity 'reflect the same transformation in dramatic character evident in early nineteenth-century drama, where the villain-hero is quickly becoming the Byronic man of melancholy grandeur,'[33] and this in turn suggests that the cultural development of Romanticism itself owes much to the 'Shadow of Napoleon', which is the subject of the chapter that follows.

This cultural shift towards a fascination with passionate indivi-duality is also intimately connected with the redefinition of female identity as seen in the plays of Inchbald and Baillie, in the novels of the English Jacobins, inspired by the opinions of Wollstonecraft, and, more significantly in the context of this chapter, in the ambiguous attraction of Sarah Siddons. She herself was a forceful and intelligent woman, and she specialised in playing female victims with a dignity and intensity that quite eclipsed their male persecu-tors. Julie Carlson argues that, after the first flush of radical emancipation associated with Wollstonecraft's publications, the dominance of Burke's reactionary opinions reaffirmed *beauty* as the special contribution of women to cultural and political stability:

What links women, theatre and nationalism in this period and makes antitheatricalism's hostility to women a specifically romantic reaction is the new prominence of beauty as a social and political category. Burke and Schiller initiate the trend in their epistolary reflections on the French Revolution by advocating beauty as the remedy to social upheaval. Whereas reason, now contaminated by France, undermines the nation because it dehumanizes and terrorizes individuals and a warring body politic by grounding social cohesion in affect rather than rationality.[34]

Sarah Siddons' acting skill, tragic presence and striking appearance had been appreciated ever since her first triumphant London season of 1782, when she had performed, almost exclusively, Augustan 'She Tragedies' such as *Jane Shore* and *The Fair Penitent*, whose images had inspired Reynolds to paint her as the Tragic Muse in 1784. The Shakespearean roles she took up to partner her brother, who joined the Drury Lane company in 1783, like Isabella in *Measure for Measure*, Constance in *King John*, and Katherine in *Henry VIII* were similarly wronged women, whose just protests inspired respect in proportion to the pity evoked by their unjust treatment. Her emotional discharge in these roles ignited a passionate response in her audiences and James Boaden saw this as the chief validation of her genius:

I well remember (how is it possible I should ever forget?) the *sobs*, the *shrieks*, among the tenderer part of her audiences; or those *tears*, which manhood, at first, struggled to suppress, but at length grew proud of indulging. We then, indeed, knew all the LUXURY of grief; but the nerves of many a gentle being gave way before the intensity of such appeals; and fainting fits long and frequently alarmed the decorum of the house.[35]

After quoting this description, Jeffrey Cox argues, more or less in accord with Carlson, that the irrational and passionate nature of her performances of oppressed women was more suited to the terror of Matthew Lewis' characters than the independence of Inchbald and Baillie's: 'She did not purge pity and fear but provoked tears and terror. She was the perfect actress for the Gothic drama, for she was at her best in the two stances the Gothic demanded of women: women were either terrorized and mad or stoic and indomitable, but they were always passive.'[36] He even argues that her conception of Lady Macbeth was equally 'passive – she is a seductive object, not a manipulator of the action'.[37] However, Siddons wrote her famous analysis of the role long after her retirement, when antitheatrical critics such as Charles Lamb were arguing that no flesh and blood actor could match their imaginations in creating ideal interpretations of Shakespeare.[38] It is also possible that she intentionally described Lady Macbeth in her essay on the character as 'most captivating to the other sex, – fair, feminine, nay, perhaps even fragile',[39] in contrast to her own appearance – dark, imposing and even masculine – because she recognised that powerful or dangerous women do not necessarily have to be 'unfeminine'. Mmes Roland, Tallien and Charlotte Corday had amply demonstrated this during the Revolution. Certainly Siddons' comments suggest she considered Macbeth's 'activity' weaker than his wife's 'passivity': 'Observe that he (I think pusillanimously, when I compare his conduct to her forbearance) has been continually pouring out his miseries to his wife.'[40]

Modern feminists tend to sound a little disappointed when discussing both the cultural images and the material reality of women of this period, that few struck out for complete independence along the lines of Mary Wortly Montagu, who left her husband to travel the world in the 1740s and 1750s. But a consciousness of oppression needs to precede liberation – as in the case of Wollstonecraft's *Maria* – and the excited response of female auditors to Siddons' persecuted heroines – as to Mrs Litchfield's Captive – suggests an intense identification with situations of entrapment. As yet, however, the stage provided few examples of genuine emancipation. Not only was Lady Macbeth clearly evil in her domination of her 'amiable husband',[41] but Siddons felt she had to distance herself from the moral position of the adulterous Mrs Haller in Kotzebue's *The Stranger*. She 'thought the sympathy of my fair countrywomen in this case dangerous to their best interests'.[42] But, whatever effect Siddons intended in her portrayal of such characters, the interpretation put on them by her 'fair countrywomen' suggests they sympathised with them more as betrayed than as fallen women. However moral her own attitude was to the characters she played, Siddons' personal grandeur and the intensity of her emotional involvement were seized upon by susceptible audiences as a validation for independence and even infidelity. As Kemble commented on her portrayal of Elvira in *Pizarro*, 'My sister has made a heroine out of a soldier's trull.'[43] It would seem that it was not just 'beauty' that was given an uncritical value in the post-Revolutionary period, but 'passion' – the Romantic fallacy that depth of emotion can justify any moral lapses.

Such a view was expressed in Baillie's *De Monfort* when Jane, passing judgement on her brother, asserts:

> Who, but for one dark passion, one dire deed,
> Had claim'd a record of as noble worth,
> As e'er enrich'd the sculptu'd pedestal.   (Act 5, scene 4)

Like Siddons commenting on Mrs Haller, Baillie dissociated herself from her character's opinion in a footnote to this speech:

The last three lines of the last speech are not intended to give the reader a true character of De Monfort, whom I have endeavoured to represent throughout the play as, notwithstanding his other good qualities, proud, suspicious, and susceptible to envy, but only to express the partial sentiments of an affectionate sister.

Baillie's reference to 'reader' rather than audience suggests that her plays were rightly assigned to the closet, as, in the theatre – and particularly when delivered by a Sarah Siddons – such a moral conclusion could hardly be qualified. Jeffrey Cox argues persuasively that Baillie intended Jane De Monfort to be a morally impeccable and resolutely independent woman, particularly as her description of Jane was so precisely based on Siddons herself, and that she 'sought to disenchant the conventional image of woman as passive responder that Siddons embodied'.[44] I suspect that in performance Siddons was the more persuasive, because the very power of her emotional response to the death of De Monfort directed the audience away from an unqualified condemnation of the murderer:

> JANE. The voice of praise was wont to name us both:
>   I had no greater pride.
> *Covers her face with her hands, and bursts into tears. Here they all hang about her;*
> FREBERG *supporting her tenderly;* MANUEL *embracing her knees, and old* JEROME
> *catching hold of her robe affectionately.*

Thus the attractive yet forbidding personality, the imperious yet pathetic sentiment, and the occasionally immoral yet emotionally persuasive behaviour of Siddons on stage raised the temperature of sexual politics without providing any clear ideological guidance. Indeed, the contradictory responses inspired by Siddons' performances are analogous to the ambiguous reactions we have noted to events across the Channel: the principles may be exemplary, but the passion is disproportionate – the emotions understandable but the behaviour inexplicable. Edmund Burke made use of this ambiguity when he modelled his depiction of Marie Antoinette on Sarah Siddons' persecuted queens,[45] as did Edward Eyre in *The Death of the Queen of France*. When persecution in France began to extend to whole branches of society, the British reaction became increasingly determined by emotional identification rather than by political analysis, and this development was paralleled by the increasing use of pathos and terror in the theatre at the expense of argument or demonstration. This is seen not only in the 'spectacularising' of the dramatic repertoire, as discussed in the previous chapter, but in the demonstrative passion of performers.

Indeed sometimes passions were depicted without any dramatic context at all. One theatrical form created during the Enlightenment was the 'monodrama', which combined music and solo speaking with a particular emphasis on the expression of the passions. Rousseau is usually credited with its creation in *Pygmalion*, also often cited as the first *mélodrame*, which was performed in Lyons in 1770. He intended it as an exemplary corrective to the artificiality of operatic recitative, demonstrating that the speaking voice and expressive gestures could, with musical accompaniment, be more affective than the decorative trills of baroque opera or rococo ballet. This experiment was similar to Noverre's drive towards the more natural expression of emotion in *ballets d'action*, and both forms owed much to the flourishing art of pantomime. Moreover, just as Rich and Weaver anticipated elements of Noverre's ballet, so 'Odes for Music' were performed in England, where, even if the speakers did not actually take on a role, they used the recitation to give physical embodiment to a variety of passions. A favourite piece for solo performance in the second half of the century was William Collins' *The Passions*. First performed in the Sheldonian Theatre, Oxford in 1750 with music by William Hayes, it was presented on the professional stage in different arrangements by Benjamin Cooke (1784) and James Sanderson (1789). In 1797 W. Seward described Hayes' original version: 'The music . . . was excellently well adapted to the words. The choruses were very full and majestic, and the airs gave completely the spirit of the Passions which they were intended to imitate.'[46] This suggests some of the poem was sung – as it may well have been in the first Oxford version. However, the recitations by non-singers such as Cooke, Kemble and Siddons gave purely verbal and mimetic expression to each separate passion. In 120 lines thirty passions were mentioned, although some like Mirth and Laughter were introduced as contributory expressions to the predominant emotion of Joy.[47] David Garrick, who made a powerful effect with his *Ode on Shakespeare* at the Stratford Jubilee of 1769, may even have used it as the silent prompt for his famous mime of passions observed by Diderot.

Categorising passions as separately identifiable states, each with its own recognisable physical expressions, had been an aspect of psychological orthodoxy since Descartes, and of artistic practice since le Brun. But with the growing emphasis on emotion as the major determinant of personal identity during the post-Revolutionary period, the art of the actor became increasingly one of displaying – and indulging – the passions. As with Romantic culture as a whole, there was a parallel emergence of analysis and scientific categorisation, as in J. J. Engel's *Mimick* of 1785 – translated in 1822 by Henry Siddons[48] – and Charles Bell's *Anatomy and Philosophy of Expression as Connected with the Fine Arts* (1806). Both works drew on the principles of Lavater's *Physiognomical Bible* (1772)[49] and Mesmer's Animal Magnetism.[50] A third aspect to the cultural expression of emotion was the Classical Revival. Although the Gothic age may have provided writers with situations of emotional excitement, pre-Renaissance visual art seemed strangely inexpressive. Classical sculpture and the newly discovered frescoes of Pompeii seemed to provide far more emotive models, as was expounded in Lessing's analysis of the Laocöon statue (1766). They also inspired the living sculpture of Emma Hamilton's 'Attitudes'.

During the late 1770s George Romney had employed Emma Hart as a model for a number of classical characters, and to portray idealised emotions. Under his instruction she began posing before audiences of appreciative art lovers. In 1784 she became the mistress of Charles Greville whose uncle, Sir William Hamilton, British ambassador to the court of Naples, was so struck with her beauty that in 1786 he took her to Italy to emulate his collection of Roman antiquities: 'She is better than anything in Nature. In her particular way she is finer than anything that is to be found in antique art.'[51] The nephew's mistress soon became the uncle's wife. In 1787 Goethe saw and admired her 'Attitudes', and in 1794 they were illustrated by Frederick Rehberg. Although these esoteric delights seem a far cry from our subject of the French Revolution, Hamilton's poses captured exactly the combination of emotionalism and classicism that typified the Revolutionary art of Chénier, Talma and David, and inspired Kemble and Siddons – visually antiquarian in terms of costume and setting; apparently scientific in the depiction of reified psychological states; and revealing an underlying sense of transience and anxiety. Horace Walpole recognised one of the contradictions in the performance of 'Mrs Hart, Sir W. Hamilton's pantomime mistress – or wife, who acts all the antique statues in an Indian shawl. I have not seen her yet, so am no judge, but people are mad about her wonderful expression, which I do not conceive, so few antique statues having any expression at all – nor designed to have any.'[52]

Of course the neoclassicism of the 1790s could not precisely recreate Greece or Rome; it was shot through with the sensitivity and ideology of contemporary revolution and reaction. However, Emma's living statues seemed to Hamilton, Goethe and Walpole too, when he finally saw her, a true embodiment of the tremulous purity of classic art, especially in her attitudes of vengeance (Medea) and grief (Niobe). In turn she influenced the cultural image that Napoleon wanted for his court as typified by Mme Récamier, who performed shawl dances *à la Greque* directly inspired by Hamilton's 'Attitudes'. It is a historical irony that when Lady Hamilton herself was too stout to be convincing as a Greek statue, she won the heart of Napoleon's nemesis, Horatio Nelson. She certainly encouraged him in developing the performative power of his own personal image![53]

The Captive by Monk Lewis has already been cited as a highly emotive example of Gothic drama, but its monodramatic form owed much to the development of Musical Odes, that were not only recited on the English stage but were a central feature of Revolutionary *fêtes*. The style of its acting may also have been effected by the German influence that critics attributed to Lewis' plays. Goethe and Iffland were developing a 'chaste' style of performance at Weimar,[54] which looked for inspiration to Talma, and, after Goethe's visit to the Hamiltons in Naples, to the art of Attitudes.[55] We have already noticed the effect of Mrs Litchfield striking attitudes of grief, anguish and stupor in *The Captive*. That she drove her audience into hysterics suggests that this statuesque style, that seems so 'cool' in the salon performances of Hamilton, and in Goethe's 'Rules for Actors' of 1803, could be deeply disturbing when incorporated into a narrative of Gothic entrapment.

It is more difficult to identify changes of style and technique in comic acting – perhaps because the form is less idealised than tragedy. However, the tendency was for plays to shift from the polished social realism of Manner's Comedy towards the exaggerated situations of farce, and for characterisation to become stereotyped into a series of stock roles. In the performance of melodrama, actors specialised as heroes, villains and victims – often using the passionate technique already discussed – so in comedy actors either became stereotypically typecast or developed a particular skill in transforming themselves into a range of eccentrics who were superficially amusing but seldom deeply motivated. Although it is difficult to tell how actual techniques of personification changed in detail during the post-Revolutionary period, one or two differences can be identified by comparing the performers of that most successful comedy of manners, Sheridan's *The School for Scandal* (1777), and Thomas Morton's *Speed the Plough*, the hit comedy of 1800. The comparison made in the introduction above between *The Jealous Wife* and *John Bull* also applies to these two plays – the one of upper-class matchmaking the other of middle-class money-making – but here I wish to compare them as performance vehicles.

Sheridan cast his play with the best actors in a fine Drury Lane company, each good enough to enable Dutton Cook to dedicate virtually all the first volume of his *Hours with the Players* to them as representing the whole Georgian period.[56] It has also been claimed that 'all the characters in *The School for Scandal* [were] deliberately fashioned by Sheridan around the known temperaments and personalities of the performers who would play them'.[57] Tom King, who had been groomed by Garrick to take over the management of Drury Lane, was cast as Sir Peter Teazle, and he played the role for fifty-four years until his retirement in 1802, when it 'was the fashion to say that Sir Peter Teazle had quitted the stage with King . . . the actor had completely identified himself with the character'.[58] Lady Teazle was Mrs Abington, who had often played opposite Garrick, and she acted the part 'as a woman of fashion, in full possession of all the manners, characteristics, and even affectations, of society'.[59] Her interpretation, however, was eclipsed during the 1790s by Mrs Farren's beauty, and Mrs Jordan's emphasis on the rural origins of Lady Teazle: 'she quarrelled with her old rustic petulance, and showed her natural complexion; her rouge and her finesse she reserved for artificial life'.[60] Like the Teazle of Tom King, the Surface brothers were identified with their performers for the rest of their lives. William 'Gentleman' Smith created Charles Surface at the age of forty-seven, and, by the time he retired at sixty-eight, he had missed only one performance of the play at Drury Lane. 'Plausible Jack' Palmer seemed so ideally suited to his part that 'there must often have been doubt as to whether *Joseph Surface* was playing John Palmer, or John Palmer was playing *Joseph Surface*'.[61] But, although he could only have seen the later performances, Charles Lamb's description of Palmer's demonstrative style suggests more than just type-casting:

He downright *acted* the part . . . He was playing to you all the while that he was playing upon Sir Peter and his lady. You had the first intimation of a Sentiment before it was on his lips. His altered voice was meant for you, and you were to suppose that his fictitious co-flatterers on the stage perceived nothing at all of it . . . Jack had two voices, both plausible, hypocritical, and insinuating; but his secondary or supplementary voice still more decisively histrionic than his common one. It was reserved for the spectator . . . the sentiments of Joseph Surface were thus marked out in a sort of italics to the audience.[62]

On the contrary Jane Pope as Mrs Candour, who was the last of the original cast to survive, and could still play her role in 1805, when she was seen by Leigh Hunt: 'her affected sentiments are so inimitably hidden by the natural turns of her voice, that it is no wonder her scandal carries perfect conviction'.[63] Dodd, who played Sir Benjamin Backbite, and Parsons, who played Mr Crabtree, also kept their roles for the rest of their careers, but Cook recorded that they were very much actors of their own time: Dodd 'was the last of the fops whose line commenced with Colley Cibber . . . His fops and fribbles were essentially creatures of the eighteenth century.'[64]

This catalogue suggests a group of players who worked together with a strong sense of ensemble and integration, and with an equally strong personal relationship with their audience. To a great extent this corporate identity can be attributed to their early experience under the direction of David Garrick – all were considered to be part of the Garrick School – while their rapport with the audience had been learnt in the smaller theatre of Garrick's time. Although Drury Lane had been enlarged in 1775 to the design of Robert Adam, it was not until Henry Holland's rebuilding of 1794 that it lost its Georgian intimacy. Nevertheless, the sense of confidence that infused Sheridan's text was shared by the actors who played it, and it seems to reflect the 'enlightened' certainties of the pre-Revolutionary society. It was a society that might have been sensitive to imbalances between wealth and social status, and could be disturbed by vicious scandal or by the hypocrisy of a Joseph Surface, but it was not a society under threat. It could share with its favourite actors a sense of ironical humour because they all shared a sense of civilised security. Leading actors at Drury Lane were at the top of a respected profession, and most were at home in the social circle they were satirising.

The actors of Morton's *Speed the Plough* suggest a greater sense of insecurity, not just because the play itself was a hotchpotch of genres and styles, but because each actor seemed to be either trapped in a line of business that did not quite fit their personality, unlike King, Palmer and Smith, or were more self-consciously transforming themselves into unrealistic social stereotypes. They were no less talented but their profession was less secure, and their art was under harsher critical scrutiny. The range of characters, socially and psychologically, was perhaps wider than required by *The School for Scandal*, but their depiction was less subtle and there seems to be a diversity of acting methods which matched the variety of dramatic genres within the play. Several critics were disturbed that the play was 'composed of one half broad farce, the other half tragedy', though the *Morning Post* concluded this was because of the influence of 'those German Dramas so highly favoured'.[65] Morton had indeed based the melodramatic part of the plot on Kotzebue's *Der Graf von Burgand*,[66] but the play's main attraction was the perceptive conception and portrayal of the good-hearted Farmer Ashfield, his wife and daughter, and the satirical caricature of the inventor Sir Able Handy and his son Bob, who believes he is expert in everybody else's business. If the social conversation was crude when compared to Sheridan's witty interplay of insinuation and repartee, there was wider reference to developments in society, such as the proliferation of novelties spawned by the Industrial Revolution, and a respectful, rather than superior, depiction of the interaction between rural and urban interests. With this breadth of reference, Morton's characterisation owes more to 'humours' than to 'manners', and, although the variety of acting techniques displayed by the original cast cannot be explained solely by the range of demands made by the script, the ensemble integration that had typified Sheridan's company no longer existed at Covent Garden. This was partly because the repertoire as a whole had been transformed from the simple alternatives of comedy or tragedy by mixed-genre pieces, but also because the economic stability of the patent-house system had been undermined by the success of minor-house competition. This was leading to more commercial exploitation, to the passing of the

Garrick School of actors before the emergence of star performers, and to changes in audience composition and expectations, which in turn had led to the architectural challenge of the newly enlarged auditorium.

The senior members of the cast, Thomas Knight as Farmer Ashfield, Mrs Davenport as his wife, and Alexander Pope as the melancholy villain, Sir Philip Blandford, were traditional enough in their approach – though Knight could employ his native Dorset dialect. More indicative of the variety of styles within the acting company was the casting of Harry Johnston and his wife as the romantic leads, Henry and Miss Blandford. Boaden identified them as 'melodramatists of much consequence', with Harry Johnston able to 'convey sentiments, and describe the passions, unaccompanied by that useful assistant, speech'.[67] An example of his pantomimic use of passionate attitudes is seen in Morton's stage direction, when the sensitive subject of his parentage is innocently mentioned: 'HENRY, *in an agony of grief, turns away, strikes his forehead, and leans on the shoulder of* ASHFIELD' (Act 2, scene 4). Leigh Hunt was unimpressed: 'He indulges himself in all the cant of the stage, he rolls his eyes, frowns most terrifically, looks downwards on one side with a swelling front and in an attitude of stiff contempt.'[68] Sir Able Handy and his son Bob were played by two of the finest comedians of the time, John Fawcett junior and Joe Munden. Fawcett's father had played Moses in *The School for Scandal*, and the son had inherited his skill in character acting. He was the acting manager at the Haymarket, under Colman, and specialised in broadly characterised servants and eccentrics. As Sir Able Handy he combined the stereotype of the hen-pecked husband with that of the incompetent enthusiast. Thomas Dutton claimed that 'Broad farce and caricature are well adapted to [his] genius; but in the sentimental he is entirely out of his element.'[69] Joe Munden, who played Bob Handy, shared Fawcett's skill for low (or rather broad) humour, and has been immortalised for 'mugging' in Lamb's extravagant eulogy: 'There is one face of Farley, one face of Knight, one (but what a one it is!) of Liston; but Munden has none that you can properly pin down and call his. When you think he had exhausted his battery of looks, in unaccountable warfare with your gravity, suddenly he sprouts an entirely new set of features, like Hydra.'[70] Hunt, however, considered his skill as 'an innumerable variety of as fanciful contortions of countenance as ever threw woman into hysterics: his features are like the reflections of a man's face in a ruffled stream'.[71] If John Palmer's acting 'in italics' was signalling to the audience how they should react to the invidious Joseph Surface, Munden's relationship with the audience was 'droll' rather than ironic. His virtuosity in varying his exaggerated responses to comical situations, and his ability to use theatrical props – Bob Handy cannot leave anything alone and breaks everything he touches, spoiling Dame Ashfield's embroidery and smashing his father's patent plough – was shared with the audience with the wide-eyed innocence of a natural clown.[72]

Although comparing only two comedies is not the most thorough method of analysing changes in acting styles, the snapshot provided by *Speed the Plough* does suggest a very different ethos of playing than that employed in *The School for Scandal*. If the effectiveness of Sheridan's pre-Revolutionary company came from social poise and professional confidence, that of Covent Garden in 1800 lay in the mastery of individual 'lines of business'. Each actor may have had his or her moment to hold the stage, but there was less of the give-and-take of genuine ensemble playing. And, if there was competition for attention within a single play, this only reflected the increasingly entrepreneurial nature of the profession. Although eighteenth-century actors had travelled from London to Edinburgh and Dublin for short seasons, the early nineteenth century saw the start of star touring, which was to typify British theatre in the railway age. Individual actors visited provincial theatres for a week at a time and performed their favourite roles with the unrehearsed support of the local company. However, the principle of the ensemble company had not yet been intentionally discarded. In 1847 the 'Old Playgoer' William Robson could look back at the Covent Garden company in *John Bull* (1803) with nostalgia for its monopoly in legitimate comedy:

Harris was rich and could afford to keep a company round him that could play anything. I care not a rush for all the volumes that have been written against the monopolizing patents; the real play-goer had never seen a piece perfectly filled in all its parts since respectability was taken from the profession, and talents that could make two theatres brilliant and efficient were diffused over twenty.[73]

Perhaps the most telling example of the way things were going was the brief, but shocking, career of Master Betty, which started in Belfast in 1802 at the age of ten. He had seen Siddons perform, and thus inspired, had so impressed William Hough, the prompter of the

Belfast theatre, with his recitations that Hough decided to train the
boy in a number of star roles. In 1803 his precocious talent led to
engagements in Dublin, Edinburgh, Birmingham and other provincial theatres, and to a debut at Covent Garden on 1 December 1804,
as Achmet in *Barbarossa*, a long-neglected play by John Brown. Now
aged fourteen, Master Betty was engaged by both patent houses, and
not just for appropriate roles such as Young Norval and Romeo, but
Rolla, Hamlet and Richard III, which were the virtual property of
Kemble and Cooke. His vast and enthusiastic audiences were led by
the social glitterati of the day, including the Royal Princes, William
Pitt and Charles James Fox, and the Duchesses of Devonshire and
Bessborough, who invited him to their fashionable soirées.[74] Mrs
Inchbald's account of the packed first night provides a sensible and
professional assessment of Betty's accomplishments and the contra-
dictions in the audience's reception:

I saw his first performance, and was so disgusted by a monotony, a
preaching-like tone, that I gave up my place at the end of the third act, and
walked behind the scenes, where myriads of critics were gathered to listen
to their remarks. Here some vociferated that Garrick was returned to the
stage; whilst others whispered, 'The Bottle Conjuror' is come again. But as
all that is said for him is in a *loud* voice, and all against in a *low* one, praise
must go forth, and criticism be scarcely heard. Indeed on returning to my
seat, in the fifth act, I found he had great spirit, great fire in the
impassioned scenes, which gave variety to his tones, and made me say,
'This is a clever boy'; and had I never seen boys act, I might have thought
him extraordinary.[75]

Giles Playfair's 1967 biography compares Bettymania with Beatle-
mania. By analysing the blatant marketing, or 'puffing', of the boy
by his father, his tutor Hough and the theatre managers, he
concludes, firstly, that it 'must have been basically, however disgui-
sedly, a sexual phenomenon', and, secondly, although 'History says,
the public went temporally out of its mind, [it] was, on the contrary,
the result of a carefully planned appeal to Fashion . . . though
Fashion is notoriously capricious, its taste is not by definition
deluded.'[76] This analysis is unexceptionable, but, identifying Bettymania as primarily a showbiz construction, tends to underestimate
the political significance of 'Fashion' – and not only in the way that
clothing can be analysed as ideological, with which I started this
chapter. By claiming that 'at the beginning of the nineteenth century,
Fashion could be defined as the collective will of the aristocracy',

and that 'the rich suffered little from [the Napoleonic wars] in blood, and less than nothing from them in treasure',[77] Playfair fails to recognise that Master Betty functioned as a source of regressive escape from the genuine anxiety engendered amongst the upper classes by the emergence of the upstart Napoleon from out of what they saw as a decade of political chaos in France. It was, at least, an extraordinary example of coincidental synchronicity that the diminutive Betty was gaining his metaphorical laurels at the same time that Napoleon was planning his coronation. A Dublin journalist noted of the public media that, 'Young Roscius, as he is called, exclude almost every other matter from the columns of the London newspapers. Buonaparte, and his Invasion, and his Coronation, are alike forgotten and discarded', and the Duchess of Devonshire likewise commented of society circles that, 'though every day an account of Buonaparte's coronation and Russia's decision [to join Pitt's Third Alliance] is expected, nothing is hardly ever seen or talked about but the Young Roscius'.[78]

In a significant confirmation of Julie Carlson's claim for the 'new prominence of beauty as a social and political category',[79] William Betty's appeal was as much aesthetic as it was as a 'natural genius'. James Northcote, who painted several portraits of the boy, described his attraction to Hazlitt: 'It was such a beautiful effusion of natural sensibility; and then the graceful play of the limbs in youth gave such an advantage over everyone about him.' And Oziah Humphrey said that 'He had never seen the little Apollo off the pedestal before.'[80] This last remark, coming from a colleague of George Romney, suggests an aesthetic link with Emma Hamilton's recreation of classical statues. Indeed Playfair quotes a highly evocative letter from the Countess of Bessborough, describing a party at Lord and Lady Abercorn's on 5 March 1805:

Ly. Hamilton did her attitudes beautifully, not withstanding her enormous size – at least, the grave ones; she is too large for the Bacchantes. Roscius was there – very shy but amused with the attitudes. When his father insisted on his repeating something, he came up to me & said: 'You are so good natured: do beg me off, for I hate it.' However it was insisted on . . . He did repeat some things wonderfully, but was very indignant at Ly Hamilton kissing him, and colouring up like scarlet said: 'I'm too old to be kissed, Ma'am', as if he was resenting the greatest insult.[81]

At one level this was an absurd social occasion with entertainment provided by a superannuated beauty and a pubescent boy, but, when put into the context of the politics of this extraordinary year, the performers take on an iconic significance, both in the subject matter of their performances – Hamilton's classical attitudes and Betty's canonical soliloquies – and in the incongruity of their embodiment. Three months before, on the day of Betty's debut, Bonaparte (small of stature and of obscure origin) had crowned himself in Notre-Dame; in the previous month the king had once more to be restrained in his straight-jacket; in April, William Pitt (once himself 'the boy wonder' of politics) was to return to Downing Street, replacing the incompetent Dr Addington; and within seven months Hamilton's lover Nelson (also a hero of small stature) would die at Trafalgar.

How then should we read the 'cultural politics' of Bettymania? Of course there was no intentional political programme behind his exploitation. While his managers had their eyes firmly on the box office (Kemble and Siddons wisely refrained from acting throughout the period of his popularity), his devotees were astonished at his 'genius', delighted by his beauty and, perhaps, excited by his sexuality. But also one of their recurrent claims was that he was the reincarnation of a more glorious past – the new Garrick, the young Roscius. The images he performed were thus of classical perfection, whilst his personal image was of innocence and inspiration. What better distraction from the new-fangled armed ideology of France? What better validation for the naturalness of cultural nostalgia and for the innate creativity of the British? Beauty, nature and tradition were the icons of aristocracy and the cornerstones of Burkean conservatism. The court of Napoleon was artificial, a fantasy constructed on bourgeois pretension and the force of arms, hypocritically eliding professions of liberty with nationalistic aggrandisement, but in Britain we had the real thing – the purity of the child and the genius of nature. Such an interpretation must have been very tempting, but it was not one that could last for long.

The first doubts were raised when Betty attempted Richard III on 8 May 1805. Betty was doubly disadvantaged: firstly, in March 1805 his father had dismissed William Hough,[82] which doubtless undermined the boy's proficiency, and, secondly, Richard was the role in which George Frederick Cooke powerfully evoked the danger and fascination of the Corsican adventurer. The performance was greeted with some hisses and was never repeated. The *Daily Advertiser*'s reviewer implied the first hints of heresy:

Many may with great propriety, perhaps, insist upon his inferiority to Cooke in the same character; but there were some strokes of genius which appeared inimitable. Viewing it as a whole, it was a very wonderful performance; but we seldom forget that it was *Master* Betty's Richard, the marvellous working of a VERY EXTRAORDINARY BOY.[83]

Two weeks later Kemble returned to the stage as Othello with Cooke playing Iago. Playfair observes that they 'received a tremendous ovation. The Bettys sat, with a 'large party', in a stage box, watching, had they realised it, a bloodless counter-revolution. The King was restored to his throne.'[84]

Betty was re-employed for the 1805/6 season, but already his magic was wearing thin. Although people still came to see him in considerable numbers – particularly during his provincial tour between London engagements – it was with a more critical and inquisitive attitude. The young critic, Leigh Hunt, started a crusade to ridicule 'Rosciusism', and he was assisted by Kemble's own subversive strategy of bringing out another, less talented, child actor. Miss Mudie, aged eight, appeared in *The County Girl* three weeks before Master Betty's return to Covent Garden, and the absurdity of her lover having to embrace her on all-fours caused her to be hissed off. Similar prodigies were soon sprouting up in theatres throughout the provinces, and Betty himself became subject to Hunt's withering common sense, when he discussed his appeal as if it were past history:

Those who call themselves the friends of Master Betty insisted that he acted like a man and should be applauded as a man; his opponents insisted that all this was a gross absurdity . . . the more cool observer, who understood the caprice of the multitude, and the intrigues of the theatre, smiled at both parties, and . . . foresaw that it was exhausted novelty and that empty benches alone in a little time would cause the retirement of infancy from the stage.[85]

Betty's second season began on 23 November 1805, two weeks after the news of Trafalgar and the death of Nelson reached London, and nine days before Napoleon's victory at Austerlitz. Two months to the day after Betty's first night, Prime Minister Pitt died, and William Cobbett warned pretenders to Pitt's mantle that, 'The taste of the people has changed. They will never bear a second heaven-born Minister, any more that they will a second Roscius.'[86]

That one of the most dangerous years of the French Wars was marked in the main London theatres by the apotheosis of a fourteen-year-old boy could be taken as evidence of its complete irrelevance to the politics of its time. I prefer to think of it as a sign that people do indeed turn to the theatre in times of crisis, not necessarily to see their concerns enacted, debated or rehearsed, but to escape from anxiety. Nevertheless, the form that such escapism takes has deep significance, if examined properly, for it needs to make emotional, even if not rational, sense of the stresses in its audience. The Master Betty interlude presented a very precise, though negative, image of the concerns of the day. A little boy dressing up and showing off, a child inhabiting the classic roles of the national drama, provided a *metaphorical* critique of the upstart across the Channel, and fulfilled an unconscious desire to believe that the emperor, dressed in his new clothes, was no more threatening than a cautionary fairytale.

CHAPTER 6

The shadow of Napoleon

Much of the subject matter of this chapter is excellently covered by Gillian Russell in *The Theatres of War*,[1] and she in turn acknowledges the insight of Linda Colley into how the French wars forced Britain to redefine the social agencies attacked by the Revolution: royalty, aristocracy and patriotism. Earlier in the century England had fought France with relatively small armies over specific political issues. In Europe these had been questions of dynastic succession effecting the balance of power; across the rest of the world the issues had been trade and imperial territory. England had tended to win the colonial conflicts because of her naval supremacy, while gaining the epithet 'Perfidious Albion' for failing to support her European allies. The American War had been different, not only in that the British navy failed to guarantee victory, but that American Independence raised ideological issues that were to have serious internal repercussions for both England and France, as discussed in earlier chapters. The wars of 1792–1802 and 1803–15 were similarly ideological, but, being fought on home territory, they were even more challenging to the political systems and social structures of the participants. For the French, the campaigns of 1792–4 determined the survival of the Revolution, but only with an internal policy of terror. In England this distortion of Revolutionary ideals and the war itself, discredited the moderate reform movement, and seemed to vindicate Burke's alarming predictions. He had described the Revolutionary Army as 'an armed doctrine' and the British establishment set out to match its ideology with patriotic speeches, journals, pageantry and plays.

I have discussed earlier how much of this effected the theatre, but primarily in terms of the official censorship of subversion and the apparently unconscious adoption of 'mixed genre' entertainments that provided metaphorical, rather than overt, expressions of political attitudes. In this chapter I intend to consider the self-conscious celebrations of the patriotic struggle and how far they shared in the less conspicuous aspects of sociocultural expression already identified. As patriotic dramas advocated hegemonic principles they avoided controversy and asserted normalcy in simple narratives of the triumph of the natural and familial, the common-sense and typical, over the crafty, sophisticated, perverted and un-British. Patriotic fervour is ever thus, but during these wars the specific dialectics of rational Enlightenment and individualistic Romanticism pervaded even the banalities of the patriotic pageant.

Before considering traditional plays of plot and character, note must be taken of the proliferation of quasi-theatrical events, which used image and spectacle without – apparently – any narrative structure. Some, like military parades and naval reviews, seemed no more that a formal display of power, but even these incorporated a narrative directly contrary to those of the Revolutionary *fêtes*. At the Feast of Federation, Louis XVI was forced to participate in the ritual action and to repeat an oath of loyalty to the people, at the Portsmouth Review and at Bagshot camp George III was cast as the supreme spectator in whose honour the cheers were raised and the anthems sung. That he received these tributes with casual modesty, and without any declarations, confirmed him as the natural and respected leader of his people. This patriarchal image of George III was perhaps due as much to accident of temperament as conscious image manipulation, but it served the cause of British patriotism well. His image as a long-suffering parent afflicted by recurrent mental illness meant that personal sympathy augmented the inflation of royal dignity seen in the increasing splendour of Windsor Castle and Buckingham House.[2] Similarly his visits to the theatre combined greater ceremony and larger retinues with an impression of personal simplicity – George loved farce and could be visibly moved by pathos and sentiment.[3] Linda Colley comments on how 'the king and his ministers [determined] to make some attempt at emulation' of the Revolutionary *fêtes*:

The Naval Thanksgiving [December 1797] the *Morning Chronicle* judged was a 'Frenchified farce', not least because it broke with normal British practice and copied Revolutionary French precedent (and advertised the Royal Navy's return to loyal obedience after the recent mutinies at Spithead and Nore) by including in its ranks 250 ordinary sailors and marines. The king himself had been responsible for this innovation and for the initial decision to hold a thanksgiving.[4]

However in 1806 he did not attend the state funeral of Lord Nelson because 'such national marks of gratitude . . . should be exclusively paid to royalty',[5] which suggested a symbolic superiority over even his most honoured subjects.

Similarly patriotism itself was divorced from actual political issues and reified into an *abstract* virtue of loyalty to symbolic images of king and country. In the 1770s 'patriotism' had been castigated by Dr Johnson as 'the last refuge of a scoundrel'[6] claimed by Whiggish radicals to excuse their disloyalty to the king's government, but now that radicals could be arraigned, like Thomas Holcroft, for treason against the crown, patriotism was appropriated by the establishment. They propagated it to encourage the populace to join the fighting forces:

When the Bastille shattered in 1789, the British army was 40,000 strong. By 1814, it had expanded more than sixfold to some quarter of a million men. The Royal Navy, bedrock of defence, aggression, empire and trade, grew faster still. Before 1789 it had employed 16,000 men. By 1812, it employed over 140,000 . . . Mobilising these civilians presented an enormous challenge to the nerve and ingenuity of those in power. It was simply not enough anymore to maintain civil order and obedience by way of professional soldiers, barracks, surveillance and sermons. Nor was it even enough to foster loyalty by means of an intensive campaign of propaganda and patriotic ceremonial. In the face of economic distress, social upheaval and the lures of French Revolutionary doctrines, a major effort had to be made for almost a quarter of a century to encourage large numbers of men from a wide range of social backgrounds to take up arms.[7]

The existing system of militia, with a month's training each year, was hardly sufficient to counter the threat of invasion – a reality in 1797 with an army under Bonaparte mustered in Normandy – never mind mount expeditionary forces against the Continent. In 1796 and 1797 the militia were mobilised, 'gentleman volunteers' encouraged and military camps set up between London and the south coast. In 1798 a systematic effort was made to identify the number of able-bodied men and their readiness to 'volunteer'. Linda Colley's analysis of the 1798 and 1803 Defence of the Realm surveys suggests, contrary not only to the expectations of the government but the assumptions of subsequent historians, that a greater proportion of urban poor were prepared to be conscripted than 'loyal' countrymen – mainly because 'the urban artisan, because he had been acculturated, because he was more easily reached by propaganda and recruiting parties, and because, crucially, he was not tied to the land, could be a more useful citizen in time of war than the solitary ploughman'.[8]

As London was particularly vulnerable to the threat of invasion its citizens were the most susceptible to propaganda, and the theatres were well positioned to bring the war home to them:

For many people war was experienced not as a written text – newspaper account, pamphlet literature, the broadsheet, or handbill – but primarily as a communal event. Any assessment of the cultural impact of the French Wars has to take this into account. The response to the conflict was played out in the streets, commons and theatres of Britain, as much as it was in the printed media of the period.[9]

Chapter 2 described how the Fall of the Bastille was dramatised at the leading minor houses, and in 1793 there were a similar rash of popular spectacles. On 3 November 1792 Covent Garden mounted William Pearce's *Hartford Bridge; or, The Skirts of the Camp*, which, like Sheridan's *The Camp* of 1778, concentrated on the sightseers coming to watch the drilling and parades, although a song listing the terrors of war for a new recruit was 'omitted in representation'. Philip Astley, who had been a regular soldier during the Seven Years' War, was present as a volunteer at the capture of Valencienne by the Duke of York on 28 July 1793 (the day before Robespierre joined the Committee of Public Safety), and on his return to London he reconstructed the siege at the Amphitheatre. The stage was set with a view of the fortifications, while the circus ring was used for cavalry manoeuvres with a canon actually captured from the French.[10] Covent Garden already had several pieces in their repertoire that had been written for earlier conflicts: O'Keefe's *Love in a Camp* and *The Poor Soldier*, Bickerstaffe's *Thomas and Sally*, General Burgoyne's *The Maid of the Oaks*, and a ballet/pantomime by James Byrne now renamed *The Shipwreck; or, French Ingratitude*.[11] Performed on 27 May 1793, this last piece was accompanied by the nautical ballads of 'Black Eyed Susan' and 'Farewell to Old England', as well as Storace's new song 'Captivity', 'supposed to be sung by an Unfortunate Queen during her Confinement', all performed by Charles Incledon, a Cornishman who specialised in playing sailors. In 1794 there were more original pieces: John Cartwright Cross' *British Fortitude and Hibernian Friendship; or, an Escape from France* (Covent Garden, 29 April), Thomas Hurlstone's *To Arms; or The British Recruit* (Covent Garden, 3 May) and the anonymous *Fall of Martinico*, 'with the storming of the Fort' (Covent Garden, 24 May). The first two afterpieces were farcical comedies including Incledon as the sailor, Munden as a frightened but resourceful servant, and Jack Johnstone as a comic Irishman. These stereotypes were to be repeated many times, and can be interpreted as encouraging the lower orders to follow their masters into danger and the Irish to avoid nationalistic subversion, as well as celebrating the 'natural heroism' of the seaman.

Harris, the manager of Covent Garden, where all these plays were performed, was a loyal supporter of the Tory government, but Sheridan, proprietor of Drury Lane, was compromised by his early support for the Revolution and continuing commitment to reform.[12] The parliamentary Whigs had by now been reduced to a tiny minority and the pressure of war inevitably undermined their overt sympathy for the French. However, on 2 July 1794 Sheridan collaborated with James Cobb and Stephen Storace in a celebration of Admiral Howe's naval victory, *The Glorious First of June*. The performance was mounted as a benefit for the families of those who had died in the battle, which implied sympathy for the victims rather than unqualified support for the war. The plot too was open to interpretation. William has deserted from the navy in order to support the family of his dead shipmate Henry Russet. He has also to protect Henry's sister Susan from the designs of lawyer Endless, who wants their landlord, Commodore Chace, a decent retired naval officer, to foreclose their tenancy for unpaid rent. When the commodore learns that William is a deserter, his sympathies are torn, but on hearing that he has returned to sea he cancels the debt. After the subsequent naval victory William returns a hero ('I have gone to my post and shared your danger and your glory') and Commodore Chace condemns lawyer Endless to a ducking for 'the worst Act of Oppression – in grinding a poor Sailor's family'.[13] Elements of the play were drawn from Prince Hoare's farce *No Song, No Supper* and others referred to Dibdin's popular ballad 'Black-Eyed Susan'. It even anticipated Jerrold's famous play of the same name. All these characterised the typical sailor as one whose emotions and generosity lead him to break heartless regulations. Perhaps Sheridan was demonstrating that he himself ought not be considered unpatriotic just because he opposed the war policy.

On 28 June 1794 the King attended a great naval review at Portsmouth, and this led to two entertainments at the Haymarket. On 18 August James Roberts' *Rule Britannia*, Act 1 ended with 'A Grand View of the British Fleet and the French Prizes entering

Portsmouth, and an appropriate Procession. The Piece to conclude with a representation of the Town &c. of Portsmouth, as illuminated on the glorious day. With a Transparency of Earl Howe.'[14] Two days later Robert Benson's *Britain's Glory; or, Trip to Portsmouth* contained a new mechanised panorama of the review itself. The plot was mostly patriotic bluster in praise of Howe and his jolly tars, but it also contained an attack on an able-bodied civilian selling souvenirs:

> What a shame it is that a Man, especially an Englishman, should stand behind a Counter to hand out Ribbands and Topknots when hundreds of our Countrywomen want employment. Ah! no wonder there are so many unfortunate Girls at a loss for a comfortable Berth and founder'd on the Quick Sands of distress when such lazy lubbers as you prevent their making an honest livelihood by taking up a Business which they only ought to pursue, and which is beneath the character of a man to follow.

It also made a more specifically political reference to the constitution than normally Larpent would have excised, but given the occasion and the sentiment it is not surprising that he passed it:

> RUDDER. Britannia is as noble a vessel as was ever launch'd and I think the Constitution is a well constructed little Frigate too.
> CAPT. FREEMAN. Well said my lad and you all shall drink a Bumper to that frigate. Charge your Glasses – may the English Constitution never have a Rotten Plank, but live in spite of every Squall of Faction and sail down the Current of Time the wonder of the World.[15]

That sailors rather than soldiers were used to express such sentiments of British Liberty reflects their greater popularity with the public. Ever since the Commonwealth people had feared the use of the army to oppress rather than defend traditional liberties.[16] Thomas Paine wrote that soldiers were 'shunned by the citizens as apprehensive of their being enemies to liberty, and too often insulted by those who commanded them',[17] which was the opposite to Leigh Hunt's portrait of the sailor on leave as 'a conqueror taking possession. He has been debarred so long, that he is resolved to have the matter out with the inhabitants . . . treading in a sort of heavy light way, half waggoner and half dancing master'.[18] The sailor's swagger, brawny arms and sunburnt complexion compared impressively with the physique and restrictive uniform of the barracks-bound soldier. Receiving their pay and prize money in a lump sum at the end of a voyage, sailors seemed more liberal and good-natured than soldiers who, on brief leave from their barracks, appeared either brutish or subservient. Sailors were certainly enthusiastic play-goers, while their pay lasted, calling for the orchestra to give them hornpipes and sea shanties. The prolific Charles Dibdin responded to this demand by writing dozens of nautical ballads, many of which were sung 'between the acts' at Covent Garden by Incledon, 'in the character of a sailor'. His most popular song was the unaccompanied 'Sea Storm', which was introduced at Munden's benefit at Covent Garden (3 May 1793) in a programme of Holcroft's *Road to Ruin*, with Munden as Goldfinch, and Hurlstone's *To Arms; or The British Recruit*, in which he was drilled by Johnstone's Irish sergeant-major. The contradictory signals of a programme that included a comedy by a notorious French sympathiser, an afterpiece gently satirising the military, and a solo song glorifying sailors suggests that the patriotic fare was produced because it was genuinely popular rather than because it was part of a co-ordinated policy of propaganda.

If Incledon was the classic noble-hearted tar, Mrs Jordan made a more oblique appeal to nautical popularity. In *The Spoilt Child* (Drury Lane, 22 March 1790), probably by Isaac Bickerstaffe, who had gone into exile in 1772 after being accused of homosexuality, she played the young boy, Little Pickle, and sang its most popular air 'What Girl But Loves the Merry Tar' dressed as a cabin boy.[19] Gillian Russell uses this performance, and Dibdin's popular lament for young 'Tom Bowling', to reflect on the homoerotic image of seamen, suggesting that in Jordan's mischievous boy,

cross-dressing was not being used to draw attention to the female body but instead to create an image of androgyny – the adolescent sailor as 'masculine-feminine'. The fact that the stage-sailor could represent a congruence of so many strands of erotic desire – both heterosexual and homosexual – is an indication of the powerful fascination exerted by the navy upon Georgian society.[20]

In 1797 this sympathetic fascination was put to a severe test. On 14 February Sir John Jervis had thwarted French invasion plans by destroying the Spanish fleet off Cape St Vincent. However, this victory was followed by naval mutinies, at Spithead in April and at the Nore in May. There was considerable sympathy for the Spithead sailors, and Lord Howe guaranteed redress of their grievances, but at the Nore, under the leadership of an Irish radical, Richard Parker, the demands went beyond better living conditions and the mutiny was put down viciously, its ringleaders hanged.[21] The very real fear of invasion and of stress amongst normally dependable sailors during 1797 and 1798 sparked off another wave of patriotic manifestations, which like the reviews of 1792/3 were reproduced on various London stages, though Covent Garden still presented more than Drury Lane.[22] Of these, two deserve special notice. John Cartwright Cross drew together the conventions of the history play and the contemporary patriotic review in a spectacular ballet/pantomime, *Joan of Arc; or, The Maid of Orleans* (Covent Garden, 12 February 1798). Following Shakespeare's propagandist model of *Henry VI*, Joan was portrayed as a witch selling her soul to the Devil, but, more originally, the play concluded with a pageant of British triumphs presided over by Britannia, including Caractacus, Richard Cœur de Lion, Magna Carta, Edward and Eleanor, the Black Prince and Agincourt – the whole an illustrated version of Burke's interpretation of history.

Of the few topical pieces at Drury Lane, Adam Franklin's *A Trip to the Nore* (Drury Lane, 9 November 1797) was similar in many ways to other dramatisations of civilian citizens flocking to view military celebrations, in this case a naval review to celebrate the Battle of Camperdown, in which the Dutch fleet had been defeated. It had the usual cast of national and social types, but Gillian Russell's interpretation of its opening crowd scene has particular political relevance:

[It] is significant for the way that it attempts to theatricalize the energy and potency of the Georgian crowd – the piece begins with the scene direction '*Enter a Mob of People, shouting and running.*' This representation of the people is closer to Paine's 'open theatre of the world' than to the disciplined, choric masses of pageantry. However, the energy of the mob in *A Trip to the Nore*, once theatrically realized, is directed towards the enhancement of patriotic values, rather than their deconstruction, as Paine was suggesting.[23]

Although the piece ends safely with civilians and sailors singing the usual anthems, just for a moment we see that London could produce a mob as vital as that of Paris. Russell argues that the levels of signification in this performance, and others like it, 'are manifold':

an audience watching a topical afterpiece that in turn represented the audience's own participation in an event – a military review rendered as theatrical spectacle – which was itself an example of the theatricalized commemoration of war (One might go further and claim that the battle of Camperdown, governed by the rules of naval engagements, was itself a kind of theatre). The worlds of war, civic space, and the theatre are here synthasized, made inseparable, as are the actions of spectatorship and participation.[24]

It would thus seem that this piece submerged the individuality of crowd members into a 'mob', perhaps for the first time since the Bastille plays of 1789/90. Most patriotic plays individualised civilian crowds on stage, even though their characterisation was usually stereotypical, to differentiate the amiable British crowd from the anonymous masses involved in the violent *journées* of Paris. The military too was dramatised as composed of individuals – even incompetent or reluctant individuals like Munden in *The British Recruit*. The use of this convention is easily recognised as political in popular drama, and such a reading suggests that the subjective individualisation of characters and creators that we have seen to be typical of Romantic culture had an equally strong, though less conscious, political imperative. This thought leads me to expand on Russell's analysis of the theatre being used as a homogenising process. She describes a fight in *A Trip to the Nore* between the sailor Bowsprit and the cowardly tailor Buckram, who claims that, at least, he had subscribed to the government's Voluntary Contribution scheme and had attended patriot benefits at Drury Lane, and she recognises that here, as in most patriotic pieces, the climactic singing of 'Rule Britannia' is constructed as a *compromising* resolution to the drama. The individuality expressed in earlier scenes of personal conflict, and in the ridiculing of social types, is now put aside as an act of duty towards the symbolic authority of crown and country. In this respect the British anthems are used differently from the *Marseillaise* in the Paris *fêtes*, or the *Internationale* during the Russian Revolution, which expressed the revolutionary principle that achieving a community of interests is not just a 'sinking of differences' but the finest manifestation of human aspiration. Thus, while the *Rule Britannia* boasted of 'never being slaves', the emphasis of the *Marseillaise* was less on individual liberty than the fraternity of the people of France marching towards a future of equality.

Playing the national anthem often caused theatrical disturbances across the country. The military insisted that it exposed the treasonous disloyalty of radicals and the discontented.[25] During the Spithead mutiny, the Portsmouth theatre was a vital meeting place for both sides, and soldiers dared not attend in uniform, until a body of officers went *en masse* to demand the singing of 'God Save the

King.'[26] In Belfast, not long after the United Irishmen had been brutally put down in 1800, army officers beat up a man who failed to remove his hat for the anthem. Such disturbances were only a minor symptom of the actual discontent felt across the country during the wars. Political reform may have been rendered a dead letter for the duration, but social resentment and economic distress could not be magically transformed by a sea shanty or national anthem. Not surprisingly plays trying to demonstrate the unifying power of patriotism did not always ring true, and relied on simplified stereotypes and farcical action before building up to a climax of symbolic spectacle, accompanied by various patriotic melodies.

After the fall of Robespierre, power in France passed to those financial classes that had been the originating force of the Revolution. They had allied with the discontented nobles in 1789, and deployed the urban poor in tumultuous *journées*, but after the coup of Thermidor (28 July 1794) the Convention consolidated around its liberal bourgeois principles. It retreated from the levelling policies of the Jacobins, restricted the power of the Sections in the Paris Commune, used regular troops to put down the last sansculottes' demonstrations of Germinal (23 May 1795), and, after the establishment of the executive Directory (31 October 1795), decisively suppressed Babeuf's communistic challenge to the principle of private property. Although – or perhaps because – the Directoire was essentially counter-revolutionary, the Revolutionary Army became increasingly successful under their administration. Paul McGarr describe how in this period,

the revolution had its greatest impact abroad through the war moving from the defensive to the offensive – ranging from Italy to Germany to an attempted invasion of Ireland. Though the Directory was internally reactionary, it was forced in its expansive wars to uproot aspects of the old order in a string of countries across Europe to achieve its goals. This process was continued under Bonaparte. Often this was done with the support of local 'patriots' (i.e., bourgeois revolutionaries) though they were strictly subordinated to the aims of the French and often suppressed when their national ambitions came into conflict with French plans. Republics were created such as the Cisalpine, Roman and Parthenopæan in Italy or the Batavia Republic in Holland.[27]

In 1797, once he realised that the British navy could indefinitely thwart a direct invasion, Bonaparte conceived a plan to attack Britain's trade route to the east, which the Directory approved partly from fear of his mounting reputation and influence.[28] In May 1798 the Toulon fleet set sail for Egypt with Bonaparte's army complete with engineers planning to build a canal through the Suez Isthmus. Avoiding Nelson's Mediterranean patrols, they reached Egypt in July. The Egyptian adventure, though ultimately unsuccessful, made a huge contribution to the Napoleonic myth. Antoine-Jean Gros' huge painting *Bonaparte Amongst the Plague Victims of Jaffa* (1804) depicts him touching a sick Arab, while his *aides-de-camp* cover their faces with handkerchiefs. Thus the European genius was shown connecting with the exotic and suffering Orient with a Christ-like gesture of healing – though the theatrical stance and atmospheric lighting equally suggested Romantic bravado. There was certainly no hint that Jaffa was the scene of a massacre, in which Bonaparte had 2,000 prisoners shot in cold blood, after his officers had been reluctant to sack the city without quarter. It also became generally believed in England that Bonaparte, rather than sharing the dangers of plague, as depicted by Gros, ordered those of his own men who were too sick to embark to be poisoned with laudanum.[29]

The visual construction of Bonaparte as the 'Man of Destiny', seen at its most panoramic in Gros' battle scenes, had begun in 1800, when, after returning from Egypt he led an army over the St Bernard pass to reconquer Italy at the Battle of Marengo (14 June 1800). On his return to Paris, David, who had painted his portrait in 1797 and had been invited to join the Egyptian expedition, depicted him crossing the Alps. This equestrian portrait, one of the cult images of Romanticism, was 'painted according to Napoleon's own wishes and not to those of David'.[30] David's *Oath of the Horatii* had inspired the Tennis Court Oath, his *Death of Marat* commemorated the sacrifice of the Revolution, and now he – and his pupils Gros, Girodet and Gericault – helped construct the unmistakable image of Napoleon and his empire. Historians ever since have perceived Napoleon in visual and dramatic terms – his stage, his tragedy, his presence and performance – even his costumes, the imperial robe embroidered with bees and the plain grey overcoat and turned-up hat. Typically, John Holland Rose, writing in 1904, described the Egyptian expedition as 'a melodramatic enterprise, intended to exalt the fame of Bonaparte at the expense of the unpicturesque mediocrities who then ruled at Paris; and as such it was an unqualified success'.[31] However, it is ironic and revealing that David's bread-and-butter portraits of these 'mediocrities' – merchants, bureaucrats and professionals – were painted with a personal sensitivity lacking from his rhetorical history paintings:

> On the one hand, he paints contemporary subjects, whether portraits or what might be called portrait journalism, with a lack of doctrinal preoccupation, which corresponds to his most innate sensibilities. On the other hand, he makes cumbersome attempts to get back to a state of aesthetic grace . . . by undertaking immensely complicated Antique subjects, seething with incident and full-length figures, their surfaces deadened by the slowness with which he worked.[32]

In this 'bifurcation of his style', David reveals that behind the extraordinary ambition, achievement and display of the Napoleonic adventure lay the mundane and materialistic power of money. The consulate and empire might have replaced the Directoire, but the French middle classes saw the change as one of retrenchment rather than divergence, they believed of Napoleon that the gains of the Revolution (their gains) were safe in his hands.

Certainly the theatre under Napoleon was 'rescued' from ideological conflict and uncontrollable competition, and became tamed and regulated along sound business lines. For bourgeois audiences liberty and equality in the theatre had meant anarchy and vulgarity, and they looked back nostalgically to the stability and tastefulness of the pre-Revolutionary theatre. Chapter 3 above described how extreme Jacobins had tried to encourage politically motivated dramas and enforce republican imagery in performance. This had caused particular stress for the Comédie-Française, splitting the company, moving its premises, changing its names, rebuilding its theatre and eventually causing its actors to be arrested.[33] Upon their release after Thermidor, the Comédie actors returned to the Théâtre du Nation rebuilt as le Théâtre de l'Egalité with pit, boxes and gallery unified into a single amphitheatre, with allegorical statues and busts of Revolutionary martyrs around the auditorium. In 1795 they moved to the more traditionally designed Théâtre Feydeau and in 1798 joined forces with Talma's company from the République, thus virtually reconstituting the old royal company. Of the once 'illegitimate' theatres of the Boulevard du Temple and the Palais-Royal, the companies that thrived in the post-Robespierre period were also those which had pre-Revolutionary origins: the Italienne was now the Opéra-Comique housed in the Théâtre Favart, Nicolet's Grandes-Danseurs was the Gaîté, Audinot's was still the Ambigu-Comique, as was the Délassements-Comiques, and

Montansier's theatre, which had started as the Beaujolais in 1784, was now the Théâtre des Variétés and the fashionable resort for the *jeunesse doré* of the Directoire.

Root-Bernstein argues, and the statistics of Kennedy and Netter confirm, that the repertoire of these theatres changed less during the height of the 'cultural revolution' than was suggested in the earlier histories of Hamiche and Carlson, and that after 1795 there seems to have been a greater homogeneity of audiences for the various genres offered at different theatres. It would also seem that, although this generic specialisation of drama, opera, musicals and variety was now determined by market forces rather than by the regulations of the old regime, there was less of a clear split between élite and popular cultures than was once thought. Kennedy and Netter come to a very clear conclusion:

Despite the theatrical innovations of the Revolutionary theatre – *faits-historiques*, *pièces-patriotiques*, *vaudevilles*, *mélodrames* – the main Revolutionary thrust was continuity with the Old Regime and resistance to Revolutionary politicization. Nothing proves this better than the list of the fifty most performed plays of the 1790s and a similar list of top authors. For some reason, difficult to identify, a substantial segment of theatregoers, most likely the majority, remained attached to the pre-Revolutionary repertory . . . This points to two possible interpretations: (1) many sansculottes (taken here in a social rather than political sense) were dissatisfied by the Revolution and sought solace in the theatre; (2) many sansculottes (in the radical political sense) sought diversion in the evening from taxing political commitments of the day. [In either case] its entertainment world proved more Rabelaisian than Robespierrist.[34]

Although it is difficult to argue with the statistical evidence for such an interpretation, I would like to raise two points not much considered in these recent studies. Firstly, they do not analyse apparently non-political plays in the way I have interpreted the metaphors of English drama, which was produced under direct ideological pressure to maintain a non-political, nostalgic repertoire. As I will argue when considering the genre of melodrama, which originated on the French stage, there was often a more disturbed and subversive agenda concealed behind its apparently simple manichean morality. Secondly, neither Root-Bernstein nor Kennedy emphasise the increasing power of bourgeoisie capitalism, which may not have been visible on the streets of Paris but was a determining factor in the economic and social policies of even the Robespierrist Jacobins. One might have expected merchants and industrial entrepreneurs to have had more in common with the Girondins than the puritanical Robespierre, but, until the rule of Terror and Virtue developed into personal paranoia, his ruthless pragmatism was more to the advantage of economic stability than the idealism of the Girondin intellectuals. The capitalists' Revolutionary hero was Carnet, the 'architect of victory', and just as he survived purge after purge, so the essentially bourgeois agenda of resistance to the dead hand of privilege allied to the expansionism made possible as the war became offensive continued to guide the Revolution between the shoals of royalist reaction and the storms of mob rule. These capitalist principles were not always a declared policy, but they were acknowledged by most leaders as economic and political 'necessity'.

This interpretation of the Revolution as an essentially capitalist process cannot be argued in detail in a study of this kind, but it owes much to the Marxist analysis of McGarr and Callinicos. The latter, having addressed the revisionist arguments of the 1970s and 1980s as to the class nature of the Revolution, points out that defining 1789–1802 as a 'bourgeois revolution' is not a matter of identifying specific details of policy, but of considering the original impetus for, and the ultimate results of, a long and contradictory pattern of events:

Bourgeois revolutions exist at the intersection between objective historical processes and conscious human agency. As 'episodes of convulsive political transformation' they involve collective action, including the intervention of political organisations of various kinds. But bourgeois revolutions also arise from and contribute to 'the increasing predominance of the capitalist mode of production'. As such, they tend to involve a gap between the intentions of the revolutionary actors and the objective consequences of their struggles.[35]

However, it was not always an invisible tendency. The bourgeois position was starkly spelt out by Boissy d'Anglas when he introduced the legislation to set up the Directory in September 1795:

A country governed by men of property belongs to the social order, whereas one governed by men of no property reverts to a state of nature. [The Convention] must guarantee the property of the rich [and resist] the fallacious maxims of absolute democracy and unlimited equality which are without doubt the most serious threats to true liberty.[36]

Thus after Thermidor sansculotte populism was suppressed, but those who had gained most from the Revolution were equally resistant to any royalist revival. Having purged the National Guard of working-class activists, the Directory used the regular army, not only to drive the English, with their baggage train of émigrés, out of Quiberon (June 1795), but also to deliver the 'whiff of grapeshot' that scattered the royalist demonstration of 13 Vendémiaire (5 October 1795).

Eventually the army became so involved in maintaining the internal stability essential for offensive campaigns that Bonaparte, returning from Egypt to find the Second Coalition gaining ground in Italy and Germany, led the coup of 18 Brumaire (10 November 1799) to overthrow the Directory and establish the Consulate. In December his domination was confirmed by his being appointed first consul. Bonaparte's achievements as ruler of France were to be as remarkable as his military victories. But, just as these victories were marked by a ruthless disregard for casualties, as much as by strategic brilliance, so his civic achievements were at the expense of the venal promotion of his own family, the extravagant creation of an imperial court and the ruthless suppression of political opposition from both left and right. Nevertheless, he did give shape and permanency to the main achievements of the Revolution, as Eric Hobsbawm concluded:

Admittedly most – perhaps all – of his ideas were anticipated by the Revolution and Directory; his personal contribution was to make them rather more conservative, hierarchical and authoritarian. But his predecessors anticipated: he carried out. The great lucid monuments of French law, the Codes which became models for the entire non-Anglo-Saxon bourgeois world, were Napoleonic. The hierarchy of officials, from prefect down, of courts, of university and schools, was his . . . He brought stability and prosperity to all except the quarter-of-a-million Frenchmen who did not return from his wars; and even to their relatives he brought glory.[37]

Yet the little Corsican had come from nowhere, and this made him both inspirational and frightening. In his personal demeanour, and his taste of reading, art and theatre, he seemed unexceptional, a rational product of the Enlightenment: 'in a word, he was a figure every man who broke with tradition could identify himself with in his dreams'.[38] Yet there was a nightmare version of Bonaparte that was to find expression on the stages, not only of England, his mortal enemy, but also of France, in the villains and *banditti* of Romantic melodrama. However, before considering the ideological implications of melodrama, I shall resume the narrative of British drama and the war.

The conclusive victory of the Egyptian campaign was not Bonaparte's but Nelson's destruction of the French fleet at the mouth of the Nile (1 August 1798). This not only ensured the expedition's eventual failure after Bonaparte's return to France (9 October 1798), but encouraged the reconstruction of the coalition of England, Austria, Prussia and Russia, and inspired Italians to claim independence from both Austria and France. Nelson spent several months assisting various Italian uprisings, including that in Naples where Lady Hamilton nursed the wound he had received at the Nile.[39] These momentous events inspired an anonymous play, or 'dramatic poem on the model of the Greek Tragedy' entitled *The Battle of the Nile*, published in 1799. Though not intended for the stage, it is interesting theatrically as being inspired by Greek rather than Roman drama. The preface claims it was a 'free imitation of the conduct, rather than a servile Copy of the Sentiments, of Aeschelus', and it follows the pattern of *The Persians* very closely, as if to equate Nelson's victory with that of Salamis. As in Aeschelus, the action is set amongst the defeated, with the ghost of Louis XVI returning like that of Darius. A chorus of old men deplore the hubris of the Directors and their chosen hero, Bonaparte:

> August Directors, plac'd upon a Throne
> Higher than e'er was reached by Kings, to you
> France bends. Your will is law . . .
> Before them rode, mounted on a steed
> Richly caparison'd, a royal Gift,
> Bearing upon his Helm a stately Plume,
> The Hero, who hath rais'd the fame of France,
> Italia's dread. All eyes he draws, yet pass'd
> Proudly unheeding on.

The Messenger, bringing news of the Nile to the distraught Directors, describes the very different demeanour of Nelson:

> Ne'er did Man, with such bright Glory cloth'd,
> Bear him so meek. To god he gave the praise,
> Owning himself his humble Minister.

As the Directors despair of invading England, more Messengers arrive with news of attacks from Prussia, Turkey and the Russian hoards of Poles, Siberians, Tartars, Kalmucks, Finns and Kamschadals. Ships are lost in the Channel, Belgium is in revolt and the chorus predicts the same in Spain and Switzerland. Into this scene of disaster enters, not the saviour Bonaparte, but the Ghost of Louis, 'Martyr once, now Saint in Heaven', who bewails the folly of his subjects:

> O my People . . . perplex'd
> In error, from right reason far and god
> Ye stray, by proud conceits and fancies wild,
> Offsprings of minds vain and misled, enslaved . . .
> Ye hop'd to build your realm on Britain's fall'n.
> As easy might ye the vast Earth-bound Rock
> Pluck from the Deep, or stay the rolling Sphere,
> As over Britain Conqueror stand. She rules
> In Justice, and the weal of all the world
> Seeks in her Councils.

Not having being performed, little can be said of the impact of this poem, except that it displays, free from the Licenser's pencil, a classical image of Britain comparable to that of David, Talma and the Romanised Consulate, and it indicates that patriotic fervour was not just the fare of popular audiences. While this poetic effusion was being composed, a more influential piece was being prepared by which Richard Sheridan was to make amends for the scarcity of patriotic pieces in the repertoire at Drury Lane.

In December 1798 the *Monthly Mirror* gave advanced notice that he was combining two plays by Kotzebue, *Die Sonnenjungfrau* (1788) and *Die Spanier in Peru, oder Rolla's Tod* (1796), which were both playing at the Imperial Theatre, Vienna. Benjamin Thompson had already translated *The Spaniard in Peru* for his collection of German drama, while Matthew Lewis' version, intended for Covent Garden, was forestalled by Sheridan's *Pizarro*. Cecil Price concludes that Sheridan actually worked from the translation by Anne Plumtre.[40] The production on 24 May 1799 had all the artistic support Drury Lane could muster: Barrymore as Pizarro the Spanish conquistador, Siddons as his mistress Elvira, Jordan as the Inca heroine Cora, wife to Charles Kemble's Alonzo, a Spaniard who has joined the Incas, who are led by Rolla played by John Kemble. Michael Kelly arranged the music, and Loutherbourg was persuaded back to the theatre to provide designs realised by Alexander Johnston, the theatre's chief machinist.[41] Pizarro's tent, the Inca Temple of the Sun and the climactic mountain gorge were all greatly admired.

Sadly, as was often the case, Sheridan's script was too long and unfinished until the last minute, and was thus under-rehearsed on the first night.[42]

However, despite a mixed critical reception, the play proved a huge success with the public, taking, according to Frederick Reynolds, £30,000 in sixty nights.[43] This success should be no surprise as Sheridan managed to bring together virtually all the characteristic features of the period. Like *Inkle and Yarico*, and other anti-slave trade plays, it showed the persecution of innocent natives by a colonial force. The venerable Las Casas, from whose account the history of Peru's invasion was drawn, evokes the natural morality of the so-called savages: 'A People, who, children of innocence received you as cherish'd guests with eager hospitality and confiding kindness . . . you repaid by fraud, oppression, and dishonour . . . as Gods you were received; as Fiends have you acted' (Act 1, scene 1). In the second act, after a Rousseauesque procession of priests and virgins that recalls Robespierre's ceremony in honour of the Supreme Being, Rolla the Inca general delivers a speech in the Temple of the Sun that was much expanded from Kotzebue by Sheridan to compare their constitutional purity with the illegality of Pizarro's invaders:

> THEY, by a strange frenzy driven, fight for power, for plunder, and extended rule – WE, for our country, our altars, and our homes. – THEY follow an Adventurer whom they fear – and obey a power which they hate – WE serve a Monarch whom we love – A God whom we adore . . . THEY will give enlightened freedom to *our* minds, who are themselves the slaves of passion, avarice, and pride. – They offer us their protection – Yes, such protection as vultures give to lambs. (Act 2, scene 2)

This last image Sheridan borrowed from his own tirade against Warren Hastings.[44] However, Rolla's speech was received, as intended, as a call to Britons against the threat of Bonaparte and his Army of Invasion. I will return to the more subtle political implications of the speech later.

Sheridan expanded Kotzebue's original Elvira, Pizarro's mistress, to give Siddons a role which ennobles the fallen woman, who, more like Jane De Monfort than Mrs Haller, asserts herself when excluded from the 'manly business' of the Spaniard's council: 'O Men! men! ungrateful and perverse, I shall not retire!' A line Siddons delivered with 'a dignity and resolution, which even shook the tyrant'.[45] Later, more like Jane Shore than Jane De Monfort, she lets her own 'crime' enflame her hatred of the man who had betrayed her love: 'Thou [who] wouldst defy the world in that extremity! – come, fearless man – now meet the last and fellest peril of thy life – meet! and survive – an injured woman's fury, if thou canst.' Finally, she appears dressed in a nun's habit,[46] and distracts Pizarro, who believes her dead, from his duel with Alonzo, and Alonzo runs him through. The image and its result could have been lifted straight from Lewis' *Castle Spectre*.

This comparison is amplified by the portrayal of Pizarro himself, not only as a bloodthirsty conqueror, personally vindictive and vengeful, but also, like other Romantic villains, suffering from self-generated despair. He is discovered in his tent tossing in guilty sleep like Richard III, and when finally affected by Rolla's generosity he cries in hopeless remorse: 'I would I cou'd retrace my steps – I cannot – wou'd I could evade my own reflections! – No! – thought and memory are my Hell' (Act 5, scene 3). Equally typical of the period is the escape scene, in which Rolla takes the place of his friend Alonzo so that he can return to his wife and child – the wife Cora being the object of Rolla's own devotion. Finally the scene of Rolla's escape and death reproduces the scenic machinery of many sensational dramas: '*The back ground wild and rocky, with a torrent falling down a Precipice, over which a Bridge is formed by a fell'd Tree*', by which Rolla escapes with Cora's child snatched from the arms of the tyrant, and, though mortally wounded, '*tears from the rock the tree which supports the bridge, and retreats by the back ground, bearing off the child*' (Act 5, scene 2).

These typical ingredients ensured the play's success with all sections of the Drury Lane audience. The transparency of its metaphorical reference to the recent history of France gave it extra potency, and that it was Sheridan's first full-length production for thirty years gave it extra piquancy – particularly as his own attitude towards the French had been so controversial. In 1798 he had tried to dissociate his own opposition to Pitt from the disloyalty of the naval mutineers, and the emergence of military rule in France had disillusioned him even more than the dominance of Robespierre – then France had been fighting for its survival, but under the Directory defence had turned to aggression. Indeed, rather than equating the Incas with the English, a more subtle interpretation of the play is to think of them as the Girondins of 1792 – perhaps naïve, but pure in their dedication to the earliest principles of the Revolution.[47] In April 1792 Sheridan had proclaimed himself a Friend of the People in opposition to Burke's pessimistic prophesies, but by 1799 Burke seemed to have been vindicated. Perhaps in Rolla's death Sheridan saw the passing of his early hope for radical reform – English as well as French – though in death Rolla saves the child who might, in more propitious times, revive that hope.

John Loftis too argues that the play is more than patriotic propaganda, or the 'U-turn' of a tired politician, and that Alonzo's declaration – 'I have not warred against my native land, but against those who have usurped its power' (Act 3, scene 3) – need not be read solely as the justification of an émigré:

Alonzo's declaration of principles, appearing in a play by a man who had long been second only to Fox in the force of his criticism of the government's policies, may not be free of Whig innuendo . . . He had long been a leading participant in the parliamentary debates, consistently opposing the repressive measures Pitt had undertaken in response to the French Revolution . . . Sheridan might not unreasonably have thought that the Prime Minister had abandoned the humanitarian principles that they had earlier shared.[48]

Even more to the point than his Whiggish opposition to ex-reformer Pitt was Sheridan's defence of Arthur O'Connor, leader of the United Irishmen, who was certainly involved in the treasonous plan of an armed uprising to coincide with a French invasion. When O'Connor was arrested in 1798, Sheridan negotiated on his behalf with Dundas, Secretary of War, and in the House, while denying knowledge of plans for an uprising, castigated those 'wicked ministers who have broken the promises they held out . . . who have given that devoted country to plunder . . . and abandoned it to every species of insult and oppression'.[49] In the light of such sentiments might not the Peruvians also be read as the oppressed and ridiculed Irish?

A further parallel between Sheridan's real-life sympathies and those within the play is perhaps more fanciful, but it may have had an influence, at least subconsciously. Ever since the days of the Regency Crisis, Sheridan had been the chief political advisor and drinking companion of the Prince of Wales. During 1798 Sheridan and Fox had discussed Irish issues at Carlton House, and hoped to involve the Prince of Wales in opposition to the government's crushing the rebels, but on 24 June the Earl of Moira warned George against making any public 'avowal of your sentiments'.[50] Although it was never in Sheridan's interest to express dissatisfaction with the prince, he must have often felt private frustration at his unreliability, and, since George's loveless marriage to Caroline of Brunswick in 1796, sympathy for his long-suffering Roman Catholic mistress Mrs Fitzherbert. This feeling may have found its way into Elvira's condemnation of Pizarro, especially when expressed by a fellow Catholic Sarah Siddons: 'Beware the desperate libertine who forsakes the creature whom his arts have first deprived of all natural protection – of all self-consolation! What has he left her! – Despair and vengeance' (Act 1, scene 1).

That so many political parallels can be read into the play perhaps confirms Loftis' judicious conclusion that, although its underlying principles were Whig and it 'celebrates the social and political philosophy of the Opposition to Pitt', Sheridan 'did not write an allegorical play, except in the generalised sense that the title character represents Napoleon Bonaparte'.[51] However, Fintan O'Toole does describe it as Sheridan's intentional attempt

to dramatise his own public career . . . a kind of emotional coup, to gain the high ground of imaginative sympathy so that the failures of his powers of reasoned persuasion might be overlooked . . . a very deliberate appeal to patriotic sentiment, and it worked. But instead of surrendering his radical principles in the process, he instead sought to claim the force of patriotic and loyalist sentiment for the same radical causes he had always espoused. The more perceptive of the Tories understood this perfectly well.[52]

George III attended a performance on 5 June, his first visit to Drury Lane for four years, and although he praised Rolla's famous patriotic oration, he probably noticed Sheridan's deliberate description of the Peruvian monarchy: 'the throne we honour is THE PEOPLE'S CHOICE'. As far as George III was concerned, the phrase implied the Revolutionary principle of the Sovereignty of the People. However, my concern is less with Sheridan's personal or political intentions, than with how audiences responded to the play. It would seem that its success stemmed from the variety of dramatic effects it pulled off, the essentially patriotic nature of its sentiment, and the enjoyment of seeing a dangerous tyrant being refuted by Las Casas, his virtuous advisor, harangued by Elvira, his feisty mistress, shamed by Rolla a noble Indian, and destroyed by Alonzo, a decent husband and father. That the tyrant Pizarro could be recognised as an exaggerated portrait of Napoleon Bonaparte gave greater satisfaction to the excitement.

While Pizarro was thrilling audiences and provoking political discussion, a far more subtle mind than Sheridan's was engaged in constructing a dramatic portrait of Bonaparte on the basis of a more sophisticated German drama than Kotzebue's. Coleridge started translating Schiller's *Wallenstein* trilogy in 1799, before visiting Germany with Wordsworth on completion of their *Lyrical Ballads*. Schiller had come to write his plays after several years of historical research on the Thirty Years' War. The ideological confusions and pragmatic conflicts of that period inspired him to write a dramatic critique of Kant's philosophy of the 'categorical imperative', questioning how any action can be considered truly moral or just. He also recognised parallels between Germany's great civil war and the political developments in post-Robespierrean France. Completing *Wallensteins Tod* in 1798, Schiller was hardly aware of the impact Bonaparte was to make on these politics, but Coleridge saw very clear parallels between the two generals, each thrown by circumstance into determining the fate of their respective countries.

However, both Schiller and Coleridge were more interested in the personal motivation of their hero than in the impact of his actions. Julie Carlson argues that they were both drawn to the poetic introspection of Wallenstein, seeing him as 'a Hamlet in military trappings'. By tracing the process of Wallenstein's reluctance to take decisive action, Schiller's trilogy evoked a number of contemporary principles:

Wallenstein's indeterminacy counteracts three erroneous systems of action that figure prominently in the play and contemporary cultural debates: necessarianism, Kantianism, and Burkean traditionalism. The first because it pictures a world governed solely according to the laws of nature [and] denies human agency . . . [Kantianism] is censured for its inhumane silencing of the heart . . . [and] Burkean traditionalism comes under fire for the collective passivity it sanctions . . . Wallenstein distances himself from all of these tendencies by existing in the middle state of the aesthetic mode. His unwillingness to act constitutes his heroism and his only just claim to rule.[53]

When Schiller's hero eventually takes action it leads him into treason and brings worse mishap upon his followers and himself. In Coleridge's plays the movement from contemplation to disastrous action is almost reversed. Having been disillusioned by the Jacobins, it would seem that Coleridge welcomed the 'commanding genius' of Bonaparte to give form and stability to the aspirations of the early revolutionaries. He had written journalistic portraits of Pitt and Washington but failed to complete one of Bonaparte because he felt that his Wallenstein depicted Napoleon's 'Character'.[54] However, as Coleridge's play was rejected for theatrical production I am not going to analyse it in detail, except to note, firstly, that the rejection deterred him from completing his translation of Schiller's full trilogy.[55] And, secondly, that the preference for a contemplative poetic genius that emerges from Schiller's plays is precisely the attitude with which Coleridge, and other Romantic intellectuals, increasingly distanced themselves from both the political and theatrical worlds into a poetic detachment that, despite its philosophical and aesthetic sophistication, tended towards Burkean conservatism. By 'detachment' I do not mean that Coleridge lost interest in drama or performance – indeed his revised version of *Osorio*, rejected in 1797, was produced at Drury Lane as *Remorse* in 1813 – but that his regret for the passing of literary drama, his prioritising of the poetry of Shakespeare over his theatricality, and his critical attacks on the sensational and 'jacobinical' Gothic drama, led him, like Lamb and Hunt, to adopt a position of patronising superiority with regard to popular theatrical success.

The philosophical debate between the 'commanding genius' of the soldier and 'absolute genius' of the poet that informed Coleridge's *Wallenstein*[56] was too sophisticated for London audiences in fear of an actual invasion. More to their taste was the knock-about satire of John Cartwright Cross' *John Bull and Buonaparte; or, a Meeting at Dover* presented at the Royal Circus, 8 August 1803, in which Mr Slader 'a ballet Actor' plays a comical 'Boney' along the lines of Gillray's demonising caricatures:

> Morbleu! I'm a Corsican born, blood and bones!
> So wildly I make the globe fear me!
> In murdering its people, and plundering its towns,
> The devil in fame can't come near me:
> 'Tis true, me respect not religion or law,
> My justice cuts keen as a razor!
> Makes widows and orphans wid glorious éclat,
> And wherever I go, I'm a Caesar
> I take de gold, I take de silver, I take de diamond
> and I take a de – snuff,
> Vive la fortune la guerre! ca ira! ca ira!
> Wherever I go I'm a *Seizer*![57]

He boasts of how he has ransacked Holland, Spain and Italy for artworks, and also, in a reference to the allegation that soldiers who contracted the plague at Jaffa were shot: 'at Egypt I take – I *take away my own people's lives*. Vive la fortune la guerre!' Returning from Egypt, he commands the Army of England

> Fort bien! me think shortly the whole world to seize,
> And be of that world grand dictateur!
> But first, if my good friend, John Bull, it shall please,
> I'll, like Cromwell, *be his Lord Protecteur!*
> But, begar, me know well, that is out of my power,
> And me and my troops in a maze are!
> For John proudly swears, If I land on his shore,
> He'll prove that 'tis he is the Caesar!

Ah! pauvre John Bull! he has no politesse! he vont let me take away de guinea, nor de roast beef, nor de plumb pudding, nor de ladies, and begar, if he catch a me he vont let me take away myself!

> Vive la fortune la guerre, ca ira! ca ira!
> JACKEY KETCH may of me be de SEIZER!

This provocative caricature is answered with a number of patriotic tableaux and songs with, as finale, 'The British lion's rous'd':

> Boney over the channel, a huge bridge of boats
> Means to throw, he has given his pledge;
> He may think what he will of our salt-water moats,
> John Bull will throw him o'er the bridge.

An even more conventionalised image of Bonaparte was that in Andrew Cherry's pantomime *The Magic of British Liberty; or, Disgregation of Bonaparte*, performed in York on 20 December 1803. Having been conjured up from Pluto's Dominion and manhandled by demons with fireworks, Bonaparte, 'Jaffa's murd'rer, fair Italia's plunderer! / The Swiss destroyer, the *wou'd-be* thund'rer!' is transformed for the Harlequinade into a 'humble Scaramouch':

> *When the vaunting Corsican presumes to point out to his followers 'The Road to England',* BRITANNIA *unexpectedly appears to him and speaks.*
> BRITANNIA. Hence, thou dark agent of Gallia's pow'r! . . .
> *Here* BRITANNIA *waves her Spear, and the* GATES *of* CALAIS *change to a view of the* BRITISH METROPOLIS: – *Then follows the* METAMORPHOSIS *of* BONAPARTE, *and the various whimsical distresses that befall this doughty hero – wherein many mechanical changes and entertaining transformations are exhibited* . . .

After the total Downfall and Disgrace of Citizen Bonaparte, BRITANNIA, *in the*
TEMPLE OF LIBERTY, *addresses her people:*
. . . While shame and vengeance on our foes are hurl'd
Shall ENGLAND reign the MISTRESS of the WORLD!

A very different play, *The Invasion of England – a Farce* was also
published in 1803, by J. Whiting 'for the author'. As a prose drama it
could not have been intended for a minor house, but would certainly
not have been passed by Larpent for performance at a Theatre
Royal. It is remarkable in that it dramatises what might happen if
the planned invasion was successful. Where popular pieces lampoon
the French, and legitimate drama transports them back into history,
this play is as realistic in its treatment of French policies and strategy
as any of the London journals. When Bonaparte complains that
England has ended the Peace of Amiens, Tallyrand replies:

> I thought, indeed, to have lulled them asleep a little longer, but they
> were afraid of the opposition party at home. That Pitt carries a great
> sway in England, whether in or out of place; – he did not like the peace
> and has been watching us ever since . . . It hurts an Englishman to
> touch the liberty of the press – they think all depends on that – their cry
> is Liberty – but where is their liberty when men are pressed to man their
> fleets, and others are drafted for militia, as soldiers? (Act 1, scene 1)

This last comment suggests that the author is not as blindly patriotic
as most playwrights, which is confirmed when he dramatises the ill-
prepared British defences:

> COL. TRUSTY. I am an old soldier and have never disgraced my colours –
> but I should not wish for a trial; – the French troops are not to be
> laughed at . . . It is highly proper to encourage a spirit of enthusiasm
> among the men, but should the French attempt a landing, we should
> have our hands full . . .
> RECRUIT. I never fired a gun in my life – I am paid for being a substitute – I
> hope we shall never fight, for I should not like to be killed.
> CAPT. FLASH. Nor I either; but if we kill them they can't kill us; and if they
> should kill us once, they can't again; and another man will take our
> place.
> RECRUIT. But that man who takes my place in the field, won't take charge
> of my wife and children. (Act 2, scene 1)

Although there is an artificial subplot, in which Trusty's daughter
joins the regiment in disguise to follow her lover, and the satire of
frightened London merchants is broad enough to earn the description 'farcical', the economic points made by Tallyrand and Mr Rich

indicate that the author had a genuinely radical insight into the politics of the invasion scare:

TALLYRAND. That the French have as good geniuses cannot be denied, but our individuals want capital: – an English manufacturer will lay out 20, 30, £40,000 on machinery, and will do the work of 500 men with a few women and children – none of our tradesmen have such money to advance. (Act 1, scene 1)

MR RICH. Why then we are ruined. I must sell out immediately, and save something. The Bank will be the first thing they will lay their hands on. (Act 1, scene 2)

GENL. MASSENA. Let the English camps revel in luxury while we march on London. If we can get their bank, we shall all be stock holders and carry more guineas over with us than we brought louis. (Act 2, scene 4)

In Act 2 the French have arrived in Sussex, and, if the author is critical of the English merchant classes, he is hardly a champion of the French, for, as well as threatening the Bank of England, they discuss employing the strategies adopted in Holland and Italy – laying waste the land and refusing to take prisoners. Finally, the navy destroys the flat-bottomed invasion ships in which Massena's army arrived and the stranded French are 'reduced to live on grass and roots they find in the fields – they die in numbers every day through want – we won't receive them nor let them escape' (Act 2, scene 5). All in all, the play presents a very realistic assessment of the probable results of a French invasion, even anticipating in this last description the fate of Napoleon's Russian campaign, and it does so without any of the rhetorical jingoism of the patriotic pieces being performed in the London theatres. Although not produced, this short play demonstrates the shallowness of most of those that were, and which failed in, or were prevented from, dramatising seriously the French invasion threats of 1798 and 1803.

That drama could be used to give expression to genuine fears is seen again in an 'amateur' drama, *Buonaparte; or, the Free-Booter*, also published in 1803 by John Scott Ripon, who, according to the preface, was due to rejoin his regiment. Not intended for performance and thus free from the restraint of censorship, Ripon turned to the model of *Richard III* to express his hatred and fear of the French adventurer. Bonaparte is found on board ship returning from Egypt, haunted like Richard by dreams of his victims – especially 'A pale spectre, with leaden steps and smeared with blood [who] said 'remember Jaffa! aye remember Jaffa!' – I started from my couch!

the lamp burnt blue.' When he orders a lieutenant to assassinate the ship's captain, the young man refuses and accuses the general of enslaving his conquests and poisoning the sick soldiers at Jaffa. Bonaparte stabs him. The captain enters and he also is killed. The next scene is set on-board a British man-of-war which preparing for attack. In Act 2, after the sea battle, Bonaparte is discovered in his tent on the coast of England. He reflects:

> Had I landed a few years ago perhaps I might have succeeded. Nay, that would have been uncertain. Though the English are disaffected among themselves, and not unfrequently mutiny to redress some apparent grievance, yet when a foreign enemy would invade their rights, parties become extinguished, and they firmly unite under one banner, and bravely enlist in the common cause.[58]

In Act 2 the local inhabitants unite to defend their lands under the leadership of an old soldier and a bellicose mother of three sons. In the final act General the Duke of – (York?) prepares for battle. Meanwhile Bonaparte, continuing to behave like a psychopath, is faced with a mutiny in his own ranks. He attempts to stab one soldier for murmuring, and condemns another with a cry of, 'Off with his head this moment.' He can only control the army by promising them unrestrained pillage. In the battle that follows a young English officer confronts the tyrant, like Young Siward facing Macbeth.

BUONAPARTE. Ha! dost thou threaten beardless boy? 'tis Buonaparte whom thou darest; hear that name and tremble.
OFFICER. Were I a gallic slave I should tremble, but I am a free-born Briton, and can hear it without dismay.

He then kills the tyrant, and the Duke of – concludes the play with a paraphrase of Henry V's speech of thanksgiving after Agincourt.

Although the quality of this script is banal in the extreme, it provides clear evidence that, when confronted with real fear and anger against the aggression of Napoleon, people turned to Shakespeare to provide words and images to express their emotion. Plays more sophisticated than Ripon's paraphrased Shakespeare's language, and Shakespeare's own plays were interpreted in the light of contemporary circumstance. I have already described Cooke's *Richard III*, and how Kemble had changed the emphasis of *Coriolanus* in 1796 to suggest a parallel between the Roman tribunes and the Jacobin leaders. However, he did nothing, even in the 1806 revival, to suggest a specific parallel between the Roman general and the French emperor. That France was now under autocratic rule did not automatically make democrats of the English. Kemble's Coriolanus could be interpreted as either an aristocratic émigré, driven from his country by revolution, or as a British nobleman maintaining his dignity and redefining his role as propounded by Linda Colley.[59] Nevertheless Kemble's desire to emphasise the aristocratic nobility of the role may well have been read differently by some of his auditors, as an autocrat scornful of the people's 'voices' – certainly when he stood firm against the demands of the O. P. rioters in 1809.

As this is a study of the Revolutionary period, I do not intend to extend my narrative into Napoleon's imperial reign. However, as the threat of direct invasion lasted until Trafalgar, I will consider the theatrical depiction of Napoleon's heroic rival, Nelson. The plays celebrating the Glorious First of June, Cape St Vincent and Camperdown had been mainly set on shore, dramatising the return of the sailors and reactions to the news of victory, with scenic depictions of the battles, or the reviews held to celebrate them, being introduced as grand finales. These final tableaux usually included illuminated portraits of the victorious admirals, Howe, Jervis and Duncan, but Nelson's image was of more than just a successful commander. The respect and affection in which he was held by his officers and regular seamen enhanced his reputation as approachable, his preparedness to give evidence on behalf of Colonel Despard of the United Irishmen delighted the radicals, and his scandalous liaison with Lady Hamilton excited interest with all levels of society. Small of stature, he invited comparison with Bonaparte, but whereas Napoleon's imperial pretensions were deemed vulgar, Nelson's delight in titles, decorations and braided uniform was generally forgiven as well-deserved vanity, while his empty sleeve and blind eye testified to personal courage and sacrifice.[60] In 1800, on his return after the Battle of the Nile, Nelson went to see *Pizarro* and was given a hero's welcome, and when the news came of his death at the decisive Battle of Trafalgar there were several theatrical responses, as well as the grand public demonstration of his funeral procession to St Paul's.

The battle took place on 21 October and the news reached London on 5 November. Two days later Covent Garden mounted an interlude by Thomas Dibdin entitled *Nelson's Glory*, which claimed to include a 'representation of the battle'. This could only have been a swift reassembly of models and scenic pieces used for similar earlier celebrations including the usual portrait of the victorious admiral accompanied by a specially altered verse of *Rule Britannia*.[61] On 11 November, within a week of the news, Drury Lane produced *An Occasional Attempt to Commemorate the Death and Victory of Lord Viscount Nelson*, a 'Melodramatic Piece' by Richard Cumberland. Although Nelson's body was not to reach England until 23 December, one of his ships was depicted arriving:

> *[After 'Rule Britannia' music] now takes the strain corresponding to the approach of a Vessel, discov'd at Sea, which lands a Captain with his boat Crew.*
>
> SEA CAPT. We bring thee trophies, nobly, hardly earn'd
> Torn from the Vanquish'd foe, but bath'd, alas!
> And all o'er red with thy dear Children's blood,
> The best, the bravest blood that ever flow'd
> From human veins, and mingled with the waves . . .

After the tenor Braham sang 'In Death's Dark House, the Hero Lies', a comparison between Nelson and Napoleon led into a patriotic chorus, which emphasises once again the message that Napoleon was a brigand who has enslaved the French, and that Britain was fighting to protect her ancient liberties:

> There is a man the Scourge of present times,
> A living monument of human crimes.
> He triumphs over liberties and Laws,
> He lives – but Nelson dies in freedom's cause.
> GLEE. Praise to the dead! with joyous triumph greet
> The living Heroes of your conquering fleet!
> They come, they come! Let France command her slaves,
> Freedom is ours, for Britain rules the waves.[62]

A similar solemn entertainment was mounted at the Haymarket, *The Naval Victory and Triumph of Lord Nelson*, 7 December, but the King's Theatre's version of the battle was criticised as being inappropriate as 'circumstances were too recent and too sorrowful for theatrical representation'.[63]

The funeral itself took place on 9 January 1806 following a procession by water from Greenwich to the Admiralty and thence to St Paul's. In her analysis of the event, Gillian Russell notes a deliberate suppression of new theatrical representations – Cumberland's piece for Covent Garden was denied a licence and Drury Lane merely performed music by Handel – although the minor Sans Souci theatre produced *Nelson's Arrival in the Elysian Fields* on

18 January. Russell argues that the funeral itself was organised as a national pageant in which Nelson was accorded honours usually bestowed on royalty,[64] but during which many spectators and some of the participants contributed spontaneously to the ritualistic theatricality:

> The crypto-royalism of the funeral ritual had been a deliberate attempt on the part of the organizers to revive the pomp and circumstance of monarchical spectacle with all this implied in political terms. To an extent this was unsuccessful because the élite was . . . unprepared to make a king out of Nelson. But it was also unsuccessful because the audience had been unwilling to play a passive, subordinate role in the spectacle and had imposed one of its own instead. The most notable example of this occurred when Nelson's flag was about to be lowered into the grave. In a premeditated act, of which the organizers of the funeral had been unaware, 'the sailors who assisted at the ceremony with one accord rent [the flag] in pieces, that each might preserve a fragment while he lived'. The decorum of the funeral rite was violated as these sailors imposed their own rite, one which expressed the significance of Nelson as a popular hero rather than a pseudo-monarch.[65]

In a way, the death of Nelson was as powerful symbolically as his victory was militarily, for it inspired the nation to engage in acts of communal grief for an extraordinary person who had risen through his profession with the individual initiative so admired by the middle classes, had been accepted into the ranks of the newly invigorated aristocracy responsible for the war effort, and who was respected by the lower classes who considered the common sailors, devoted to their dead commander, as their most potent representatives in British civic life. This communality was not the creation of the theatre as such, but the theatricalisation of the war as a spectacle, its leaders as dramatic protagonists and its progress as a dramatic narrative, owed much to the patterns of entertainment within the theatre, even if it found its most effective expression in the public rituals of royal pageantry and, as on this occasion, the funeral of a national hero.

On 16 May 1806 Covent Garden was allowed to present a 'Grand Burletta Spectacle', *The Nation Gratified; or, Nelson's Funeral*, which, by dramatising the funeral's spectators in the style of Franklin's *Trip to the Nore* (1797), gave a voice to the popular feelings that had been allowed only symbolic expression during the funeral itself. As in so many of the patriotic plays, Incledon played the sailor, Ben the boatswain, while Emery, as John Lump from Yorkshire, took over the plebeian Munden role. Fawcett as Old Caleb gave voice to the mercantile interest in the war:

> Little Bony declares, and he stamps, and he stares,
> And he wishes it told the whole nation
> That he wants some more ships to take West Indian trips
> And get Commerce and Colonisation,
> But I think it will give him vexation
> When he first receives information
> That his Fleet, when combin'd, ran leaving behind
> Twenty ships for the English Nation.[66]

Despite earlier disapproval of the depiction of actual events, this piece included views of the funeral procession both by water and by land. It inevitably concluded with *Rule Britannia*.

However, in 1806 the war was by no means concluded, and precisely because of the danger of theatricalising my own narrative I want to conclude it, as it were, in the middle of Act 4. If I were to take it through to 1815 and bring the curtain down after the Battle of Waterloo, all would seem neatly concluded with the villain Napoleon despatched and the hero Wellington receiving the praise of a grateful nation. But history is seldom so theatrically contained, nor can the fate of nations be symbolically encapsulated in the personal narratives of individual players, even when of such star quality as Napoleon Bonaparte. I have chosen therefore to halt my narrative at an act-drop rather than at a final curtain, dropping it on the ambiguous spectacle of Nelson's funeral. The nation seemed for a moment united in grief, but with one battle won the war was not yet over, and the questions raised for the British by the French Revolution were far from resolved.

This was particularly true for those who had seen the Revolution – as most Westerners today regard it – as a moment of great change, when patterns of religious, political and philosophical belief were challenged and, for a moment at least, appeared to have been transformed for ever. And yet this 'progressive' interpretation of events seemed to have been proved wrong, the Revolution had changed France into an aggressive military dictatorship, while in England reform had been halted, the 'Old Corruption' reinforced, and the privileged elements of civic society – royalty, nobility and the established church – seemed to have been strengthened. In Britain under an old mad king, a decadent regent and the political turncoats Pitt and Burke, inspired only by a flawed hero, Lord Nelson, it would seem that, just as in France under Napoleon, the ancient regime had been restored stronger and more dangerous than ever in a Europe that was being torn apart by nationalistic wars of unprecedented extravagance and viciousness. History might eventually prove the accuracy or inaccuracy of such a perception, but in 1805 many people must have felt a deep sense of disappointment and anger – what in my introduction I described as a state of cultural crisis, and in the next chapter will define as alienation.

CHAPTER 7

Theatre and alienation

When trying to recapture a past time, its events, experiences, thoughts and feelings, historians used to conjure up a Spirit of the Age. This romantic concept has since been replaced by the more objective analysis of belief systems and their expression as ideology and culture. Within a generation of the Revolution, Marx posited a causal relationship between the social realities of economic power and the conceptual superstructure of politics, law, religion and art. This simple equation of base and superstructure has long been problematised, but it would be extremely foolish to reject Marx's essential argument about the dialectical relationship between cultural production and economic circumstances: 'Men are the producers of their conceptions, ideas, etc., . . . Developing their material production and their material intercourse, [they alter], along with this their real existance, their thinking and the products of their thinking. Life is not determined by consciousness, but consciousness by life'.[1]

Yet the idealist thesis, the subject of Marx's attack – that concepts determine progress – was precisely that which had inspired the Enlightenment, and had been adopted by the Romantics in their belief that the individual imagination can encompass all possible experiences. I have endeavoured throughout this book to argue for the influence of circumstance over agency and that the process of Revolutionary events was far from what had been originally envisaged by those involved. Indeed, there was a very disturbing disjuncture between good intentions and evil effects. This was partly because real power was not in the hands of those politicians and artists who believed they were responsible for the events and for the rhetoric and images of the period, and partly because those with the power – capitalist entrepreneurs and military leaders – followed a different agenda, even though they professed, and perhaps thought they believed, the slogans and propaganda of the 'idealists'. The majority of the working classes were certainly without power, and they must have felt – as eventually, I propose, did many politicians and artists – to be the thwarted and confused victims of some malevolent genie that, for the want of a better name, might be called the 'Spirit of the Age'.

Before exploring in detail how this confusion, both conscious and unconscious, and which I refer to as 'alienation', found its expression in theatrical culture, it is necessary to tease out its various meanings and applications as an analytical concept. Having started the chapter quoting Marx, it is perhaps sensible to continue by citing his definition of *economic* alienation. Naturally, it finds its classic application with reference to the alienation of labour, and, not surprisingly, he reached it by observing the conditions of the industrial proletariat emerging across Europe. Alex Callinicos usefully expounds the concept with particular reference to the 'dual revolutions' of France and industrial England. He also explains how Marx believed that a lack of economic control and responsibility leads to a lack of emotional control and personal identification with society – and even nature:

He controls neither the products of his labour, nor his labour itself. What should be his 'life-activity', through which he affirms his humanity, or 'species-being', becomes a mere means to an end. And because he has thus become alienated from his own human nature, the worker is also alienated from nature, for it is through labour that he transforms nature, and thus humanises it, and he is also alienated from other human beings. This condition of alienated labour gives rise to the relationship between worker and capitalist, in which a non-worker controls, and profits from, the labour of others.[2]

Marx's analysis of the Revolution, Callinicos argues, demonstrates that the shift from the oppression of the *ancien régime* to that of the capitalist nineteenth century was, as far as the mass of the population was concerned, essentially cosmetic:

The Revolution swept aside the remnants of feudalism which had clogged up society, and which had interfered with the efficient pursuit of profit. And it created a powerful and centralised bureaucratic state, capable of providing capital – the new trading and industrial wealth – with the services it required and of crushing any threat from below. So the result of the 'dual revolution' was paradoxical. On the one hand, the principle that every member of society, however lowly his position, was entitled to equal rights of citizenship, even if not fully realised. (One person, one vote is an achievement of the twentieth, not the nineteenth century.) On the other hand, the differences in wealth and economic power remained vast. The industrial revolution merely changed the form of social and economic inequality – to lord and peasant was added capitalist and worker. The essence remained the same.[3]

To which one might add that the most alienated workers of the period were the conscripts and impressed sailors. They were certainly subjected to the most efficient propaganda – the duty of fighting, and possibly dying, for the glory of France or the protection of their homeland. In this respect, at least, the alienation of the 'hands' was addressed by their masters, and the patriotic drama discussed in the last chapter was a major part of the ideological manipulation that was aimed at giving the warring masses a sense of purpose and identity. From this 'patriotism' was to develop that most destructive of ideologies, 'nationalism.' It was to turn the tables on Napoleon from 1810 onwards, but has perpetuated European discord ever since.

If, however, during the Napoleonic Wars, patriotic nationalism gave people some sense of purposeful identity, the transformation of peasant into proletarian seems to have been entirely alienating. For every single individual who left the land and prospered by their enterprise, there were scores who exchanged their traditional poverty for a new kind of oppression. Here Marx's simple equation between economic dependency and personal alienation needs reassessment. The peasant, though poor, had known little different over generations – the rich man in his castle and the poor man at his gate had seemed inexorable and only natural – but, when you had left home in order to make a fortune or to survive in different employment, and when you saw others no better than yourself succeeding where you were failing, there was a new awareness of the circumstances within which your personal history was being made. Add to this awareness a disappointment with the promises made by radicals, on whose behalf you had risked your life and/or livelihood, then alienation becomes not just an unconscious state of powerlessness, but a clear sense of betrayal.

Thus the dungeons, that on the stages of 1789 had symbolised the Bastilles of the *ancien régime*, and, in 1795, a repository for those on their way to the guillotine, had, by the 1800s, become the prisons of repressive governments, the bowels of satanic factories or those newly constructed panoptic gaols, the workhouses.[4] And, if the symbolism of the drama continued to evolve unnoted, in 1809 the clash of economic interests in the English theatre found very public expression in the riots demanding the reinstatement of Old Prices at Covent Garden. John Kemble, driven to despair by the financial drain on Drury Lane of Sheridan's continuing extravagance, went over to Harris at Covent Garden in 1803, and, when that theatre was rebuilt after the fire of 1808, he had to defend, as acting manger, the economic reforms introduced to pay for the new building. As the patent rights had originally been granted by the crown, the rioters argued the theatre was in a very real sense a national institution, its profits a privilege due only because it provided the populous with entertainment. Thus the battle fought in France against theatre regulation, which led to Chapelier's decree of 1791 establishing free competition, was now being fought in England – two years after Napoleon had re-established theatrical monopoly in Paris.[5] After two months the management gave way on the main principles of the rioter's demands, but, although force *majeure*, combined with arbitration and legal precedent, won the battle, economic imperatives led the management eventually to regain more gradually what they had publicly forgone.[6] The whole incident was shot through with contradictions. The O. P. rioters adopted the carnivalesque techniques of a Paris *journée* or *fête* with songs, slogans and symbolic images, but were demanding traditional rights, which, they believed, had been granted by royal prerogative. Kemble was depicted by delighted cartoonists as confronting the rioters from the stage in the roles of either Macbeth or Coriolanus, and, thus, cast as the Napoleonic tyrant. Yet he, like Napoleon himself, presented a heroic image that disguised less-than-heroic commercial interests. Although the principle that a national theatre has social obligations was upheld, the O. P. struggle opened the question of to whom the Theatres Royal were ultimately responsible, and the answer in post-Revolutionary times was inevitably, 'to the share-holders'.

If by 1805 it was clear that the result of revolution in both France and England was reaction and repression, then Marx's economic alienation was the lot of theatre workers as well as of much of the general population. A kind of *social* alienation too was on the increase for the cultural workers of the time. Like the quasi-feudal peasants in the pre-Revolutionary period, artists during the Enlightenment were often dependant upon personal patrons, and, although they could experience extreme humiliation in such a personal relationship, patronage bestowed a certain protection and identity denied to those who relied solely on public sales and the commercial interest of publishers and managers. In the theatre during the eighteenth century membership of a Theatre Royal gave actors a sense of status as royal servants, and, as most minor houses and provincial circuits tended to employ whole families rather than just individuals, there was a sense of communality within the profession. When David Garrick, and even Sheridan, won recognition beyond that of a theatre worker, they became patrons themselves and their status was to an extent shared by the profession as a whole. The story of Master Betty demonstrated how fragile such stability had now become in reality, as does the contempt with which 'respectable society' responded to the disorderly genius of Cooke and later Kean. Moral attitudes towards the theatre, which had been somewhat relaxed during the later eighteenth century, were resuming the puritanical stance of Collier's *Short View of the Immorality and Profaneness of the English Stage* (1698). The Methodists and other Evangelicals, including Wilberforce, were reviving traditional charges of lewdness and artificiality. We have already seen how critics and intellectuals like Coleridge and Lamb deplored Kotzebue and the German drama, and the response of Sir Thomas Bertram in Jane Austen's *Mansfield Park* (1814) to the proposed amateur production of Inchbald's translation of Kotzebue's *Lovers' Vows* suggests that antitheatrical prejudice was deeply ingrained in the middle classes.[7] The nineteenth century was to see a further decline in the reputation of the acting profession, so that Macready, looking back from his retirement in 1851 to his decision to leave Rugby school in 1810 to act in his father's company, wrote:

I was not aware, in taking it, that this step in life was a descent from the equality in which I felt myself to stand with those of family and fortune whom our education had made my companion. I had to live to learn that an ignorant officer could refuse the satisfaction of a gentleman on the ground that his appellant was a player, and that, whilst any of those above-named vocations [law, church, army and navy], whatever the private character, might be received at Court, the privilege of appearing in the sacred precincts was too exclusive for any, however distinguished, on the stage.[8]

If the acting profession had long been aware of social exclusion, Pitt's antiradical legislation, backed by the unofficial aggression of church and crown mobs, forced several intellectuals into isolation, and in the case of Thomas Holcroft, the so-called Jacobin play-wright, into actual exile. His friends Godwin and Wollstonecraft had encouraged their readers to recognise the unacknowledged oppressions of marriage and social dependency, which, though not new, became more emotionally affective once they had been identified. The upper classes too, though not under immediate threat, were made aware of the precariousness of what they once considered as a natural right to rule, by the arrival on the London scene of their French counterparts as émigrés. At the other end of the social spectrum, the forcible displacement of black slaves became a vital political issue rather than an invisible fact of life. All these material experiences help explain the potency of the cultural depiction of wandering, homeless 'aliens' and the 'alien' societies of the Orient, the Indies and the past. I have already cited examples of Gothic drama that presented images of both entrapment and estrangement. I will address plays dealing specifically with slavery later in this chapter.

The material experience of exclusion and oppression inevitably effected patterns of thought and emotional expectations. So, although it is impossible to provide statistics to prove an increase in mental distress – or even agree terms between our definitions of stress and those of the time[9] – it is not irrelevant to the study of cultural expression to consider the nature of *psychological* alienation. As Marx suggested, economic alienation effects a person's self-perception, and more recent definitions of psychic alienation also centre on the breakdown of a mature self-image. Joel Kovel provides a concise description of the condition:

The normal person, be he good or bad, experiences a certain integration between self, body and society – or it may be more accurate to say that he takes the unity for granted and goes about his business without a second thought . . . In the neurotic, on the other hand, this seamless pattern fails to hold. Fissures appear early on in the ground of experience, allowing the lava of the unconscious to break through . . . The alienation within neurosis is one of its most essential features. In reality, though we are not all One, we are all interconnected; and the notion of the absolute self, free from deep linkage with the rest of humanity, is but a peculiar fiction . . . Not so for the neurotic, who experiences an alienation within himself, and so between himself, society and nature.[10]

Mario Prax's analysis of Romanticism as a virtual pathology is now considered too extreme,[11] but it is true that many creative intellectuals of this period felt deep anxiety over their own mental stability, and Linda Colley suggests that the 'massive strain on the lives, nerves and confidence of the British élite' explains an extraordinary incidence, not only of drunkenness and early death but suicide amongst public figures engaged in 'the expanding volume and diversity of domestic and imperial government'.[12]

However, alienation is not necessarily a state of psychopathology, though the imaginings of de Sade, Fuseli, Blake, Coleridge and Goya suggest that Romantic introspection, especially if combined with drug abuse, brought several artists close to clinical madness. Melanie Klein's classic definition of alienation proposes it is a reversion to a state of childhood, when dependency upon the parent expresses itself as either a self-absorption, in which everything external to the self seems to be an extension or incorporation of the self, or a self-negation, in which all one's fears, wants and responsibilities are projected on to an other – that other taking on the power of the parent to either punish or protect. Thus in adult alienation, as in normal infancy, the self is experienced as either invulnerable and omnipotent or intangible and fragmented, and both these states of mind found frequent expression in Romantic art and poetry. The concept of man's contingency on nature was also at this time embedded in the philosophy of Kant, for whom the very existence of nature external to the self depended upon its experience by the self. If this existential concept did not derange everybody, as it did Kleist, then his moral philosophy, which also insisted on the individual's validation of general principles, was a receipt for anxiety and stress that was much exercised in Schiller's drama and a variety of Coleridge's work.[13] Thus intellectual relativity rejected the 'common sense' that was the cornerstone of Enlightenment thinking, for experiences of 'common non-sense', which at times seemed like a state of psychic alienation when the 'lava of the unconscious' arose from the abyss of those 'caverns measureless to man' that Coleridge dreamed of beneath the golden palaces of Zanadu.

To insist on the analysis of a corporate psychology of the times would be to revert to the discredited Spirit of the Age historiography, but when considering the extraordinary originality of the new theatrical genres of the time, a psychoanalytic approach does help explain the widespread satisfaction that their essential irrationality provided. Take for instance the structure of the classic English pantomime. Its form had of course evolved long before this period, but never was its popularity so great. It provided one of the basic forms on which the illegitimate theatres relied, and was performed in the respectable patent theatres for up to thirty nights a season. Although new pantomimes tended to be presented at the patent houses in the Christmas season,[14] they were not intended as children's theatre. The narrative structure invariably started with a 'naturalistic' storyline, which was changed into a harlequinade by the magical transformation of the main characters into the roles of Harlequin, Columbine, Pantaloon and Clown. In his authoritative work on pantomimes between 1806 and 1836, David Mayer summarises the nature and appeal of the genre:

Pantomime before and during the period of Grimaldi's domination had two characteristics: treatment of a wide range of comic subjects in a single dramatic piece and the capacity to reuse the chief pantomime characters endlessly . . . Its structure enabled fleeting comedy or satire to be directed at many topics without requiring that they be shown in a logical or plausible sequence . . . [It was] by its nature an imperfect instrument for recording history, for the greatest of its faults was a refusal to discriminate between the worthy and the paltry . . . when confronted with the more complex issues it became tentative and hesitant.[15]

In the context of discussing self-image, projection and transference, the illogicality and lack of discrimination of the genre may actually account for its appeal, rather than provide a source of dissatisfaction. As in dreams, the action of the play involved a fluidity of personal identity, with characters mutated into stock types who behave like automaton, the magical transformation of objects and settings, the unrelenting chase, and the terrors of the 'dark scene'. That all turns out well in the end at the wave of a magic wand was not so much escapism as psychic reassurance for people who felt alienated from their own society. Entering a fantasy world, in which not only does true love win fair lady – as it also does in traditional comedy – but 'real life' is transformed magically into a set of characters, familiar since childhood, whose conflicts and dangers are emotionally distanced by their very artificiality, provided audiences with archetypal metaphors for confronting parental authority with either childlike omnipotence or comical subversion:

The relationships between parent, suitor, and daughter evoke conflicts in which youth and genuine affection is to be sacrificed for another's wealth, power, self-aggrandisement. The father, encountering his daughter's mute obstinacy and learning of her preference for another man, takes steps to have the young lover killed or banished or imprisoned, frequently trapping the lovers as they elope. When the father is on the point of forcibly separating the lovers a benevolent agent sympathetic to the lovers, usually a fairy or supernatural being and almost invariable female, intervenes.[16]

Although topical references were continually being made, particularly by Clown when performed by Grimaldi, the lack of precise or consistent satirical application probably contributed to the drama's curative power as an annually repeated ritual. Mayer describes the comedy as 'retributive', providing 'a vicarious release from society's strictures and taboos. It is mutiny made harmless and even pleasurable, protest without injurious consequences to the protester. Each act is wishful thinking, the enactment of revolt against order and authority.'[17] But this I think underestimates the reassurance provided by such release and mutiny. The ability of the unchanging Harlequin characters to rekindle the same laughter, excitement and relief year after year suggests a potency rather more affective than the merely 'harmless' and 'pleasurable'.

Although Joey Grimaldi had been building a reputation as the Clown of Sadler's Wells, with winter appearances at Drury Lane, his performance at Covent Garden on 29 December 1806 in *Harlequin and Mother Goose; or, The Golden Egg*, by Thomas Dibdin, marked a major development in the nature and popularity of the genre. By shifting the emphasis of the drama from Harlequin's mute agility – the quality first established by Rich and Weaver in the early eighteenth century and exhibited since 1787 by Jack Bologna – to the subversive comedy of the *zanni*, or servant character, Grimaldi enhanced the democratic potential of the form. He usurped the magic of Harlequin's bat, the slap of which cued the mechanical transformation of scenes and props, with the inventiveness of his own imagination. He transformed objects not literally but by the way he used them. Buckets became boots and barrels became horses, not by supernatural intervention but by the exercise of Fancy. By inserting into his songs apparently improvised patter of scurrilous or nonsensical commentary (which would have been technically illegal at the Wells), he enlarged the scope of the script to make topical references and of his own character to relate to the audience. But Grimaldi's Clown remained a fantasy figure. Even though he might don the clothes of realistic characters – as in *Harlequin in His Element* (Covent Garden, 26 December 1807), when he stole a watchman's cape, hat and booze – he kept his extravagant make-up and costume and his physical capering and tumbling. On stage he provided a consistent and renewable identity that could steal, binge and mock – and be punished for it – with an impervious invulner-ability, which could absorb all the anxieties his audience might project upon him.

My final example of how the term *alienation* can be usefully applied in the post-Revolutionary or Napoleonic period is for a particular strategy of cultural production – much as Brecht used the term.[18] However this distancing of the representation from its subject matter was seldom done in the spirit of Brecht's own dialectical dramaturgy. There were a variety of reasons why plays continually used indirect means to address the issues of their day. Clearly the artificiality of pantomime is one example, and the increasing popularity of musical theatre as a whole – opera, ballet and musical comedy – tended towards a formal distancing or mediating of the material subject matter of the drama. But perhaps more significantly than these differences of genre, each of which had its own aesthetic attraction, was the almost universal practice of setting the drama in an 'alien' culture. I have discussed this tendency already, with reference to history plays and the exotic spectacle of Oriental scenery. To an extent it was to avoid censorship, and also to break or uphold tradition as part of the Revolutionary debate, but I have also suggested that cultural expression went further in ex-ploring the Other than legal or even political considerations alone would justify. To quote Marx again, for his insight that to change history one must confront history – and that sometimes history wins the confrontation:

Men make their own history, but they do not make it just as they please; they do not make it under circumstances chosen by themselves, but under circumstances directly encountered, given and transmitted from the past. The tradition of all the dead generations weighs like a nightmare on the brain of the living. And just when they seem engaged in revolutionising themselves and things, in creating something that has never yet existed, precisely in such periods of revolutionary crisis they anxiously conjure up the spirits of the past to their service and borrow from them names, battle-cries and costumes in order to present the new scene of world history in this time-honoured disguise and this borrowed language. Thus Luther donned the mask of the Apostle Paul, the revolution of 1789 to 1814 draped itself alternately as the Roman Republic and the Roman Empire.[19]

Insofar as Girondins, Jacobins and Bonapartists began to believe their own myths and classical rhetoric, they became alienated from the immediate issues at stake and were led into dangerous attitudinising and unrealistic ambitions. The stakes in England may not have been as high as in France, where the attitudes were struck on the scaffold and the imperial dream led to the fateful Russian campaign, but here too the centrality of history to the arguments of Paine and of Burke became blurred into a generalised nostalgia. The hard questions of legal precedent and constitutional traditions that had informed the history plays of the 1790s became slicked over with either the pallor of Gothicism or the glamour of Orientalism. The Adams brothers had used the discoveries at Pompeii to enliven their designs, just as Chippendale had incorporated motifs of chinoiserie, but these Enlightenment artists never let decoration dictate function, whereas at the regent's Brighton Pavilion the spectacular reconstruction of the Orient ran riot.

The inspiration for George's seaside palace may well have been the 1811 revival of Colman's *Blue Beard*, the 1798 production of which was discussed in chapter 4 above. In 1971 George Steiner, discussing Bartók's opera *Bluebeard's Castle*, described the door into the final chamber as a leap into an unknowable future, essentially threatening and anarchic, and related it to the 'squandered utopia' with which science, in his opinion, threatened the late twentieth century.[20] In the context of 1798, the door of Colman's *Blue Beard*, opening into a chamber of death, perhaps implied that for him too the rational hopes of the Enlightenment for a better society had been squandered. Steiner, whose essay reflects on the 'collapse of hierarchies [and] the end to classic literacy',[21] found some hope, however, in the music of Bartók's *Bluebeard*. He argued that music is a 'language outside the world', without the ideological dogma that is embedded in the very words of literature: 'With the mendacies of language brought home to us by psychoanalysis and the mass media, it may be that music is regaining ancient ground, wrested from it, held for a time, by the dominance of the word.' And he asks a rhetorical question particularly apt to the period of the present study, 'Is there a lie, anywhere, in Mozart?'[22] But, however pertinent Steiner's speculations may be to postmodern culture, in this particular passage they reflect an essentially Romantic response to alienation, a retreat from words into sounds and from explanation into imagery. This suggestion might apply equally to the classical operas of Mozart, Beethoven, Gluck and Paisiello, and the popular musical extravaganza of Kelly, Arnold, Reeve and Shield. The intellectual and emotional content of both the highbrow and the popular was not to be found in verbal debate or rhetorical exhortation but in the inarticulate power of music, the suggestive power of visual images and the ritualistic substructure of myth and folk-tale. In particular, the unimaginable terrors of the secret dungeon could reflect *both* the instinctive fear of the conservative *and* the dashed hope of the radical, as the bright dawn of revolution, which had promised rational enlightenment and benevolent sensibility, descended into the dark horrors of the midnight tocsin and the perverted efficiency of Dr Guillotine's death machine.

Although Coleridge, like Steiner, might consciously probe the culture of his time for a rational explanation of what I describe as alienation, most people's anxiety was focused on the more immediate issues of the war, employment and personal relationships. Even today, when the theories of Marx and Klein are in the public domain, alienation is seldom consciously recognised. Psychiatry knows well the defence mechanisms of such avoidance – denial, repression, transference and projection. Though they had not yet been defined, all these can be seen in the post-Revolutionary period. The most obvious strategy was that of replacing dashed hopes for political and social change with the loud and insistent demands of patriotic duty. But cultural production too developed more subtle methods of avoiding reality. And here their use of 'alienation' or 'making strange' differed fundamentally from Brecht's *Vefremdung*. He wanted his audience to question the differences between past and present circumstances, and to consider implications for the future, whereas the exotic experiences of Romantic drama were created as 'escapism', a controlled thrill of horror or an opportunity to laugh in the face of terror. Nevertheless such contrived experiences had their cathartic effect – indeed it was that purging of anger and distress that caused Brecht to attack what he called the 'Aristotelian drama'. And, in the post-Revolutionary period, all the various theatrical experiments described so far found, as it were, their consummate realisation in *melodrama* – the classic reactionary genre.

It is a rather sad irony that the playwright attributed with introducing 'real melodrama' to the London stage was that champion of radical enlightenment, Thomas Holcroft, whose arrest was described in chapter 4 above. In 1796 his bitterest dramatisation of the corrupting power of money, *The Man of Ten Thousand* (Drury Lane, 23 January), a reworking of Shakespeare's *Timon of Athens*, received only seven performances. The following year his novel *Hugh Trevor* was published, but did not achieve the popularity of *Anna St Ives*. The year 1798 saw a mere six performances of his adaptation of two Goldoni plays as *Knave or Not?* (Drury Lane, 25 January), and, although his translation of Goethe's *Clavigo* as *He's Much to Blame* (Drury Lane, 13 February 1798) received a respectable twenty-one performances, a comic opera, *The Old Clothesman* (Covent Garden, 2 April 1798), collapsed after two. Finally, when *The Inquisitor* (Haymarket, 23 June 1798) achieved only three performances, Holcroft realised, that despite the readiness of the managers to produce his plays, his radical reputation had cast a blight on his ability to attract audiences. During 1798, when fear of invasion was at its height, the United Irishmen were suppressed, the persecution of English radicals was intensified, and several of Holcroft's political friends were imprisoned. Not surprisingly then, in July 1799, having married a new wife, Louise, daughter of Louis Sébastien Mercier, whose version of *Le Déserteur* was discussed in chapter 1 above, Holcroft sold his library to clear his debts and left for Germany. After spending a miserable few months in Hamburg, he finally went to Paris in January 1800.

According to Marvin Carlson, 'the minor houses of Paris declined under the Directory. Suspected by the police, prostituted by unscrupulous speculators, driven to the most absurd expedients in their competition for audiences, over half those houses still open as 1797 began had disappeared by the following fall.'[23] In a new atmosphere of bourgeois sociability, pleasure gardens were beginning to take over from the minor theatres as places of fashionable resort. The patriotic pieces mounted during the period of Bonaparte's Italian and Egyptian campaigns were similar to English ones, but French audiences had grown tired of ideological and nationalistic bombast. However, Emmet Kennedy claims that liberation from the political censorship of the Jacobins allowed the period 1795–9 to be theatrically 'the most innovative':

It is after the Terror that the idea of a good and bad revolution is born: that the period just ending has nothing to do with its beginnings, nor even with the Republic. It truly required putting a parenthesis around the reign of the Committee of Public Safety . . . In the months that followed 9 Thermidor, theatre played a political role by placing the responsibility for the Terror on the heads of a few misguided men. But it was a matter explained inductively and not deductively, in order to propagate the new institutions . . . The style and the staging were, however, profoundly reworked.[24]

Kennedy cites how *Cange, ou Le Commissionaire de Saint-Lazare* (1794) personalised the oppression of the Terror, resurrecting the figure of the benevolent governor to defeat the ruthless Jacobin, *Les Suspects, ou L'Interieur des comitées révolutionaires* (1795) ridiculed the vainglory of ignorant sansculottes in positions of power, and *Madame Angot, ou La Poissarde parvenue* (1796, Théâtre d'Emulation, the old Gaîté, soon to be so renamed) was the first of a string of comedies in which an old fishwife tries to disguise her vulgar origins. These plays seem fairly traditional, but it was not in the 'realistic' dramatisation of actual events that traumatic experiences found their most effective expression. One must agree with Kennedy's assertion that during ten years of Revolution, theatre had 'proved itself an imperfect instrument of education and propaganda . . . [it] followed the evolution of society rather than the other way round'.[25] Thus early *mélodrames* provided a reflection rather than an inspiration. And they did so by developing models from England that the earlier Revolutionary playwrights, Mercier and Chénier, would have considered as 'barbaric' as Voltaire had Shakespeare.

In 1797 the English Gothic novels of Radcliffe and Lewis were first published in Paris and they inspired a flush of 'horror plays', typified by *Le Moine* by Cammaille-Saint-Aubin (Théâtre de la Gaîté, 1797) which was performed 116 times in two years. Guilbert de Pixérécourt based his *Château des Appenins* (Ambigu-Comique, 9 December 1798) on Radcliffe's *Mysteries of Udolpho*, and Gothic themes were to permeate much of his subsequent work. These plays were presented on the Boulevard and took the form of *pantomimes dialoguées*, which Carlson describes as 'a form now very close to the earliest melodramas',[26] though Pixérécourt's *Victor, ou L'Enfant de la forêt* (Ambigu-Comique, May 1798) was the first to formally adopt the description *mélodrame*. Although Holcroft's arrival in Paris in 1800 coincided with the first flush of *mélodrames*, his first translation was of Jean Bouilly's *L'Abbé de l'Epée*, which when sent to Drury Lane was produced under the pseudonym of 'Herbert Hill' as *Deaf and Dumb; or, The Orphan Protected* (24 February 1801). The play purports to dramatise the experience of a real-life philanthropist, in much the same way that Inchbald's *Such Things Are* presented the prison reformer John Howard in 1787.[27] Charles Michel de l'Epée had died in 1789 and the

National Assembly memorialised him as a benefactor of mankind, for his creation of a sign language for deaf mutes.[28] The play would seem then to accord with Holcroft's long-held belief in the power of rational education as the true source of enlightened principles, as the Abbé de l'Epée declared:

> The bare thought of prompting to the forgetfulness of nature; of calling forth the faculties of mind; this one persuasion gives strength, courage, and perseverance, to accomplish miracles . . . Judge what are my sensations, when, surrounded by my pupils, I watch them gradually emerging from the night that overshadows them . . . till the full blaze of perfect intellect informs their souls with hope and adoration. This is to new-create our brethren. What transports to bring man acquainted with himself! (Act 3, scene 2)

However, this celebration of enlightening the darkness of the inarticulate is embedded in a story more appropriate to the new melodramatic genre. A deaf mute has been robbed of his inheritance and left for dead, and de l'Epée helps him reclaim his noble estate from the 'petty trader' who has usurped it. When the usurper's son discovers his father's villainy he takes the guilt upon himself, crying:

> My own father the perpetrator! Saints of heaven, guard my soul from desperation! Already the licentious rabble point at me as I pass; I hear them cry – 'There goes the monster, the unnatural villain, who contrived to rob his noble kinsman!' (Act 4, scene 2)

In the light of the sequestrations that took place during the Revolution such agitation on the return of émigrés would not have been unknown. The last act of the play is concerned with persuading the villainous father to repent and return the estate without having to face public denunciation, and, although Holcroft, perhaps sensibly, refrained from staging the actual conversion, the off-stage recantation brings the play to a happy close. Of course, most credit for the play must go to the French author Builly, but it would seem that, as the Revolutionary War came to a close, Holcroft had offered London a morally and politically engaged drama consistent with the radical optimism that he had maintained throughout ten years of political turmoil.

However, in the following year the Treaty of Amiens (25 March 1802) allowed him to return to London himself, bringing with him a translation of Pixérécourt's *Cœlina, ou l'enfant du mystère* (Ambigu-Comique, 2 September 1800). It was produced at Covent Garden as *A Tale of Mystery* (13 November 1802) and was the first play on any

British stage to be billed as 'a melodrama'. No doubt Holcroft was delighted by the financial success of both translated plays, but there is a curious symmetry in his bringing *Cœlina* across the Channel just as he had brought *The Marriage of Figaro* eighteen years before. The attack on aristocratic privilege in *Figaro* had foreshadowed the Revolution, while *Cœlina* was a prime example of the essentially reactionary drama engendered by the Revolution.

To describe melodrama as reactionary is of course provocative, as there were many generic elements that were as hostile to privilege and élitism as in *Figaro*. Pixérécourt was personally dedicated to providing drama for the people, claiming he wrote 'for those that cannot read'.[29] But, by examining a few examples of the new form, I will demonstrate how it restrained, and even defused, the radical impetus for change. To an extent this can be explained by the re-regularising of the Paris theatres. Even before Napoleon reintroduced theatrical monopolies in 1807, market forces had closed down a swathe of small minor houses. The commercial pre-eminence of the giants of the Boulevard, the Gaîté and the Ambigu-Comique, was further consolidated by César Ribié, who had replaced Nicolet in 1797, and Labanette Corsse, who took over Audinot's theatre in 1798, by their capitalising on the new vogue for melodrama.

The conventions of melodramatic performance have been analysed thoroughly by several theatre historians, so I will restrict myself to its earliest manifestation and to making comparisons with the theatrical forms considered in this study. This approach may well indicate that some critics of the genre have been unduly influenced by the later development of the form, as in the period of French Romantic theatre of Hugo and Dumas, the Victorian theatre of Boucicault and Charles Reade, or even the American theatre of Daly and Belasco. I am also aware that in emphasising the reactionary purpose of the genre, I am contesting radical or democratic interpretations of this particular form of popular theatre.[30] Certainly, sympathy in the plays was with the dispossessed, but in many of the early French examples this refers to returning émigrés – as I interpreted Bouilly's deaf mute – rather than to the peasant victims of grasping landlords that typified English melodramas of the 1820s and 1830s. In Pixérécourt and Holcroft's *Cœlina*,[31] although a worthy miller twice acts generously to save the two brothers, most of the characters are of noble and wealthy families or their servants. The plot is similar to that of *Deaf and Dumb* in that the mute Francisco is dispossessed by his brother, Count Romaldi (Treguelin), and once again the villain is brought to repentance by the heroic virtue of his mute brother. Although Romaldi is cornered, he spurns attacking Francisco and his daughter a second time:

> ROMALDI, *in terror, enters from the house presenting his pistol.* FRANCISCO *opens his breast for him to shoot if he pleases.* SELINA *falls between them. The whole scene passes in a mysterious and rapid manner. Music suddenly stops.*
> ROMALDI. No! too much blood is upon my head! Be justly revenged; take mine!

And then, when the forces of the law arrive and threaten to shoot Romaldi, Francisco shields the brother who has wronged him, while Selina and her guardian also evoke forgiveness:

> SELINA. Oh, forbear! Let my father's virtues plead for my uncle's errors!
> BONAMO. We all will entreat for mercy; since of mercy we all have need: for his sake, and for our own, may it be freely granted! (Act 2, scene 2)

This desire for reconciliation, despite the enormity of the crimes, marks the play as politically reactionary. Particularly because, not only must the crimes of the past be forgiven, but they must also be rendered mute. Whether one reads Romaldi as aristocrat or terrorist, or Francisco as émigré or the spirit of guillotined moderation, the subtext of the play is similar, trust must be restored – even if it is an irrational trust in the nobility of the aristocrats and the benevolence of the bourgeoisie.

Significantly, Holcroft added a scene in which the housekeeper Fiametta forces Bonamo to beg forgiveness for distrusting his son and friend, when they try to convince him of the innocence of his niece Selina and her true father the dumb Francisco. Simon Shepherd and Peter Womack point out that here Holcroft is less 'conservative' than his original:

> Against [Bonamo's] documentary evidence, and his social rank, she asserts her instinctive belief and her personal experience . . . While thunder rumbles in the distance, the female housekeeper compels the male owner to fall to his knees, in front of his own son and most trusted male friend, and repent his unjust mistake . . . The housekeeper . . . is one of the disenfranchised to whom radical melodrama not only gives a voice, but also, by summoning up the special facilities of the stage, amplifies that voice with reverberations of distant thunder.[32]

But this one scene fails to give a 'radical' tone to the play as a whole, although it does suggest how melodramatic conventions might be adopted in the cause of reform at a later date. Shepherd's analysis,

however, is more perceptive when he discusses the political implications of Francisco's dumbness, and associates it with a proliferation
of 'mutilated' heroic victims in melodrama:

The emotion of the moment of speaking out is something very different
from the frustration experienced when the dumb man cannot speak to
clear himself. Being able to acclaim the truth is the opposite of being
trapped into a false truth. Melodrama may be said to construct excitement
out of the possible alternation between being trapped in circumstances and
being able to change them.[33]

This, he suggests, is related to Marx's dialectical concepts of
determination and *agency*. Idealistic rhetoric overcomes apparently
impossible obstacles, and familial virtue, on behalf of a traditional
status quo, triumphs unrealistically over the dynamism of those who
have tried to change things in their own interest. Thus tradition is
painted as innocent and change as evil. And, because in the
dramaturgy of melodrama there can be no compromise between the
two, this rigidity actually contradicts the mechanics of Marx's
dialectical process of change.

Inflexible Manichaeism, Peter Brooks argues, is the dominant
feature of melodrama, and the one that it bequeathed to a whole
branch of nineteenth-century literature:

Good or bad, characters are notable for their integrity, their thorough
exploitation of a way of being or of a critical conjuncture. They exist at a
moment of crisis as exemplary destinies . . . bringing alternately the victory
of blackness and whiteness, and in each instance giving a full enunciation
of the condition experienced.[34]

He too identifies 'muteness' as the innocent opposite to the rhetoric
of hypocritical virtue or blatant villainy. Of course, developing from
the dramatic pantomime, the language of gesture is an unsurprising
theatrical convention, and mute stage business accompanied by
music typified the climax of spectacular pageants as well as melodramas.[35] But, the employment of an unspecific and unmediated
expression of feeling can be seen as an attempt to disguise the bitter
logic of moral contradiction and political disillusion, which could
not be escaped if it were expressed in words.

Mute gesture can . . . most pertinently be considered as a trope and
analyzed on the plane of rhetoric. It is a sign *for* a sign, demanding a
translatio between two signs. It hence resembles metaphor, the transference
or displacement of meaning . . . whose tenor is a vaguely defined but

grandiose emotional or spiritual force that gesture seeks to make present without directly naming it, by pointing at it.[36]

Throughout this study I have emphasised how the drama of the period ought to be read metaphorically, direct references proving too dangerous in a period of political censorship. However, in melodrama all the indirect methods of history plays, Gothic sensationalism, mime, dance and music were brought together in an aesthetically coherent art form. Inevitably, however, it was not intellectually coherent, precisely because it employed *rhetorical* extremes – underarticulated gesture and overarticulated protestation – to dramatise *moral* extremes. However emotionally reassuring this might have been, it bore little relation to the realities of the age.

Melodrama's insistence on moral legibility was far from the confident assertion of the 'self-evident truths' of the American constitution of 1776, and was rather, I suggest, the 'escape mechanism' of cultural alienation. Trying to affirm absolutes of innocence and villainy in the highly ambiguous context of 1802 was blatantly a process of denial. France had agreed a fragile treaty with England, aristocrats were returning to reclaim confiscated estates, the French church was trying to re-establish its dominance, parvenu bureaucrats and profiteers were seeking to justify their newly won wealth, and Napoleon was already planning to transform the hard-won Republic into a personal empire. Equally in England the social and political scene was full of contradictions: military officers were reluctantly returning to half pay with the enemy undefeated, Dr Addington was leading a patchwork coalition, while Pitt retreated like Achilles to his tent, and the industrialisation process was advancing along its unregulated path, redistributing wealth and disrupting traditional social relationships. No wonder Brooks suggests that these early melodramas should not only be interpreted psychoanalytically, but that they were themselves a kind of psychoanalysis:

Psychoanalysis is a version of melodrama first of all in its conception of the nature of conflict, which is stark and unremitting, possibly disabling, menacing the ego, which must find ways to reduce or discharge it. The dynamics of repression and the return of the repressed figure the plot of melodrama. Enactment is necessarily excessive: the relation of symbol to symbolized (in hysteria, for instance) is not controllable or justifiable. The Evil of melodrama is reworked, only partly de-ethicalized, in the process of repression and the status of repressed content; the unconscious is ever ready to act as *le traître*. The structure of ego, superego, and id suggest the subjacent Manichaeism of melodramatic persons and indeed the characters most often put on the stage.[37]

Although Brooks is looking to the genre to explain a whole raft of nineteenth-century fiction – Balzac, Dostoevsky, Henry James – the application of a psychoanalytical perspective to the recurrent images and tropes of even the earliest melodramas suggest psychological processes for the containment and displacement of anxiety were being employed. The image of muteness has already been discussed, while that of the dungeon dates back to the fall of the Bastille. Pixérécourt introduced Gothic chambers into *Les Mines de Pologne* (1802), set in the castle of Minski 'in the Krapack Mountains', and in *Le Château des Appenins*, adapted from Radcliffe's *Udolpho*, but in several of his plays the trope of incarceration leading to liberation was replaced by that of displacement and recovery. The stories are of children lost and refound – as in *Cœlina* and *Deaf and Dumb* – and the visual sign is the limitless forest or mountain rather than the enclosed dungeon. In *Cœlina* the mountains are of Savoy and the pass of Arpennaz. Although *Tékéli, ou le siége de Montgatz* (1803) and *La forteresse du Danube* (1805) – adapted by Theodore Hook as *Tekeli* (Drury Lane, 24 November 1806) and *The Fortress* (Haymarket, 16 July 1807) – both involved castles and incarcerations, they were also set in wild and mountainous regions where characters were as likely to be lost as imprisoned.

William Dimond's version of Pixérécourt's first melodrama, *Victor, ou l'enfant de la forêt* (1798), as *The Foundling of the Forest* (Haymarket, 10 July 1810),[38] prioritises its forest setting over the Gothic castle, which has already been burnt down. Huguenots (metaphorical revolutionaries) have destroyed Valmont's castle near Albi, and his wife and son have apparently perished in the flames. He has now become a melancholic recluse, 'devoted to despair – a subtle slow despair that, drop by drop, congeals the blood of life, yet will not bid the creeping current quite forbear to flow' (Act 1). However both wife and son have survived – Florian brought up by huntsmen up in the forest, and Eugenia as a mute 'child of misfortune . . . accustomed to wander in the woods by night'. Bertrand, the henchman sent by the evil arsonist Longueville to kill Florian and so ensure his own claim to Valmont's estate, recognises Eugenia and, overcome with remorse, changes from persecutor to champion of the unfortunate woman. When she realises she is in Valmont's new castle she goes mad: 'Ha! ha! come to the altar – my love awaits me – weave my bridal crown!' (Act 2), and when her husband learns of her survival he too is overwhelmed with insane fury: '*In the delirium of his passion, he draws his sword, and strikes with it at an ideal combatant, his powers forsake him in the effort, he reels and falls convulsed*' (Act 3). In the end Florian kills Longueville and the family are reunited, as Valmont concludes: 'Our long-benighted loves at last encounter on a sun-bright course, and reach the haven of domestic peace' (Act 3). The madness of the characters makes the incredible, dreamlike coincidences of the narrative even more open to psychological interpretation. The images are of irreparable loss and displacement, which has destroyed the mental identities as well as happiness of the parental couple. The son, lost to his parents but at home in the wildness of the forest, returns to unite them as a family once again, and the play ends with the wish-fulfilling assertion that they have now reached 'a haven of domestic peace'. Taken as a 'realistic' drama, such a piece is so incredible and exaggerated that it has attracted critical scorn as mere 'escapist entertainment'. But my analysis of the anxiety in audiences on both sides of the Channel, which was itself the product of real social and ideological displacement, should confirm Brooks' suggestion that these dream dramas answered a genuine therapeutic need. And that their extravagance is comparable to the expressionism that accompanied the Great War, and the cruel visions of Artaud that reflected the rise of Fascism and the Second World War.[39]

Although dramatists attempted to give their fantasies some credibility by setting them in an identifiable historical past and remote geographical location, the experiences with which their audiences really identified were the recurrent ones of entrapment, dislocation, loss of family and the sensations of having lost voice, sight or hearing. Such experiences were so close to their actual reality that the dramas had to be distanced, or they might have prompted hysterical reactions as those that were inspired by Lewis' *Captive*. Their means of distancing were to create narrative of incredible coincidence, characters of incredible innocence or instability, and scenes of high emotion alternating with scenes of low comedy; the whole was to be acted with an extravagance of gesture and costume, and, above all, the action punctuated by music. In short, in order to express, and perhaps alleviate, *social* and *psychological* alienation, the drama adopted its own methods of *theatrical* alienation. By distancing the drama from reality it enabled audiences to recognise, and perhaps cope with, their own reality.

In addition to the containment or refocusing of emotion, the distancing effect of melodramatic conventions enabled differences in social application. In France the dispossessed mute regaining his inheritance could be read as an aristocratic émigré, regaining his wealth but not his power, but he could also be read as a rehabilitated revolutionary, who under the Directory and empire was no longer prosecuted for subversive thoughts – but only insofar as they remained unspoken. In England, however, the lost mute could evoke emotions on behalf of soldiers and sailors posted abroad, for even officers found it hard to correspond with their families while on active service. Dispossession was also the lot of many of the growing class of urban artisans, who looked back to their family roots in the countryside with a certain rosy nostalgia – which was even rosier for second-generation city workers who had not experienced the hardship of rural life. Certainly, the domestic melodramas of the 1820s onwards idealised village existence. None of these interpretations, however, were immediately applicable to the class of urban bourgeois, who on both sides of the Channel increased in number and wealth during the Revolutionary and Napoleonic Wars, and it was they who made up the majority of theatre audiences. They may well have unconsciously recognised the applicability of situation and sensation to the real-life experience of other classes, but their emotions were moved by sympathy rather than direct empathy with experience. As *imaginative* identification with the distress of others is probably the most powerful attraction of theatrical entertainment, the bourgeois audience, now as then, enjoyed melodrama as a pleasurable rather than distressing experience – however distressed the fictional characters might be. And, once this successful formula for vicarious pleasure had been created, it is no surprise that it fairly swiftly developed into a formulaic entertainment. This paradox of pleasurable distress made melodrama the outstanding cultural product of the post-Revolutionary theatre, and, precisely because the modern world has failed to recover the social coherence or the shared ideology that the Revolution swept away, so melodrama has become the dominant genre of popular, and especially screen, drama. It seems to be more appropriate and affective than the classic forms of comedy and tragedy.

By widening my discussion of the generic attractions of melodrama, and its capability to develop into forms as various as grand opera, action film and television soap, I have moved beyond identifying the earliest plays to be formally classified as melodramas. Although there were precise differences in form and technique between Gothic tragedy, historical romance, patriotic plays and Pixérécourt's *mélodrames*, all, as 'mixed genres', shared the metaphorical function I have described as peculiarly 'melodramatic'. Indeed metaphorical application has been a central concept in my whole study of how French and English theatrical cultures influenced each other. Despite being political enemies, at war for most of the period, the initiative leading towards the full emergence of melodrama shifted from side to side of the Channel. There was an impulse towards history plays in both countries before and during the Revolution, but the Shakespearean form developed by the English soon became the preferred form for France as well. Its elaboration into Gothic fantasy also started in England, and the translation of Radcliffe and Lewis into French, had a direct impact on Pixérécourt. But ultimately, the classic melodramatic form was French and its proliferation on the English stage was mainly through the translation of French originals. Holcroft's was the earliest example because he was already in Paris, as an exiled radical, but the Peace of Amiens, which facilitated his return to London, encouraged other English writers, politicians and members of high society to visit the French capital.[40]

The record of translations from the French, and especially Pixérécourt, over the next five years indicates the impact of melodramas on the English stage. Of course French plays had been translated before, but, as the nineteenth century progressed, the dependence of English playwrights on French models was to become increasingly prevalent. Theatrical economics were to make the prolixity of the Dibdins during the 1790s a general rule for later playwrights like Fitzball, Haines, Milner, Moncrieff, Peak, Planché, Pocock and Stirling.[41] In the first instance, during the earliest years of the century, which are the last years of this study, several Pixérécourt plays were presented in London with great success. They included *La femme à deux maris* (Paris, 1802), translated by James Cobb as *The Wife with Two Husbands* (Drury Lane, 1 November 1803), and two versions of *Le homme à trois visages*; Robert Elliston's *Venetian Outlaw* (Drury Lane, 26 April 1805) and Matthew Lewis' *Rugantino; or, the Bravo of Venice* (Covent Garden, 18 October 1805). Presented at patent houses, these, and other Pixérécourt plays, were swiftly pirated and adopted for the minor houses, as their use of musical accompaniment and pantomimic action enabled them to be per-formed under the legal definition of a burletta.

Pixérécourt's *Le homme à trois visages* and its English versions offer a different perspective on how melodrama could relate to political developments, because it concentrated on the hero/villain rather than on the dispossessed victims. Whereas the iron mask had tortured prisoners in the Bastille, the hero now uses masks to defeat conspiracy and champion the virtuous. Thus Vivaldi adopts a variety of disguises, the principal one being that of a Venetian 'Bravo' or hired assassin. As such he is employed by a group of conspirators whose plot he eventually exposes. He also saves the Doge's daughter from a rapacious member of the gang, which is our first hint that he is not quite as heartless as his reputation. In Matthew Lewis' version the Duke (Doge) reflects that Rugantino (Vivaldi) 'must possess such talents and such courage, as, at the head of an army, would enable him to conquer half the world' (Act 1, scene 6), when he suddenly appears, having scaled the palace walls, boasting that 'Rugantino fears not Venice; 'tis Venice fears Rugan-tino.' In Pixérécourt's original Vivaldi makes a more political and more Romantic vaunt:

> There is perhaps beneath my coarse envelope a heart more tender and a soul more generous than yours . . . These run-of-the-mill men, these beings one sees loitering by thousands through the streets of Venice resemble insects creeping beneath our feet: one crushes them, or if one spares them it is because one despises them, and one sees them expire every day without having so much as suspected their existence. Not for me the shame of such a destiny! Only what is rare and extraordinary has a claim to the esteem of our contemporaries and the admiration of posterity.[42]

He has come to demand the hand of the Doge's daughter, despite her having been officially betrothed to the Duke of Milan. Rugantino reappears equally suddenly at the climax of the Doge's masque, revealing himself to be Rosabella's true love, who had left the city at the Doge's command. He then denounces the conspirators, who are arrested, and eventually reveals he is really the Duke of Milan, who has adopted all these masks to test both the Doge and the fidelity of his daughter. Thus a ruler disguises himself as a lover, who disguises himself as a villain, who uses other disguises to escape detection. The denouement explains everything, but during the action of the play everyone is deceived by appearances.

The whole play is what Americans would describe as 'hokum', and it clearly anticipates not only the nineteenth century detective's use of disguise, but also the comic-book superhero's powers of ubiquity and transformation. In the context of my own arguments, the play provided a dream-image of, firstly, the uncertainty of personal identity explored in chapter 5 above, and, secondly, the moral confusion created by the twists and turns of the politics of the period. Robespierre, for instance, was both virtuous hero and ruthless assassin, yet seemed to be able to justify himself without hypocrisy. Similarly, Bonaparte had played many roles with extraordinary virtuosity. In 1802 he was made consul for life, having started out as an immigrant from Corsica (the home of swarthy *banditti*) and risen through the ranks; he joined the Jacobins, but put down the last popular *journées*; he became not only France's most successful general, but also master of internal reconstruction and, arguably, reconciliation. Whether people admired or feared him, Napoleon was a 'Superman', whom all Frenchmen hoped would prove a hero rather than villain.

This discussion of how melodrama, and other conventionalised forms of drama, reflected contemporary political attitudes has tended towards a rather negative emphasis on the disillusionment and reaction that followed the early years of hope and reconstruction. But any history of the Revolution must recognise the extraordinary ideological reformation caused by its unprecedented course of events. Even if both Bonaparte and Pitt, in their different ways, achieved military success at the cost of domestic repression, and even if after 1815 the predominant hegemony across Europe was a restored autocracy, and in England the anti-radical government of Liverpool, Sidmouth and Castlereagh, the concepts of the Rights of Man, and the Rights of Woman, had been enunciated and, for a while at least, under the Republic of 1792, legislated. Even if melodrama and pantomime's evocation of an 'alien Other' was in order to mediate present anxieties, an awareness of and sympathy for other peoples and other cultures had been awakened. Similarly, class fear and class conflict grew from an awareness that class structures were not immutable. Change, as epitomised by revolution, could of course be resisted, but everyone now knew change was possible.

In one area at least radical change was actually achieved. It was in an area in which England, rather than France, took the initiative and, for all its limitations and mixed motives, it was a change that heralded a worldwide transformation. In 1807 the British parliament abolished the slave trade. As an achievement, it was more important in terms of ideological perception and cultural validation than it was for the immediate relief of the hardship and oppression of the slaves themselves, but it was the first step towards emancipation and eventual civil rights.[43] In chapter 1 above I noted, with reference to Colman's *Inkle and Yarico*, that the Lord Chamberlain's censorship was exercised more lightly with anti-slave trade plays than with pro-Revolutionary reform plays, and that the English theatre played an honourable part in awakening consciousness of the inhumanity of the trade.[44] From 1792 there were several slave revolts in both the British and French West Indies. The largest one was in St Dominique, led by the charismatic Toussaint Louveture. In 1801 Napoleon tried to regain the island, but, although Toussaint was captured, the eventual result was the creation of the independent black state of Haiti in 1804.[45]

This slave war intensified interest in abolishing the trade, and in the years 1799 to 1801 a number of anti-slave trade plays were written by authors well established in the London theatres: John Fawcett's *Obi; or, Three Fingered Jack*, Philip Astley's *Kongo Kolo* and John Cartwright Cross' *King Caesar*. They may also have been influenced by *The Negro Slaves; or, the Blackman and the Blackbird*, published in Edinburgh in 1799 by Archibald McLaren, a prolific Scots author of seldom-produced plays. His was an ingeniously symbolic drama, which was performed at the Theatre Royal, Edinburgh and at Astley's Amphitheatre in London.[46] McSympathy, 'a highland Cynic', attacks the planter Rangoon for ill-treating his slaves, whilst, like all cautious radicals, emphasising his own patriotism:

RACOON. You, like the rest of your countrymen, are never happy but when you're up to the ears in politics.

MCSYMPATHY. Speak not of my country, Sir! – love and loyalty shall always be our motto; and if we should throw in a few grains of humanity into the compound, the never a bit worse will it taste.

The blackman of the title is Quako, who when asked why he released his master's caged blackbirds, replies:

Because I think too many of their colour are slaves already – Ah, master, had you seen the poor things as they lay on my hand, their hearts went pant, pant, this way; and tho' they cou'd not speak. I understood the meaning of their pant, pant, to be at liberty ... I threw them in the air, that way, and they flew to the woods. – By this time they know what Quako's heart wou'd feel, if any friendly power wou'd waft him to his native shore of Guinea.

Quako's slavery is paralleled by the capture of an English officer, Firmlove, by native Indians,[47] an experience which leads him to set Quako and his beloved Sela free: 'I present you with the brightest jewel in the British dominion – and that is your liberty.'

John Fawcett's *Obi; or Three Fingered Jack* had none of MacLaren's radical sentiments, but it demonstrated an informed knowledge of slave society. This 'Pantomimical Drama', with music by Arnold, received thirty-nine performances during the 1800 season at the Haymarket, where Fawcett was assistant manager. The 'prospectus of the drama' claimed that *Obi* was based on 'a matter of fact which occurred (*An. Dom.* 1780) in the island of Jamaica' and explains that 'Obi' was a form of black magic or Voodoo.[48] The play was hardly sympathetic to emancipation – the Christian slaves Quashee, Sam and Tuckey help the English officers to recapture Jack and his gang of escaped slaves – and although one song reflects on divided families, it merely enjoins humane treatment by the owners:

> O, it be very sad to see
> Poor Negro child and father part! –
> But if White man kind massa be
> He heal the wound in Negro's heart.

Philip Astley presented a similarly educative pantomime at the Pavilion in November 1800. Set in Africa, *Kongo Kolo; or, the Mandingo Chief*[49] depicted the war between Kolo the 'robber king' of the Mandingo tribe and the peaceable Foulahs. He plans to sell his captives into slavery to the Irish trader Felix Fagen O'Fogharty. However the shipwrecked Sidney not only frees Kolo's captives, but persuades O'Fogharty to break his whip and renounce his trade.

> These as ourselves are Men, form'd by that power
> Which gave us life – Their feelings are as ours
> Their passions too the same – and tho' this true
> Their Climate gives their skins another hue
> Yet, they are men and brothers born as free
> Tho' Tyrant Custom's lost them liberty.

O'Fogharty then sings a song in praise of Irish bravery and British liberty, which includes the line: 'Don't be telling me of your exotic Trees of Liberty'. Thus the appeal is to common decency, perceived as the special preserve of the British, as opposed to the trumped-up claims of the French with their artificial trees of liberty.

In September 1801 the New Royal Circus also presented a play that sought to strike a balance between sympathy for imprisoned slaves and fear of the self-enfranchised. At the height of the St Dominique conflict, as Toussaint Louveture united the island and prepared to repulse the forces sent by Napoleon, John Cartwright Cross based his *King Caesar; or, the Negro Slaves*[50] on the St Dominican slave revolt of Mackandal in the 1760s. The programme asserted the accuracy of the plot: 'It is but a short time since that the island of St Domingo trembled at the single name of MACKANDAL (or King Caesar). Born in Africa, he was unquestionably of high rank, for his education had been attended to with an assiduity not common among negroes.' In the play a love intrigue leads to Mackandal's stabbing his overseer –

and, grown desperate in his fortunes, at the solicitation of the *banditti*, who place immoderate faith in the power of his fetiche [fetish], he becomes their leader under the title of KING CAESAR, and from this instant begins to spread terror and devastation in the habitation of the adjacent plains, exterminating all who disobey him.

As in many a spectacular pantomime and melodrama of the period, this villain offers many possible readings: the historical Mackandal, the contemporary Louveture, or even the dreaded French emperor himself – all of whom could have been given the title of Caesar. Starting the play as a black Macheath, beloved of the ladies and scornful of the law, Mackandal is corrupted by his power into a typically Gothic malcontent:

> Abandon'd by all, what's the world now to me?
> The sun-beams but torture and lights to disgrace:
> Oh, Vengeance! – and outcast consign'd is to thee
> Vowing hatred and death to the whole human race!

These pantomimes combine a desire to give justice to the slaves with a fear of their barbaric vengeance. The issues are more complex than in *Inkle and Yarico*, but the solutions remain the same: common decency and the tradition of British liberty – with no appeal to the dangerous concepts of the Rights of Man. As in most exotic melodrama, the ominous Other was exorcised by a ritualistic, rather than an ideological, confrontation. Typically, the magical power of the Orient, as in Colman's *Blue Beard* (1798), was erotic, ensnaring women into a harem, but that of the African was more violent, threatening savage butchery. Some generous Orientals may be admired for their civility, but Africans were at best pitied for their enslavement.[51] Not only do *Obi* and *King Caesar* share ambiguous attitudes to their black characters, but they reflect the ambiguity which even reformers felt about the French Revolution. In Paris the desire to rationalise government had descended into the nightmare of the Terror, just as in the West Indies the emancipation of slaves threatened the massacres of St Dominique. As these outcomes seemed irrational and incommensurate to the power of the 'common decency' advocated by Colman, or McLaren, so the dramatisations of slavery, although better informed, became more sensational.

In July 1804 John Cross produced another slavery pantomime for the Royal Circus. The source of *Joanna of Surinam* was not acknowledged in the published songs and prospectus,[52] but, as Cross kept the same names as his original, audiences would have recognised it as a dramatisation of John Gabriel Stedman's *Narrative of a five year expedition against the revolted Negroes of Surinam*, printed by the radical publisher John Johnson in 1796. As in *Inkle and Yariko*, the hero of both the play and the memoirs falls in love with a black woman. In Stedman's own case, she was already a slave, although he had married her and she had born him a son. The plot of the play is centred on his attempts to gain her full enfranchisement. He has no money of his own, and, even after being rewarded by the Governor of Surinam for his services against an army of revolted slaves – led by Baron, 'a desperate Negro, chief of the marauding *banditti*' – Stedman is cheated by villainous Colonel Fourgeould, who wants the lovely Joanna for himself. Although the play transformed a remarkable history into a predictable melodrama – including the arrival of the British navy to impose justice – it provided its audience, most of whom were unlikely to have read Stedman's *Narrative*, with something of the complexity, as well as the cruelty, that he describes in relationships between slaves, their owners and those sympathetic to their plight.[53]

In 1807 Wilberforce's Abolition Bill was finally passed by parliament, and Drury Lane's Christmas pantomime (19 December) was *Furibond; or, Harlequin Negro*. It provides a fine example of what Paula Backscheider describes as 'Spectacular Politics', as the issues were mediated through theatrical magic and imagery rather than ideological discourse.[54] The fairy Benigna, in a display of mime, transparencies, and tableaux transforms Furibond, a Negro slave, into Harlequin:

> Be sure of all Benigna can bestow
> But weigh thy Choice, or great will be thy woe.
> *[He points to his black face]*
> What – art thou weary of they sable hue?
> I can on one condition that remove.
> Such are the terms – that fair narcissus view
> An object only to himself of love.
> *[A transparency of* NARCISSUS*]*
> Wilt thou the Beauties of the mind forgo?
> *[He objects to it]*
> I knew thy manly Nature would say, no.
> *[He asks for Power]*
> For power! – and does ambition swell thy breast?
> *[A transparency of a tyrant]*
> Try if thy wish obtain'd would make thee blest?
> *[He turns away disgusted]*
> Well may'st thou turn thee from the cruel scene
> 'Tis gone! –
> *[A transparency of* HARLEQUIN *relieving distress]*
> – View now what thou might'st have been
> Dispensing comforts to th'oppressed with grief
> Heaven's instrument of general relief.
> *The Fairy waves her Wand,*
> *the Slave changes to* HARLEQUIN
> Thou dost adopt my choice – this sword receive
> 'Tis fraught with Magic Virtues, guard it well
> Protection from thy direst foes 'twill give
> All wealth procure, all outward ills repel.
> SLAVE DRIVER *enters with Slaves in Chains,*
> HARLEQUIN *supplicates for them*
> Poor Afric's Children sigh for liberty
> Alas! – that task was not reserv'd for me.
> BRITANNIA *appears in the Clouds with the Genius of*
> *Britain and attendants. The chains of the Slaves*
> *immediately fall off. They kneel in Thankfulness.*
> See Britain's Genius from the Skies
> Listening to the Negro's Cries.

Although it falls outside the period I have set myself, a sense of symmetry takes me to the summer of 1808, when George Colman, with whose *Inkle and Yarico* I began this study, celebrated abolition of the trade with *The Africans*.[55] Like Astley's *Kongo Kolo*, it was set in

Africa and dramatised dealings between rival tribes and with the white slave traders. The actual slave-selling is presented comically, presided over by Liston as Augustus Mug, a cockney cabinet maker who came to Africa to buy mahogany but who has been appointed minister by the local tribal chief. When one of the African women protests that slaves cannot be happy – 'To make men happy you must make them free!' – Mug replies, 'Huzza, miss! That's an English sentiment: go to London and parliament will naturalize you directly!' In a more serious tone, Fawcett, who had written *Obi*, played Mandiboo, and his condemnation of a tyrannical chief reveals well how the politics of metaphor work. The setting is Africa, but his story presents in detail the patriotic English view of Napoleon:

> He is no rightful ruler; but worked and bullied himself in to power. When the troubles about liberty broke out among the Mandingoes, he was of low note among their warriors. Enterprise and good luck gave him, at last, complete sway over the fighting men; – that's everything when a nation is in ferment, and the successful upstart is active, cruel, and cunning. But what has it made him? Why the usurping king of a people who murdered their true king, because they would have no king at all; and the pillaging protector of some trembling neighbours, whom he forces to say, 'Come shoot one half of us, that the survivors may thank you for putting their property in your clutches.'

Here we see plainly how the ideology of British patriotism, forged to pursue the wars with France, appropriated the emotive issue of slavery into its armoury, just as Sheridan had used the conquest of Peru to extol the Whiggish Liberties of Britain.

Recognising these metaphorical strategies can help neutralise the potentially offensive racial stereotypes presented in many of these plays, but if, however, we distance them too far from their ostensible subject matter, we may also underestimate their material achievement. 'Spectacular politics' is not just a matter of setting forth an image – there are real politics as well as the spectacle – and the comment from the introduction to the Cumberland edition of *The Africans* might be applied to all these anti-slavery plays: 'Mr Colman has again put his axe to the root of the Upas tree of Slavery; which, to the honour of British humanity, is now grubbed up and laid prostrate for ever!'

Colman's *The Africans* may seem to bring my account full circle, in terms of theatrical developments, and it is important to recognise that all the radical and reactionary changes of the previous twenty years, in both politics and theatre, did not entirely destroy the benevolent ideology of Enlightenment that had originally inspired the desire for change. The principles of the Rights of Man, the slogans of Liberty, Equality and Fraternity and the impulses towards toleration and empowerment having been once enunciated were not lost. But the struggle to achieve these ideals was not one for a single generation, which is why I do not want to finish my history with a sense of closure, and my final chapter will not be one of conclusion, or even prediction, but will reflect instead on the processes of my own production.

Reflections towards a conclusion

When a historian reaches the end of a book he becomes acutely aware of omissions. What there has not been room for, what he has not researched and what he has not prioritised. All this is a necessary part of the craft of selection and organisation, but with this book I am particularly aware of a disparity between the ephemeral nature of my theatrical examples and the enormity of the changes taking place in politics and society. In my introduction I used the metaphor of a hot-air balloon, and I also referred to the spume on a wave. In both cases what is seen is a manifestation of something invisible – the buoyant air or the swell of the sea. The balloon makes a nice comparison because it is a man-made construction apparently entirely free from contact with the earth – just like some of the inconsequential entertainments I have described. However, sea spume is more obviously the product of the violent action of the waves – and in contrast to the driving force of Revolutionary events theatrical entertainment certainly seems a light and frothy concoction. But spume is neither constructed nor controlled, whereas many people were involved in making theatre. It was their livelihood as well others' relaxation.

And spume is not just the white plume on a rolling breaker, it is the froth that remains once the wave, and even the tide, withdraws. It can be a sad looking splodge left on the sand, turning greyish, containing bits of weed and debris. The remnants left by the crash of the wave and the surge of the tide, it is the historical evidence of once vital and terrifying events. As a theatre historian, I have had to make choices that determined my research and effected my writing; some were conscious others accidental. And as I reach the end of my book I look back to see what those choices were and what effect they might have on the way my work is read and understood. I have tried to be simple and to be open. Simple, in describing plays and

performances without obscuring the events with too much interpretation, and yet open, in suggesting that every event is inevitably
subject to interpretation. This dialectic between report and analysis
is a recurring challenge to the writer of history, and is central to
debates about historicism and methodology. These debates can get
very knotty and, if carried on throughout a book, exclude the reader
who simply wants to know what happened and why. Of course we
historians say such questions are hopelessly naïve. But as a historian
I, at least, insist that events did take place and that they were the
result of decisions taken and choices made. Although our knowledge
of historical events comes to us only through the constructed
discourse of historical reporting, history as discourse is different from
history as event, and the historian, who sifts through such reports for
traces of evidence, should know better than anyone the difference
between froth on a beach and a storm at sea.

So I am deeply aware of my omissions, and I would like my reader
to be aware as well. I also want to prioritise these omissions as much
as the examples I have included. I have tried to lift the reader's view
from the sand to the horizon, and this has lead to many unmediated
generalisations. I have mentioned without analysis great shifts in
political power, economics, philosophy, literature and social behaviour. All these deserve more attention than the space here allows,
because they are the invisible forces of the air, the winds, currents
and thermals that kept the gorgeous balloon of theatre afloat and
determined how and where it flew. But it is difficult to judge the force
of the wind from within the balloon. Was one wind stronger than the
rest? My Marxist analysis insists that this was the case. Both the
French and the Industrial Revolutions were crucially instrumental in
establishing the capitalist hegemony of the nineteenth century, and so
my greatest omission may be a detailed analysis of the finances of
theatre – as well as of the national economies of England and France.

I have, however, argued in some detail that the determining
feature of the period for the theatre was the sense of loss, a feeling
that things had changed in ways that people did not expect or want,
and that theatrical formulations reflected this in images of incarceration, dislocation and supernatural intervention. Plays looked backwards to the past in order to make sense of the present and future.
That past provided contradictory settings – cruel fortresses of feudal
power and innocent family homes in rural villages. Homes and
security that were continually threatened, but, in dreamlike happy

endings, were saved by heroic acts of restoration. But in real life, conflict and change were not resolved so neatly. If traditional powers were restored they were reconstructed in the process, and, when the reconstructions were as thorough as Napoleon's reinvention of autocracy, the factory owner's dispossession of the peripatetic clothier, or Jeremy Bentham's utilitarian reformulation of Enlightenment benevolence, then the oppression seemed worse as it had become more efficient.

However, as Marx also pointed out, although conflicts are resolved in a new transformed synthesis, this in its turn provokes new challenges. Therefore, to illustrate how the ebb and flow of the tide does not follow the same channels, I choose to end my history by considering the later lives of two characters who have featured much in my narrative, George Colman and Thomas Holcroft. Of course, as characters in a book they are my own constructions and I choose to cite their stories because they are exemplary – even metaphorical. But I am drawn to this strategy because history is not only the ground swell. It is determined by human agency. Choices that individuals make in material circumstances.

Colman was a manager before being a playwright. Once he inherited the Haymarket Theatre he used it to make money and he employed his writing facility to bring in audiences. It was a great facility, and I have used his plays to define several new genres of the age – *Inkle and Yarico*, *The Battle of Hexham*, *Blue Beard*, *John Bull* and *The Africans* – all of which were designed for commercial success rather than as personal statements. But, despite their success, Colman's income could not support his own extravagance. He aspired to cutting a dash as a dandy, a man about town, so both personal need and business interest led him to manage the Haymarket on increasingly commercial lines. In 1804 he tried to loosen his dependence on actors from the winter houses, whose longer seasons were now encroaching on the Haymarket's summer business, by creating a scratch company of provincial actors. The policy was not entirely successful, but it was a departure from the artistic principle of a permanent ensemble that was soon to become general practice across the industry. In 1805, therefore, he was forced to sell half of his share to a triumvirate of his brother-in-law David Morris, James Winston, who became production manager, and a wealthy lawyer named Tahourdin.

For the theatre's management from now on, as in *John Bull*, 'the sole interest turned upon poverty and wealth'.[1] There are many anecdotes of Morris' penny-pinching ways,[2] and Joe Cowell's description of Winston's duties vividly suggests a middle-manager rather than an artistic collaborator:

> It was his province to measure out the canvas and colours for the painters, count the nails for the carpenters, pick up the tin-tacks and bits of candle, calculate the least possible quantity of soap required for each dressing-room, and invent and report delinquencies that could in any way be construed into the liability of a forfeit.[3]

Between 1806 and 1817 Colman was restrained in the King's Bench Prison for debt, and, although he continued as chief proprietor of the Haymarket from his well appointed cell, power passed increasingly into the hands of the businessmen Morris and Winston. They tried to extend the summer season into the winter months, and Morris even tried to stop Colman selling his own plays to the more profitable winter houses. Morris was a capitalist wanting a return on his investment, but Colman too was fairly described in 1810, as 'sacrificing the interests of his own theatre to that of another . . . Ready money is the inspiring motive – the *praesena divus* – of all such persons.'[4] Colman's financial problems seem slight when compared to those of Drury Lane, but manager Sheridan was an exceptional individual and his theatre occasioned exceptional expenses, being rebuilt in 1794 and burning down in 1809. In comparison the Haymarket flourished, but even there the power of the market determined artistic policy.

Eventually, of course, investment in the minor houses was to force the ending of the patent houses' privilege, though not until 1843. Kemble foresaw the effect of their commercial competition, when Samuel Arnold attempted to establish an English opera house at the Lyceum in 1794:

> The great companies of good sterling actors would be broken and dispersed, and there would no longer exist establishments sufficiently important to maintain any large body of them; the best plays would no longer find adequate representatives in any but a few of the principal parts, the character of theatrical pieces would be lowered, the school of fine and careful acting would be lost, no play of Shakespeare's could be decorously put on the stage, and the profession and the public would alike fare the worse for the change.

Kemble's niece Fanny, who reported these remarks in 1878, acknowledged that he was an interested party: 'One of the patented proprietors, one of the monopolists . . . and therefore, perhaps, an incompetent judge in the matter.' Nevertheless, she concluded with hindsight, 'The cause went against us, and every item of his prophecy concerning the stage has undoubtedly come to pass.'[5]

These details of theatre administration and financial policy confirm my conviction that capitalism or, as it was then termed, political economy was the one ideology to emerge more confident than before from the intellectual turmoil engendered by the Revolution. What Adam Smith called the 'invisible hand' of economic competition was becoming visible. Classical economists and their political equivalents, the Benthamite Utilitarians, began to claim that the market was the only realistic force that could benefit good, and drive out bad, practice – not only in commerce, but in all organisations, civic, cultural and even charitable. E. P. Thompson claims that this period not only defined but created economic determinism:

If we turn to earlier British history . . . we find that 'economics', in the modern sense, is a notion for which there is no word and no exactly corresponding concept. Religious and moral imperatives remain inextricably intermeshed with economic needs. One of the offences against mankind brought about within full-grown market society, and within its ideology, has been, precisely, to define all compelling social relationships as 'economic', and to replace affective bonds by the more impersonal but no less compulsive bonds of money.[6]

When Thomas Holcroft returned to London in 1802 from his self-imposed exile, he revived his intimacy with William Godwin's circle, which now included the young William Hazlitt. In 1805 he published his last novel, *Memoirs of Bryan Perdue*. It was a tale of persecution and wrongful arrest that reflected his own sense of betrayal, and it contained many of the symbolic elements to be found in Pixérécourt's melodramas – incarceration, dumbness and the threat of the inexplicable. Even in novel form, Holcroft was forced to abandon the 'plain speaking' of the eighteenth century. The literary examination of man in political society could now only be dealt with metaphorically. However, despite experimenting with such 'romantic' forms, Holcroft maintained his humanist rationalism to the end. On hearing of the death of Thomas Paine in 1809 he wrote to Godwin, despite his own poor health: 'Hey for the New Jerusalem! The millennium! And peace and eternal beatitude unto the soul of Thomas Paine.'[7] He died himself on 23 March 1809, and when

Godwin visited his deathbed, 'his feelings were so overpowered; he could not converse and only pressed his hand to his bosom and said "My dear, dear friend".'[8] The playwright had been reduced to such penury that Godwin and other friends had to organise a subscription for his family.

The significance of relating these final years is that Godwin encouraged the young Hazlitt to complete Holcroft's unfinished autobiography.[9] Although Hazlitt probably considered the task a piece of hack work, the book's existence indicates a direct link between pre-Revolutionary radicalism, as professed by Holcroft, and the post-1815 radicalism associated with a new generation of rationalists that included not only Hazlitt but Francis Place and Robert Owen. Holcroft, a self-educated man, never let persecution or disappointment in the course of events undermine his belief that simple honesty could find rational solutions to political problems. In that he was probably the most consistent of those who greeted the dawn of 1789. For many of the so-called Romantics the Terror of 1793, the emergence of Napoleon's personal dictatorship and cultural triumph of bourgeois vulgarity led them to adopt a state of social isolation and intellectual denial. The new radicalism of the 1820s replaced both Holcroft's simple faith in the benevolence of man and the Romantic obsession with individual identity with a new critique of property. Owen called it Socialism.

Notes

INTRODUCTION

1 The English became aware of balloon flight with the first cross-channel flight on 7 January 1785; Maurice Quinlan, 'Balloons and the Awareness of a New Age', *Studies in Burke and his Times*, 14.3 (1973), pp. 221–38.

2 Charles Dickens, *Hard Times* (London, 1854; Oxford, 1955), p. 66 and p. 272.

3 In the 1720s and 1730s Fielding, following Gay, had ridiculed Italian opera as the progeny of Queen Nonsense, but by 1760 to prefer either Italian or English opera was a matter of personal taste not ideological conflict; see Eric Walter White, *History of English Opera* (London, 1983), pp. 151–2.

4 E. P. Thompson, *Customs and Practices* (London, 1991) and *The Making of the English Working Class* (Harmondsworth, 1968 edn).

5 J. Steven Watson, *The Reign of George III* (Cambridge, 1960), p. 327.

6 See Edward Said, *Orientalism* (Harmondsworth, 1955 edn).

7 Emmet Kennedy, Marie-Laurence Netter, James P. McGregor and Mark V. Olsen, *Theatre, Opera, and Audiences in Revolutionary Paris* (Westport, Conn., 1996), chapter 1, 'History of the Problem'. A similar conclusion is reached by Michèle Root-Bernstein, *Boulevard Theater and Revolution in Eighteenth-Century Paris* (Ann Arbor, Michigan, 1984), p. 240.

8 Kennedy *et al.*, *Theatre, Opera, and Audiences*, p. 27.

9 Charles Bell, *The Anatomy and Philosophy of Expression* (London, 1806).

10 Henry Siddons, *Practical Illustrations of Rhetorical Gesture and Action, from J. J. Engel* (London, 1807: reprint New York, 1969).

11 Marc Baer, *Theatre and Disorder in Late Georgian London* (Oxford, 1992).

12 Catherine Gallagher, 'Marxism and New Historicism', *The New Historicism*, ed. H. Aram Veeser (London, 1989), pp. 37–48.

13 Stephen Greenblatt, 'Resonance and Wonder', *Literary Theory Today*, ed. P. Collier and H. Geyer-Ryan (Cambridge, 1990), pp. 74–9.

14 Raymond Williams, 'Dominant, Residual, and Emergent', *Marxism and Literature* (Oxford, 1977), pp. 121–7.

15 Joseph Roach, *The Player's Passion: Studies in the Science of Acting* (Newark, Del., 1985); Bruce McConachie, *Melodramatic Formulations: American Theatre and Society, 1820–1870* (Iowa, 1992). For their respective theoretical

positions see Roach's introduction and editorial commentary, J. Reinelt and J. Roach (eds.), *Critical Theory and Performance* (Ann Arbor, Mich., 1992), B. McConachie, 'Using the Concept of Cultural Hegemony to Write Theatre History', in T. Postlewait and B. McConachie, *Interpreting the Theatrical Past: Essays in the Historiography of Performance* (Iowa, 1989).

16 W. Doyle, 'The Principles of the French Revolution', *The Impact of the French Revolution on European Consciousness*, ed. H. T. Mason and W. Doyle (Gloucester, 1989), p. 3.

17 P. McGarr and A. Callinicos, *Marxism and the Great French Revolution* (London, 1989), p. 124. See also their reviews of the 'revisionist' approaches of recent scholarship.

18 As well as McGarr and Callinicos, the works that have most influenced my own theoretical understanding of the French Revolution are: E. Hobsbawm, *The Age of Revolution* (London, 1962); Alfred Cobban, *Aspects of the French Revolution* (New York, 1968); Albert Soboul, *The French Revolution 1787–1799* (New York, 1975); Lynn Hunt, *Politics, Culture and Class in the French Revolution* (Stanford, 1984).

19 Walter Scott, *Essays on Chivalry, Romance, and the Drama* (London, n.d.), p. 223.

20 'E', *Literary Journal* (i, 381–2), cited J. F. Bagster-Collins, *George Colman the Younger* (New York, 1946), pp. 156–7.

I ENGLAND AND FRANCE IN 1789

1 Bagster-Collins, *Colman the Younger*, pp. 32–6; Barry Sutcliffe, *Plays by George Colman the Younger and Thomas Morton* (Cambridge, 1983), introduction, pp. 21–6 and text, pp. 65–112. It was revived at the 1997 Barbados Opera Festival, billed as 'The Barbadian Opera'.

2 For the difficulty of defining 'opera' see Jane Girdham, *English Opera in Late Eighteenth-Century London* (Oxford, 1997), chapter 5, 'Questions of Genre', pp. 123–35. Henry Harris, son of the Covent Garden manager, speculated that the French term *melo-drame* was derived from the verb *mêler* (to mix): Sutcliffe, *Colman and Morton*, p. 30, and Simon Shepherd and Peter Womack, *English Drama, a Cultural History* (Oxford, 1996), p. 194.

3 Alan Sinfield, *Faultlines: Cultural Materialism and the Politics of Dissident Reading* (Oxford, 1992), p. 40.

4 Richard Steele, *The Spectator*, 10 March 1711.

5 Sinfield, *Faultlines*, p. 32.

6 Linda Colley, *Britons: Forging the Nation 1707–1837* (New Haven, Conn., 1992), pp. 101ff.

7 *Ibid.*, p. 192.

8 S. Foote, *The Nabob* (Haymarket, 29 June 1772). It was specially reprinted in 1792.

9 The Botany Bay scheme was to found a penal colony and develop Pacific trade. Arthur Phillip's expedition reached Australia in 1788.

10 George Taylor, 'Anti-Slave Trade Drama in England: 1786–1808', *History and Theatre in Africa*, ed. Y. Hutchinson and E. Breitinger (Bayreuth and Stellenboch, 2000), pp. 9–20.

11 Cited Bagster-Collins, *Colman the Younger*, p. 50.

12 Emmet Kennedy, *A Cultural History of the French Revolution* (New Haven, Conn., 1989), p. 143.

13 Root-Bernstein, *Boulevard Theater*, p. 34.

14 See pp. 33–4 below for the Opéra-Comique's visits to London.

15 Root-Bernstein, *Boulevard Theater*, pp. 28–30 and 59–62.

16 For a thorough overview of pre-Revolutionary theatre management see Kennedy *et al.*, *Theatre, Opera, and Audiences*, chapter 7, 'Theatres and Their Directors', pp. 65–73.

17 Root-Bernstein, *Boulevard Theater*, pp. 70–1.

18 Millin de Grandmaison, *Sur la liberté de théâtre*, pp. 49–52; cited Root-Bernstein, *Boulevard Theater*, n. 14, p. 71.

19 Article 1, 13 Jan. 1791; cited Root-Bernstein, *Boulevard Theater*, p. 35.

20 *Archives parlementaires de 1787 à 1860*, ed. J. Mavidal and E. Laurent, 82 vols. (Paris, 1862–1913), 13 Jan. 1791, vol. XXII, pp. 210–14; cited Kennedy, *Cultural History*, p. 171.

21 C. Price, J. Milhous and J. Hume, *Italian Opera in Late Eighteenth-Century London* (Oxford, 1995), pp. 579–87.

22 Though from 1778 the development of *ballets d'action* marked a diversification of genres, and the engagement of a dance company, mainly French, virtually independent of the mainly Italian singing company.

23 For details of legal status see *The London Stage, 1660–1800*, 5 parts in 11 vols. (Carbondale, Ill., 1960–8), Part 5, ed. C. B. Hogan; also W. Nicholson, *The Struggle for a Free Stage* (Boston, 1906, New York, 1966).

24 For amateur theatricals see Sybil Rosenfeld, *Temples of Thespis: Some Private Theatres and Theatricals in England and Wales, 1700–1820* (London, 1978), and also G. Russell, *The Theatres of War* (Oxford, 1995), chapter 6.

25 *Gentleman's Magazine*, March 1788, cited Nicholson, *Struggle for a Free Stage*, p. 116.

26 For the Pantheon see Price, Milhous and Hume, *Italian Opera*, chapter 8; for the O. P. Riots see Marc Baer, *Theatre and Disorder*; for the Third Theatre see Nicholson, *Struggle for a Free Stage*, chapters 8 and 9.

27 John Dent, *The Bastille* (London, 1789) – Kemble/Devonshire collection 358.

28 It is perhaps significant that Copley and West were both Americans working in London in the aftermath of Independence.

29 Librairie Nepveu, *Les Animaux savant, ou Exercices des chevaux de MM. Franconi* (Paris, 1816), cited A. H. Saxon, *Enter Foot and Horse* (New Haven, 1968), pp. 31–3.

30 Georg Büchner, *Woyzeck* (written 1836–7), translation Victor Price, *The Plays of Georg Büchner* (Oxford, 1971), p. 113.

31 For changes in the legal definition of 'burletta' see Nicholson, *Struggle for a Free Stage*, pp. 282–94.

32 Girdham, *English Opera*, p. 125.
33 White, *History of English Opera*, p. 225.
34 *Ibid.*, pp. 137–70.
35 Theatre bill for Easter Monday 1781, cited by Richard Findlater, *Joe Grimaldi, His Life and Theatre* (Cambridge, 1978), p. 20.
36 David Mayer, *Harlequin in his Element* (Cambridge, Mass., 1969), p. 8.
37 *The Examiner* (26 Jan. 1817), cited *ibid.*, p. 10.
38 Jean-Georges Noverre, *Lettres sur la danse et sur les arts imitateurs* (1760); M. Hannah Winter, *The Pre-Romantic Ballet* (London, 1974).
39 Price, Milhous and Hume, *Italian Opera*, chapter 7, 'The Ballet'.
40 Frank A. Hedgcock, *David Garrick and his French Friends* (London, 1911), pp. 105–7.
41 *Ibid.*, p. 132.
42 Price, Milhous and Hume, *Italian Opera*, p. 490. Dauberval created the first *ballets d'action* on contemporary subjects: *Le Déserteur*, *L'Epreuve villageoise* and *La fille mal gardée*. Usually subjects were mythological: his *Psyché* and Noverre's *Médée et Jason*.
43 15 May 1784, cited *London Stage*, part 5, vol. II, pp. 705–6.
44 F. Reynolds, *The Life and Times of Frederick Reynolds* (London, 1827), vol. I, pp. 261–4.
45 R. Fiske, *English Theatre Music in the Eighteenth Century* (Oxford, 1973), p. 370.
46 For the scenario of the Dauberval and Gardel ballets see S. Pitou, *The Paris Opera, Rococo and Romantic* (Westport, Conn., 1985), p. 154, and Price, Milhous and Hume, *Italian Opera*, pp. 490–7. In later versions – at least in the canine drama – it seems that Henry rejoins his regiment and leads them to victory.
47 Two years later Mercier was to propose his concept of the 'playwright-legislator' who deliberately uses the stage as a political tribune. L-S. Mercier, *Du Théâtre, ou nouvel essai sur l'art dramatique* (1773), cited Scott S. Bryson, *The Chastised Stage: Bourgeois Drama and the Exercise of Power* (Saratoga, Ill., 1991), pp. 48–51.
48 L-S. Mercier, *Le Déserteur*, ed. Simon Davis (Exeter, 1974), p. 85.
49 *Ibid.*, p. xv.
50 *The What Is It; a Tragic-Comic-Pastoral-Musical Entertainment* (Royal Circus, St George's Fields, 1789).
51 Sinfield, *Faultlines*, p. 40, cited above, note 3.
52 Bertold Brecht, *A Short Organum for the Theatre*, para. 52 (1948), translated John Willett, *Brecht on Theatre* (New York, 1964), p. 195.
53 George Taylor, *Plays by Samuel Foote and Arthur Murphy* (Cambridge, 1984), pp. 4–16, and L. W. Conolly, *The Censorship of English Drama 1737–1824* (San Marino, Calif., 1976), chapter 5.
54 These included the memoirs of Voltaire and Frederick the Great; plays and children's stories by la Comtesse de Genlis (who had been inspired by the educational theories of Rousseau's *Emile*); political geography by Obsonville and Chenier, and Lavater's *Essays on Physiognomy*. For full

bibliography see *Dictionary of Literary Biography*, 89 (New York, 1989), pp. 181–4.

55 Madame de Campan, *Mémoires sur la Vie de Marie-Antoinette* (Paris, 1849), p. 203, cited Marvin Carlson, *The Theatre of the French Revolution* (New York, 1966), p. 2.

2 THE REVOLUTION

1 Reynolds, *Life and Times*, vol. II, p. 54.

2 Conolly, *Censorship*, pp. 83–112.

3 Russell, *Theatres of War* p. 74; R. Storac and K. McCreery, *Theatre as Weapon: Workers' Theatre in the Soviet Union, Germany and Britain 1917–34* (London, 1986).

4 Cited Denis Arundell, *The Story of Sadler's Wells* (London, 1964), pp. 44–5.

5 Carlson, *Theatre of the French Revolution*, pp. 15–16.

6 See Jacob Decastro, *Memoirs* (London, 1825), pp. 122–5: Edward W. Brayley, *Historical and Descriptive Accounts of the Theatres of London* (London, 1826), pp. 71–2; both cited in Saxon, *Enter Foot and Horse*, p. 3n.

7 John Dent, *The Bastille* (London, 1789).

8 Charles Dibdin, *The Touchstone*, submitted for licence November 1789, Larpent MS: LA851.

9 *London Stage*, part 5, vol. II, p. 1210.

10 *The Public Advertiser*, 4 Dec. 1789, in *ibid.*, p. 1211.

11 John St John, *The Island of Marquerite* (Dury Lane, 13 Nov. 1789), Larpent MSS: LA845 and LA848: 21 October and resubmission 4 November.

12 Reynolds, *Life and Times*, vol. II, p. 54.

13 In the scene that most resembles the storming of the Bastille the Crusading hero, like Henri Dubois, climbs the drawbridge to cut the ropes to open it, thus saving Christian victims from execution. *The Crusade* (Covent Garden, 6 May 1790), Larpent MS: LA870.

14 The censor, John Larpent, cut a speech from *The Crusade* which by putting mildly satirical comments into the mouth of an Islamic prophet, might have prompted the drawing of more parallels: 'What in England! – Oh there I prophecy wonders on wonders, nay, almost impossibilities – in 1790 the lawyers will become honourable, The Bench of Bishops charitable – The Men of fashion sensible, the physicians useful, and the two houses of parliament witty and entertaining.'

15 W. Stukeley, *Itinerarium Curiosum* (1724); Thomas Percy, *Reliques of Ancient English Poetry* (1765); Joseph Ritson, *Pieces of Ancient Popular Poetry* (1791); Horace Walpole's Strawberry Hill 'Gothic castle' (1750–75).

16 Colman's preface to the 1808 edition, as quoted by Elizabeth Inchbald, *The British Theatre* (London, 1808), vol. xx.

17 Paula R. Backscheider, *Spectacular Politics: Theatrical Power and Mass Culture in Early Modern England* (Baltimore, 1993), p. 158.

18 The essential Gothic elements had already been established in

Walpole's *Castle of Otranto* (1764) and this was dramatised in Robert Jephson's *Count of Narbonne* (1780), but until the mid-1790s it was Walpole's antiquarianism rather than his sadomasochistic fantasies which influenced most playwrights; see chapter 4 below.

19 Inchbald, 'Remarks', *British Theatre*, vol. xx, p. 4.

20 See Carlson, *Theatre of the Revolution*, pp. 21–36; Graham E. Rodmell, *French Drama of the Revolutionary Years* (London, 1990), pp. 59–86.

21 Carlson, *Theatre of the Revolution*, p. 29.

22 A. J. Bingham, *Marie-Joseph Chénier: Early Political Life and Ideas* (New York, 1939), p. 14.

23 Root-Bernstein, *Boulevard Theater*, p. 219. However her assertion that 'At the Gaité *Père Duchesne*, and its sequel at the Ambigu-Comique *The Wedding of Père Duchesne*, owed nothing to revolutionary events and made no reference to political or ideological change', may be correct in terms of form, style and superficial content, but the fact that Hérbert adopted the name of Père Duchesne for his sansculotte journal in September 1790, and that Antoine Lemaire wrote a pamphlet in 1789 entitled *The Window's Broken by Père Duchêne*, argues there were more political connotations to the 'rough diamond' character Duchesne than she suggests.

24 Jonathan Bate, *Shakespearean Constitutions: Politics, Theatre, Criticism 1730–1830* (Oxford, 1989), p. 63.

25 *Ibid.*, p. 77. The change from 'Lord Chief Justice' to Chancellor transferred the reference to Lord Thurlow. That Harris of Covent Garden recognised that Kemble intended a retrospective application to Prince Hal might explain his presentation of Ryder as Falstaff in *Henry IV, part 1* on 2 November 1789. For other depictions of Fox as Falstaff see M. Dorothy George, *English Political Caricature, 1793–1832* (Oxford, 1959), vol. I, p. 169, 198 and vol. II, p. 90.

26 See Conolly, *Censorship*, p. 126 for the prohibition of *King Lear* during the Regency after 1811. Although not presented between 15 May 1788 (DL) and 23 Nov. 1789 (CG), there was apparently no ban because of the Regency Crisis. It had not been regularly performed since Garrick's retirement in 1776.

27 *Ibid.*, p. 61.

28 *Ibid.*, p. 20.

29 James Boaden, *Memoirs of J. P. Kemble* (London, 1825), vol. II, p. 2: see also David Rostron, 'Kemble's Shakespeare', unpublished dissertation, Manchester University, 1976, p. 113.

30 Rostron, 'Kemble's Shakespeare', p. 138.

31 Inchbald, *British Theatre*, vol. v: *Coriolanus*, p. 5.

32 See below, chapter 6.

33 Philippe Fabre d'Eglantine, *Le Philinte de Molière, ou La Suite du Misanthrope* (Paris, 1810), pp. 42 and 51.

34 Edmund Burke, *Reflections on the French Revolution* (London, 1790; 1986), p. 119.

35 Paul Fussell, *The Rhetorical World of Augustan Humanism* (Oxford, 1965), pp. 228–32.

36 Burke, *Letters on a Regicide Peace* (1793), cited *ibid.*, p. 231.

37 Philip S. Foner, ed., *The Life and Writings of Thomas Paine* (New York, 1993), pp. 267–9.

38 Burke, *Reflections*, p. 183.

39 *Ibid.*, p. 211.

40 Mona Ozouf, *Festivals and the French Revolution* (Cambridge, Mass., 1988), p. 44.

41 *Ibid.*, p. 35.

42 William Wordsworth, *The Prelude* (London, 1805), book 6.

43 *London Stage*, part 5, vol. II, p. 1311. See also *A Picture of Paris*, Larpent MS: LA886.

44 *The Paris Federation; a Sketch of the entertainment now performing at the Royalty Theatre, in Two Parts; consisting of A Pantomimic Preludio and the Paris Federation. To which is added The popular French Music adapted to the Harpsichord* (London, 1790).

45 At the Haymarket Bannister performed a monologue by Colman, *Liberty; or, Two Sides of the Water*, for his benefit (13 August 1790). Following the model of the Covent Garden afterpiece, it concentrated on British travellers rather than on any political significance: 'The object of it was to give a humorous description of Mr & Mrs Bull's visit to Paris to be present at the late Grand Confederation', featuring also a Jewish peddler, a Scotsman, a 'son of St Patrick' and an English sea captain. See *European Magazine* (August 1790), p. 151.

46 See Marat, *C'en est fait de nous* (Paris, 22 July 1790).

47 See Kennedy, *Theatre, Opera and Audiences*, esp. Marie-Laurence Netter's chapter 4, 'The Great Successes of Each Year', for new 'political' plays.

3   FROM THE FEDERATION TO THE TERROR

1 *Morning Chronicle*, 20 Febuary 1792, *London Stage*, part 4, vol. II, p. 1427.

2 C. Kegan Paul, *William Godwin; his Friends and Contemporaries* (London, 1876) vol. I, p. 65.

3 Gary Kelly, *The English Jacobin Novel, 1780–1805* (Oxford, 1976), pp. 115–45.

4 The references other than to France are to the Partition of Poland by Russia, Austria and Prussia in 1790, and the 1792 campaign leading up to a renewed attempt to abolish the slave trade.

5 See Larpent MS: LA935, submitted for License, February 1792.

6 See above p. 12.

7 See Pearce Egan, *Life in London* (London, 1821).

8 Thomas Holcroft, *The Road to Ruin* (London, 1791).

9 Holcroft possibly identified closely with the extremes of disapproval and unqualified affection that Dornton displays for his son, because he had lost his own son in tragic circumstances. In 1789 William Holcroft, aged

sixteen, stole money and pistols from his father and ran away to sea. When Holcroft and Godwin caught up with him at Deal, William shot himself.

10 Cited Conolly, *Censorship*, p. 43.

11 Cumberland, *Richard the Second*, Larpent MS: LA963.

12 It was based on Antoine-Marin Lemierre, *Guillaume Tell* (Paris, 1766), which was revived in several Paris theatres in 1793 as appropriately republican, see Kennedy, *Cultural History*, pp. 283–4; see also Conolly, *Censorship*, p. 86.

13 'A Kentish Bowman', *Helvetic Liberty* (London, 1792).

14 *Ibid.*

15 Frederick Jameson, *The Political Unconscious: Narrative as a Socially Symbolic Act* (Ithaca, N.Y., 1981).

16 Root-Bernstein, *Boulevard Theater*, p. 207.

17 Kennedy, *Cultural History*, appendix A, 'Statistics on Music and Theatre', p. 394.

18 Root-Bernstein, *Boulevard Theater*, p. 210.

19 Carbon de Flins des Oliviers, cited Carlson, *Theatre of the French Revolution*, p. 141.

20 *Ibid.*, p. 142.

21 Jean Massin, *Almanach de la Révolution Français* (Paris, 1963, Club français du livre), pp. 302–5.

22 Root-Bernstein, *Boulevard Theater*, pp. 218–19.

23 Carlson, *Theatre of the French Revolution*, pp. 131–2.

24 The play *Le ami des lois* by Jean-Louis Laya (Théâtre de la Nation, 2 January 1793), was similarly condemned by the Jacobins as too Girondinist for advocating a slavish submission to the Rule of Law; see Rodmell, *French Drama*, p. 136ff.

25 Ozouf, *Festivals*, p. 106; also see pp. 108–18.

26 *Ibid.*, p. 111.

27 Kennedy, *Cultural History*, pp. xxiii–xxv.

28 Carlson, *Theatre of the French Revolution*, p. 193.

29 Rodmell, *French Drama*, pp. 36–40.

30 Cited Frederick Brown, *Theatre and Revolution* (New York, 1980), pp. 74–5.

31 Rodmell, *French Drama*, pp. 157–60.

32 George, *English Political Caricature*, vol. II, p. 122.

33 It received some provincial performances, being advertised at The Bull Inn, Hertford (25 January 1796) by a strolling company led by David Osborne. I am indebted for this information to Derek Forbes, who is currently preparing a history of theatre in Hertford and Ware. Allardyce Nicholl also lists a performance under its subtitle, *The Maid of Normandy* at Wolverhampton in 1794.

34 Conolly, *Censorship*, p. 197.

35 Huntington Library, Larpent MS: LA1413, 7 May 1804, marked 'Refused'.

36 Stephen Storace wrote two songs: 'Captivity, a Ballad supposed to be sung by the Unfortunate Marie Antoinette, during her Imprisonment in the Temple' and 'Lamentation of Marie Antoinette, late Queen of France, on the Morning of her Execution', though neither appear to have been sung in a public theatre. Whilst in Vienna Storace had been personally acquainted with the queen's brother, the Emperor of Austria. Fiske, *English Theatre Music*, p. 491.

37 H. T. Dickinson, *British Radicalism and the French Revolution* (Oxford, 1985), p. 15.

38 'Lady Eglantine Wallace', *DNB* vol. xx, p. 554.

39 Two copies in Larpent MSS: LA1093, submitted by Thomas Shaw of Margate Theatre Royal (7 September 1795), and LA1104, the printed, and unchanged, version.

40 The role reversal of servants and masters may owe something to Marivaux's *Jeu d'amour et du hasard* (1730).

41 *DNB*, vol. xx, p. 555.

42 James Boaden, *The Secret Tribunal*, Larpent MS: LA1085, also published London, 1795.

43 *London Stage*, part 5, vol. iii, p. 1763.

44 For example; *A Letter to the Reverend John Erskine, D.D., One of the Ministers of Edinburgh: On the Dangerous Tendency of his Late Sketches of Church-History: By his countenancing The Author, and Promoting the Designs, of the Infamous Sect of the Illuminati* (Edinburgh, 1798).

45 The most famous example still in the operatic repertoire is Beethoven's *Fidelio* (1802). Mozart's *Magic Flute* (1791) dramatises a process of liberation facilitated by the very Freemasonry that *The Secret Tribunal* condemns.

46 Girdham, *English Opera*, pp. 140–70 and 207–12.

47 *Lodoiska* [*Czartoriska*] Larpent MS: LA1029; published as *Lodoiska, A Musical Romance* (London, 1794).

48 See chapter 6 below for the discussion of patriotic anti-Bonaparte drama.

4 DRAMATISING (THE) TERROR

1 *London Stage*, part 5, vol. iii, *Seasons 1792–1799*.

2 Leigh Hunt, *Critical Essays* (London, 1807), cited *ibid.*, p. 1732.

3 'E' as cited in introduction above, note 20.

4 Kelly, *Jacobin Novel*, pp. 71–2.

5 *Ibid.*, p. 11.

6 Patricia Sigl, 'Elizabeth Inchbald', *Dictionary of Literary Biography*, p. 207.

7 *Ibid.*, p. 206.

8 Marjean D. Purinton, *Romantic Ideology Unmasked* (Newark, Del., 1994), p. 125.

9 Between December 1792 and April 1795 she was in France, from whence she might have been deported as British once war began, but

she claimed to be married to an American national, Gilbert Imlay. Having parted from him in 1796, a relationship ensued with William Godwin, and she died shortly after the birth of their daughter Mary in 1797. Godwin's memoir of her, published with her *Posthumous Works*, caused a violent conservative reaction against the 'free-thinking' and 'lax morality' of the whole group of Godwinian radicals: see introduction, *The Works of Mary Wollstonecraft*, ed. Janet Todd and Marilyn Butler (London, 1989), vol. I, pp. 10–13.

10 William Hazlitt, *The Life of Thomas Holcroft*, ed. Elbridge Colby (London, 1925), vol. II, 65.

11 *Ibid.*, p. 30.

12 These included as the first to be tried, Thomas Hardy, Horne Took and John Thelwall, all of whom were acquitted by an unconvinced jury on 5 November 1793.

13 Hazlitt, *Life of Holcroft*, vol. II, p. 94.

14 *Ibid.*, p. 95.

15 *The British Theatre* (London, 1808), vol. XXIV. Introduction to *The Deserted Daughter*.

16 E.g. Horace Walpole's *Castle of Otranto* (1764), Clara Reeves' *The Old English Baron* (1778); William Beckford's *Vathek* (1786).

17 *The Letters of Horace Walpole*, ed. Peter Cunningham (Edinburgh, 1906), vol. II, p. 364; cited Robert Keily, *The Romantic Novel in England* (Cambridge, Mass., 1979), p. 6.

18 Several plots resembled, and may have been borrowed from, French anticlerical plays like *Les victimes cloîtrées*, translated by Lewis as *Venoni* in 1808.

19 Marilyn Butler identifies pre-Revolutionary domestic issues influencing 'the dark vein in contemporary art . . . the disruptive, desolating aspect of change, increased mobility, loosened ties within the large old family units, [and that] urban life, however sophisticated, had made no secure advances over poverty and hunger, crime and injustice, disease and premature death'. *Romantics, Rebels and Reactionaries* (Oxford, 1981), p. 27.

20 Robert Miles, *Ann Radcliffe, The Great Enchantress* (Manchester, 1995), p. 70.

21 Keily, *Romantic Novel*, pp. 43–65.

22 Louis F. Peck, *A Life of Matthew G. Lewis* (Cambridge, Mass., 1961), pp. 11–18; and Syndy M. Conger, *Matthew G. Lewis, Charles Robert Maturin and the Germans* (Salzburg, 1977), introduction and chapter 1.

23 Keily, *Romantic Novel*, p. 34.

24 Miles, *Ann Radcliffe*, p. 44.

25 Quoted V. Sage, *The Gothick Novel: A Casebook* (London, 1990), p. 49.

26 Ronald Paulson, 'Gothic Fiction and the French Revolution', *ELH*, 48 (1981), pp. 536–7.

27 Jeffrey N. Cox, *Seven Gothic Dramas, 1789–1825* (Athens, Ohio, 1992), pp. 30–1.

28 Miles, *Ann Radcliffe*, pp. 70–1.

29 Postscript to *Adelmorn the Outlaw* (1801), cited Peck, *Life of Lewis*, pp. 112–13. See *ibid.*, p. 65 for Peck's discussion of Montague Summers' allegation that Lewis was gay, *The Gothic Quest* (London, 1938), pp. 263–7. Even if Lewis was not, the sexuality of Walpole and Beckford is undisputed, and much of the erotic imagery of the Gothic can be read as homosexual as well as sadomasochistic.

30 Cox, *Seven Gothic Dramas*, p. 18.

31 The best surveys are Bertrand Evans, *Gothic Drama from Walpole to Shelley* (Berkeley, 1947) and Paul Ranger, *'Terror and Pity Reign in every Breast': Gothic Drama 1750–1820* (London, 1991). Critics who specifically discuss the 'Revolutionary' reading of the genre include: Paulson, 'Gothic Fiction and the French Revolution' and *Representations of Revolution (1789–1820)* (New Haven, 1983); Cox, *Seven Gothic Dramas*; Peter Brooks, 'Virtue and Terror: The Monk', *ELH*, 40 (1973).

32 Adapted from Radcliffe's novel *Romance of the Forest* (Covent Garden, 25 March 1794).

33 Boaden, *Memoirs of Kemble*, vol. II, p. 206; for a study of the stage technicalities see Ranger, *'Terror and Pity'*, pp. 116–26.

34 Another precedent is Arthur Murphy, *The Grecian Daughter* (1772), Ranger, *'Terror and Pity'*, pp. 95–8.

35 'To the Reader', *The Castle Spectre* (London, 1798).

36 For details of censorship see Jeffrey N. Cox's editing of the play in *Seven Gothic Dramas*, pp. 151–224.

37 Introduction to *The Castle Spectre*.

38 Samuel Taylor Coleridge, *Biographia Literaria*, ed. J. Engell and W. Jackson Bate (Princeton, 1983), vol. II, p. 221.

39 Cox, *Seven Gothic Dramas*, p. 18.

40 Paulson, *Representations of Revolution*, p. 550.

41 M. G. Lewis, *The Captive*, *The Life and Correspondence of M. G. Lewis*, by Margaret Cornwall Baron-Wilson (London, 1839), pp. 236–41; Cox, *Seven Gothic Dramas*, pp. 225–30; and Huntington Library, Larpent MS: LA1374.

42 Mary Wollstonecraft, *Maria; or, the Wrongs of Woman* (1798; London, 1975), p. 21.

43 Baron-Wilson, *Life of Lewis*, pp. 233–4.

44 G. Colman, preface to *Blue Beard* (London, 1798), p. iii.

45 Sutcliffe, *Plays by Colman and Morton*, p. 39.

46 See above chapter 2, pp. 43–5.

47 Michael Kelly, *Reminiscences of Michael Kelly of the King's Theatre and Theatre Royal, Drury Lane*, 2 vols. (London, 1826; ed. R. Fiske, Oxford 1975), p. 190. Colman's 'reactionary' reputation was confirmed by the rigour of his censorship when he was appointed Examiner of Plays on the death of John Larpent in 1824.

48 Preface to *The Borderers* (London, 1842), cited *The Poetical Works of William Wordsworth*, ed. E. DeSelincourt (Oxford, 1940), p. 343.

49 *The Works of Charles and Mary Lamb*, ed. E. V. Lucas (London, 1903–5), vol. I, p. 99.
50 Byron to Lady Byron, 14 September 1821, *Letters*, vol. VIII, p. 210; cited Purinton, *Romantic Ideology Unmasked*, p. 60. For examples of this criticism see Richard M. Fletcher, *English Romantic Drama, 1795–1843: A Critical History* (New York, 1966); George Steiner, *The Death of Tragedy* (New York, 1963); J. C. Trewin, 'The Romantic Poets in the Theatre', *Keats-Shelley Memorial Bulletin*, 23 (1969).
51 Harold Bloom, *Romanticism and Consciousness* (New York, 1970), introduction.
52 Marjean Purinton suggests that Wordsworth renamed the character after John Oswald, a Scottish radical who threatened to lead an invasion of England in 1790 in alliance with the French. *Romantic Ideology Unmasked*, p. 35.
53 William Wordsworth, preface to *The Borderers*, *Poetical Works*, ed. DeSelincourt, pp. 345–6.
54 Alan Richardson, *A Mental Theatre; Poetic Drama and Consciousness in the Romantic Age* (University Park, Penn., 1988), p. 31.
55 *Ibid.*, pp. 38–9.
56 *Poetical Works*, ed. DeSelincourt, p. 343.
57 Samuel Taylor Coleridge, *The Fall of Robespierre* (Cambridge, 1794), in *Complete Poetical Works*, ed. E. H. Coleridge (Oxford, 1912; 1975 edition), vol. II, p. 495.
58 *Ibid.*, p. 516. Note the perversion of the Revolutionary image of the Tree of Liberty.
59 *Ibid.*, p. 519.
60 Wordsworth, *Poetical Works*, ed. DeSelincourt, p. 346.
61 Purinton, *Romantic Ideology Unmasked*, p. 27.
62 Butler, *Romantics, Rebels, and Reactionaries*; Jerome J. McGann, *The Romantic Ideology: A Critical Investigation* (Chicago, 1983); Jeffrey N. Cox, 'The French Revolution in the English Theatre', *History and Myth: Essays on English Romantic Literature*, ed. S. C. Behrendt (Detroit, 1990).
63 Daniel P. Watkins, *A Materialist Critique of English Romantic Drama* (Gainesville, Fla., 1993), p. 8.
64 *Ibid.*, p. 19.
65 Purinton, *Romantic Ideology Unmasked*, p. 39.
66 Anthony Kubiak, *Stages of Terror* (Bloomington, 1991), p. 99; see also, Alan Liu, 'Wordsworth and Subversion', *Yale Journal of Criticism*, 2 (spring 1989); Julie A. Carlson, *In the Theatre of Romanticism: Coleridge, Nationalism, Women* (Cambridge, 1994).
67 For Coleridge on Kant and Schiller see Rosemary Ashton, *The German Idea: Four English Writers and the Reception of German Thought, 1800–1860* (Cambridge, 1980), pp. 27–66, and Carlson, *Theatre of the Revolution*, chapter 2, pp. 63–93.
68 Thompson writing in 1801 identified thirty-one plays other than the eleven he had translated: Benjamin Thompson, *The German Theatre*, in

Six Volumes (London, 1801). By his death in 1841, Kotzebue had written 218 plays, vastly outstripping, in both performance and publication, Goethe, Schiller, Lenz and Iffland combined.

69 Albert William Holzmann, *Family Relationships in the Dramas of August von Kotzebue* (Princeton, 1935), p. 8.

70 *Anti-Jacobin*, 4 June 1798, p. 236.

71 *Ibid.*, p. 238.

72 Conolly, *Censorship*, pp. 98–101. The play's delayed production allowed for only a few performances, but it is possible that its lack of success was because audiences were aware that it was an emasculated version of Schiller's notorious original.

73 Jeffrey N. Cox edits together the first published edition with the Larpent MS (LA1287) and incorporates some later changes made in Siddons' own script; see *Seven Gothic Dramas*, p. 231.

74 Daniel P. Watkins interprets the hostility as class based. Rezenvelt is a parvenue who has recently inherited his wealth and position, while De Montfort is a representative of an aristocracy threatened with dispossession. Though I read Rezenvelt more as one of Colley's 'redefined élite' than as an essentially bourgeois character, I fully endorse Watkins' description of De Monfort's social alienation: 'The psychological confusion and the passion of hatred seen in De Monfort are . . . signs of a radically divided subject . . . Unable to discover the stability he desires, either in social life or in the personal world inhabited by himself and his sister (he fears she plans to marry Rezenvelt), he is cast loose upon a stream of ever-changing personal and social events within which he, as subject, is repeatedly displaced and reconstituted . . . While his specific actions are unique to his character, the passion of hatred that energises those actions is fired in the oven of rapidly increasing social change whose flames are felt not only by De Monfort.' (Watkins, *English Romantic Drama*, pp. 57–8.)

75 Joanna Baillie, *De Monfort*, Act 5, scene 1.

76 Joseph W. Donohue, Jr, *Dramatic Character in the English Romantic Age* (Princeton, 1970), pp. 81–2.

77 Boaden, *Memoirs of Kemble*, vol. II, pp. 252–3.

78 Purinton, *Revolutionary Ideology Unmasked*, pp. 161–2.

79 Ellen Donkin, *Getting into the Act: Women Playwrights in London, 1776–1829* (London, 1995), chapter 7.

80 Cited *ibid.*, pp. 166–7.

5 PERFORMANCE AND PERFORMING

1 See James Laver, *A Concise History of Costume* (London, 1967).

2 James Epstein, 'Understanding the Cap of Liberty: Symbolic Practice and Social Conflict in Early Nineteenth-Century England', *Past and Present*, 122 (1989), pp. 75–118.

3 Anita Brookner, *Jacques-Louis David* (London, 1980), p. 96; Massin, *Almanach de la Revolution*, p. 244.

4 William Hazlitt, 'On Modern Comedy', *Criticisms and Dramatic Essays*, 2nd edn (London, 1854), pp. 20–1.

5 *Ibid.*, p. 22.

6 Carlson, *Theatre of the Revolution*, p. 101.

7 Unreferenced quotation in Toby Cole and Helen Chinoy, *Actors on Acting*, rev. edn (New York, 1975), p. 179.

8 James Boaden, *Memoirs of Mrs Siddons* (London, 1827), vol. II, p. 291.

9 Much of the following discussion is drawn from Roach, *Player's Passion*, especially chapter 4, 'Diderot', pp. 116–59.

10 Diderot, *Eléments*, cited *ibid.*, p. 130.

11 Diderot, *Le neveu de Rameau*, p. 68, cited *ibid.*, p. 123–4.

12 *Ibid.*, p. 157.

13 In the mid-eighteenth century these two, with the actor Lekain, had been responsible for a change in French acting comparable to Garrick's reforms in England. Instead of relying solely on the declamation of tragic Alexandrines, they were 'actors who use the whole body in movements so violent that they are transmitted to the still rather stiff costumes; the movement of the arms and head are emphatic and a little angular, the facial expression is correspondingly eloquent.' Kirsten G. Holmström, *Monodrama, Attitudes, Tableaux Vivants* (Stockholm, 1967), p. 21.

14 Jean-Joseph Regnault-Warin, *Memoires historiques et critique sur F. J. Talma* (Paris, 1827), pp. 240–52.

15 *Memoirs of Hyppolite Clairon, the celebrated French Actress: With Reflections Upon the Dramatic Art* (1798: trans. London, 1800), cited Cole and Chinoy, *Actors on Acting*, p. 171.

16 *Memoires de Marie-Françoise Dumesnil* (Paris, 1800), cited Cole and Chinoy, *Actors on Acting*, p. 175.

17 François Joseph Talma, *Reflections on the Actor's Art* (1825), Columbia University Papers on Acting 4 (New York, 1915), p. 10.

18 Price, Milhous and Hume, *Italian Opera*, pp. 592–3. The use of castrati in opera decreased across Europe during the years of the Revolution. Rossini refused to write for them after a heated argument with Giovanni Velluti: Angus Heriot, *The Castrati in Opera* (New York, 1974), p. 192. However, the Italian church continued to castrate boy choristers well into the nineteenth century: Patrick Barbier, *The World of the Castrati* (London, 1996), pp. 235–9.

19 Herbert F. Collins, *Talma* (London, 1964), pp. 23–5.

20 Boaden, *Memoirs of Kemble*, vol. I, pp. 157–8.

21 Donohue, *Dramatic Character*, p. 244.

22 George Taylor, 'The Just Delineation of the Passions', *The Eighteenth-Century English Stage*, ed. K. Richards and P. Thomson (London, 1972), pp. 51–72.

23 W. Hazlitt, *The Times*, 15 June 1817.

24 E. and J. Goncourt, *Histoire de la Société française pendant le Directoire* (Paris, 1855), cited Collins, *Talma*, p. 104.

25 Although he was notoriously 'indisposed' and under-rehearsed in *The Iron Chest*, in later performances he performed the role with success.

26 Ranger, *Terror and Pity*, p. 99.

27 Baillie, *De Monfort*, Act 4, scene 3; in Cox, *Seven Gothic Dramas*, p. 299.

28 Walter Scott, *Quarterly Review* (1826), p. 215; cited Donohue, *Dramatic Character*, p. 250.

29 W. C. Macready, *Reminiscences*, ed. F. Pollock (London, 1875), p. 148.

30 *Monthly Mirror*, 10 (1800), p. 318, see Don B. Wilmeth, *George Frederick Cooke, Machiavel of the Stage* (Westport, Conn., 1980), pp. 125–36 for a detailed analysis of Cooke's Richard III.

31 *Monthly Mirror*, cited Wilmeth, *G. F. Cooke*, p. 134.

32 *Mirror of Taste*, 3 (Philadelphia, 1811), p. 196, quoted Donohue, *Dramatic Character*, p. 276.

33 *Ibid.*

34 Carlson, *Theatre of Romanticism*, p. 136.

35 Boaden, *Memoirs of Siddons*, vol. I, p. 327. Giles Playfair, *The Prodigy* (London, 1967), p. 32 quotes an unidentified Irish newspaper, recorded in Richard Ryan, *Table Talk* (London, 1828), parodying Boaden's claims: 'One hundred and ninety ladies fainted! Forty-six went into fits, and ninety-five had strong hysterics. The world will scarcely credit the truth, when they are told that fourteen children, five old women, one hundred tailors, and six Common Councilmen, were actually drowned in the inundation of tears that flowed from the galleries, the slips and the boxes, to increase the briny pool in the pit; the water was three feet deep, and people there, obliged to stand upon the benches, were in that position up to their ankles in tears! An Act of parliament against her playing any more will certainly pass.'

36 Cox, *Seven Gothic Dramas*, p. 53.

37 *Ibid.*

38 For Lamb's essay, 'On the Tragedies of Shakespeare, Considered with Reference to their Fitness for Stage Representation' (1811), see Jonas Barish, *The Antitheatrical Prejudice* (Berkeley, 1981), pp. 328–32, and Carlson, *Theatre of Romanticism*, pp. 168–75.

39 'Remarks on the Character of Lady Macbeth', in Thomas Campbell, *Life of Mrs Siddons* (London, 1834), vol. II, pp. 10–34; also in Cole & Chinoy, *Actors on Acting*, pp. 142–5.

40 *Ibid.*

41 *Ibid.*

42 Unreferenced quotation in Richards, *Rise of the English Actress*, p. 84.

43 Yvonne Ffrench, *Mrs Siddons: Tragic Actress* (London, 1954), p. 119, cited Richards, *Rise of the English Actress*, p. 74.

44 Cox, *Seven Gothic Dramas*, p. 53. The passage specifically describes Jane as 'So queenly, so commanding, and so noble', and dressed like Siddons, in contrast to the fashionable frippery of the Countess Freberg:

> She is not deck'd in any gallant trim,
> But seems to me clad in the usual weeds,
> Of high habitual state; for as she moves
> Wide flows her robe in many a waving fold.

45 Christopher Reid, 'Burke's Tragic Muse: Sarah Siddons and the "Feminization" of the *Reflections*' (unpublished paper) cited Carlson, *Theatre of Romanticism*, p. 153.

46 W. Collins, 'The Passions; an Ode for Music' cited in *The Poems of Thomas Gray, William Collins and Oliver Goldsmith*, ed. Roger Lonsdale (London, 1969), pp. 477–85.

47 *Ibid.*, pp. 477–82.

48 Siddons, *Practical Illustrations of Rhetorical Gesture and Action*.

49 Translated into English by Thomas Holcroft in 1789.

50 George Taylor, *Players and Performances in the Victorian Theatre* (Manchester, 1989), p. 42; see also Roger Cooter, *The Cultural Meaning of Popular Science* (Cambridge, 1984).

51 Cited Emma Hamilton, *DNB*, vol. VIII, p. 1033.

52 Walpole to Mary Berry, 17 August 1791, *Correspondence* (New Haven, Conn., 1944), p. 337, cited Holström, *Monodrama, Attitudes, Tableaux Vivants*, p. 111.

53 Lord Elgin wrote of Nelson, 'There never was a man turned so *vainglorious* . . . he is completely managed by Lady Hamilton'; quoted Geoffrey Bennett, *Nelson the Commander* (London, 1972), p. 160.

54 See Cole and Chinoy, *Actors on Acting*, pp. 269–76.

55 Programmes of Attitudes were performed in Northern Europe by Ida Brun of Copenhagen and Henrietta Hendel-Schütz of Halle (*ibid.*, p. 167 and pp. 181–6). Goethe's own monodrama *Proserpina* (1815) is described by Holström as 'a beautiful memorial' to the epoch of the classical attitude (*Monodrama, Attitudes, Tableaux Vivants*, p. 186).

56 Dutton Cook, *Hours with the Players* (London, 1881), 2 vols.

57 Philip Highfill, Jr, Kalman A. Burnim and Edward A. Langhans, *A Biographical Dictionary of Actors, Actresses, Musicians, Dancers, Managers, and Other Stage Personnel in London, 1660–1800*, 16 vols. (Carbondale, Ill., 1973–93), vol. XIV, p. 185.

58 Cook, *Hours with the Players*, p. 114.

59 *Ibid.*, p. 128.

60 Boaden, *Life of Mrs Jordan*, cited *ibid.*, p. 127.

61 Cook, *Hours with the Players*, p. 151.

62 Charles Lamb, 'On the Artificial Comedy of the Last Century', in *Works*, ed. Lucas.

63 Cited Highfill *et al.*, *Biographical Dictionary*, vol. XII, p. 83.

64 Cook, *Hours with the Players*, pp. 192–3.

65 *Morning Post*, 10 February 1800, cited Sutcliffe, *Colman and Morton*, p. 47.

66 *Ibid.*, p. 48. Alexander Pope, who acted Blandford in *Speed the Plough*, had originally adapted Kotzebue's play as *The Count of Burgundy* in 1799, but it received only one performance (Covent Garden, 2 April, 1799).

67 Both comments cited in Sutcliffe, *Colman and Morton*, p. 49.
68 L. Hunt, *Critical Essays on the Performers of the London Theatres* (London, 1807), cited *London Stage*, part 5, vol. I, p. cxxv.
69 Cited Highfill, *et al.*, *Biographical Dictionary*, vol. v, p. 200; although in 1803 Fawcett successfully created the 'sentimental' role of Job Thornberry in *John Bull*.
70 Charles Lamb, "On the Acting of Munden", *Works*, vol. II, p. 148.
71 Hunt, *Critical Essays*.
72 Taylor, *Players and Performances*, pp. 63–4.
73 W. Robson, *The Old Playgoer* (London, 1847), p. 55.
74 The Duke of Clarence, whose mistress was Mrs Jordan, took a particular interest in the boy – as long as his fashion lasted, Playfair, *The Prodigy*, p. 84.
75 Cited in Clarke Russell, *Representative Actors* (London, 1888), p. 364.
76 Playfair, *The Prodigy*, pp. 11–12.
77 *Ibid.*, pp. 12 and 75.
78 *Ibid.*, pp. 36 and 73.
79 See above, p. 140.
80 Hazlitt, 'Conversations with Northcote', cited in Russell, *Representative Actors*, pp. 363–4.
81 Playfair, *The Prodigy*, p. 91.
82 *Ibid.*, p. 23 for speculations about the relationship between Hough and his protégé.
83 *Ibid.*, p. 132.
84 *Ibid.*, p. 133.
85 *Ibid.*, p. 139.
86 W. Cobbett, *Political Register* (London, 1805), cited *ibid.*, p. 127.

6 THE SHADOW OF NAPOLEON

1 Gillian Russell, *The Theatres of War* (Oxford, 1995).
2 Colley, *Britons*, pp. 212–15.
3 There is a nice irony in the image of Sheridan, with his republican sympathies, having to walk backwards with a candelabrum to guide the king to the Royal Box at Drury Lane; Cecil Price (ed.), *The Dramatic Works of R. B. Sheridan* (Oxford, 1973), vol. II, p. 630.
4 Colley, *Britons*, p. 216.
5 Russell, *Theatres of War*, p. 82.
6 James Boswell, *Life of Johnson*, ed. G. B. Hill and L. F. Powell (Oxford, 1950), vol. II, p. 348.
7 Colley, *Britons*, p. 287.
8 *Ibid.*, p. 300.
9 Russell, *Theatres of War*, p. 18.
10 Charles Dibdin, *Professional and Literary Memoirs of Charles Dibdin the Younger*, ed. George Speaight (London, 1956), p. 26.
11 Byrnes' *Nootka Sound; or, Britain Prepar'd* of 4 June 1790, renamed (4 October 1790) *The Provocation!* was originally based on a colonial dispute

with Spain over Vancouver Island. Now the hostile characters became French: General Sanguinaire and Monsieur L'Ingrate, and the scenes included 'an Engagement between an English and French Man of War; A shipwreck; A view of an English Camp; a Naval and Military Procession', *London Stage*, part 5, vol. III, p. 1551.

12 In 1792 Sheridan and Charles Grey had founded the Friends of the People to promote parliamentary reform, and in January 1794 Sheridan attacked Pitt for provoking French extremism: 'Such has been your conduct towards France, that you have created the passions which you persecute. You mark a nation to be cut off from the world; you covenant for their extermination . . . and you now come forth with whining declamations on the horror of their turning upon you with the fury you inspired.' James Marwood, *Life and Works of Richard Brinsley Sheridan* (Edinburgh, 1985), pp. 131–2.

13 *Dramatic Works of Sheridan*, vol. II, pp. 753–74.

14 *London Stage*, part 5, vol. III, p. 1670.

15 Robert Benson, *Britain's Glory*, Larpent MS: LA1036.

16 In 1812, 12,000 soldiers were billeted in areas threatened by Luddism, which was more than were in the Peninsular Army of 1808; Russell, *Theatres of War*, p. 10.

17 Cited *ibid.*, p. 12.

18 *Ibid.*, p. 9.

19 See Claire Tomalin, *Mrs Jordan's Profession* (London, 1994), p. 109 for whether Mrs Jordan wrote the play herself.

20 Russell, *Theatres of War*, p. 103.

21 James Dugan, *The Great Mutiny* (New York, 1965); Thompson, *Making of the English Working Class*, pp. 183–4.

22 To list only patent house performances: *Bantry Bay* (CG, 18 February 1797); *Cape St Vincent* (DL, 14 March 1797); J. C. Cross, *The Surrender of Trinidad* (CG, 11 May 1797); *The Rival Soldiers* (CG, 17 May 1797); *England's Glory* (18 October 1797); O'Keefe, *Britain's Brave Tars* (CG, 19 December 1797); *A Naval Interlude* (HAY, 26 March 1798); *The Quarter Deck* (CG, 8 May 1798); *Voluntary Contributions* (CG, 12 May 1798); J. C. Cross, *The Raft; or, Both Sides of the Water* (CG, 31 May 1798); *The Starboard Watch* (CG, 28 May 1798); *Britons Roused; or, Citizen Soldiers* (CG, 16 May 1798); *Unanimity; or, War, Love and Loyalty* (CG, 4 June 1798); T. J. Dibdin, *The Mouth of the Nile* (CG, 25 October, 1798) and his *The Naval Pillar; or Britannia's Triumph* (CG, 7 October 1799).

23 Russell, *Theatres of War*, p. 65.

24 *Ibid.*, p. 66.

25 John Bohstedt suggests that 21·6 percent of theatre riots involved the military; *Riots and Community Politics in England and Wales, 1790–1810* (Cambridge, Mass., 1983), p. 14.

26 Russell, *Theatres of War*, p. 114.

27 McGarr and Callinicos, *Marxism and the Great French Revolution* p. 108, n173.

28 It took Bonaparte only three weeks after his appointment to command the Army of England to decide against the invasion (February 1798), although the pretence of preparation was kept up for several months.

29 J. C. Herold confirms the accusation and comments rather callously that 'Even if Bonaparte did order the mercy-killing of two or four dozen hopeless plague patients, surely the action was more defensible than the massacre of several thousand prisoners of war, which he had ordered at Jaffa the weeks earlier.' *Bonaparte in Egypt* (London, 1962), pp. 307–8. See J. S. Ripon, *Buonaparte; or, the Free-Booter*, below page 181, for a dramatisation of Bonaparte the murderer.

30 Brookner, *David*, p. 147.

31 J. H. Rose, *Cambridge Modern History* (1904; Cambridge, 1934 edn), vol. VIII, p. 618.

32 Brookner, *David*, p. 135.

33 For how the actors of the Comédie (Théâtre du Nation) escaped the guillotine, see Carlson, *Theatre of the Revolution*, pp. 200–2.

34 Kennedy and Netter, *Theatre and Opera in Paris*, p. 90.

35 McGarr and Callinicos, *Marxism and the Great French Revolution*, p. 126.

36 Cited *ibid.*, p. 81.

37 Hobsbawm, *Age of Revolution*, pp. 75–6.

38 *Ibid.*

39 Naples was also the site for one of his most reprehensible acts when he lent his authority to the unjustified execution of Caracciolo and other Neapolitan radicals. Bennett, *Nelson the Commander*, pp. 159–60.

40 Price, *Dramatic Works*, vol. II, p. 646.

41 A. Oliver and J. Saunders, 'De Loutherbourg and Pizarro, 1799', *Theatre Notebook*, 20 (1965–6), pp. 30–2; C. Baugh, *Garrick and Loutherbourg* (London, 1990), pp. 93–5.

42 Kelly, *Reminiscences*, pp. 252–5.

43 Reynolds, *Life and Times*, vol. II, p. 263.

44 John Loftis, *Sheridan and the Drama of Georgian England* (Cambridge, Mass., 1977), p. 129.

45 *The Oracle*, 25 May 1799, cited Price, *Dramatic Works*, vol. II, p. 660.

46 Having been condemned to death by Pizarro, she begs to die in the habit she disgraced when she first eloped with him.

47 Sheridan had been particularly close to Brissot, and shared his opposition to the execution of the French king, when other Girondins voted for it. Fintan O'Toole, *A Traitor's Kiss* (London, 1997), p. 281.

48 Loftis, *Sheridan*, pp. 129–30.

49 Quoted O'Toole, *Traitor's Kiss*, p. 340.

50 A. Aspinall (ed.), *The Correspondence of George, Prince of Wales* (London, 1963), vol. III, p. 440, cited *ibid.*, p. 341.

51 Loftis, *Sheridan*, p. 126.

52 O'Toole, *Traitor's Kiss*, pp. 344–7.

53 Carlson, *Theatre of Romanticism*, p. 75.

54 *Ibid.*, pp. 88–9.

55 In the preface to *The Death of Wallenstein* (1828 edition) Coleridge claimed he had chosen not to translate Schiller's short opening play *Wallenstein's Camp* because it was 'not necessary as a preliminary explanation', merely 'a lively picture of the laxity of discipline, and the mutinous disposition of Wallenstein's soldiery' (*Coleridge's Poems*, vol. II, p. 724). This removed Schiller's emphasis on Wallenstein's reluctance to take action.

56 Carlson, *Theatre of Romanticism*, pp. 21–6 and 79–82.

57 J. C. Cross, *John Bull and Buonaparte* (London, 1803).

58 John Scott Ripon, *Buonaparte; or the Free-Booter* (London, 1803).

59 Rostron, 'Kemble's Shakespeare', pp. 132–50.

60 G. Jordan and N. Rogers, 'Admirals as Heroes: Patriotism and Liberty in Hanoverian England', *Journal of British Studies*, 28 (1989).

61 Bennett, *Nelson the Commander*, p. 285.

62 Huntington Library MS: LA14465.

63 *Monthly Mirror*, 20 (1805), p. 407, cited Russell, *Theatres of War*, p. 83.

64 For example, his coffin lay in state, heralds broke their staves as when in a royal funeral the cry goes up 'The king is dead, long live the king', and the whole event inspired memorial exhibitions and souvenirs. G. Jordan, 'Admiral Nelson as Popular Hero', *New Aspects of Naval History* (Baltimore, 1985), cited Russell, *Theatres of War*, pp. 81–2.

65 Russell, *Theatres of War*, p. 87; her quotation is from Robert Southey, *The Life of Nelson* (London, 1909), p. 260. The crowds lining the streets were remarkably silent and doffed their hats as the procession passed, while the sailors in the procession were heard to raise a 'low wail'. See above, p. 158, for George III's instructions for the inclusion of common seamen in the ceremony – and his own absence.

66 Huntington Library, MS: LA14486.

7 THEATRE AND ALIENATION

1 Karl Marx, *The German Ideology* (1846; ed. C. J. Arthur, London, 1977), p. 47.

2 Alex Callinicos, *The Revolutionary Ideas of Marx* (London, 1983), p. 70.

3 *Ibid.*, p. 42.

4 The infamous Speenhamland System had started in 1795. Outdoor Relief was restricted to the home parish, which resulted in the forceful deportation from towns and villages of impotent paupers, as well as the depression of rural wages. Its failure signalled a movement towards the repressive Poor Laws of the 1830s and the virtual persecution of 'the undeserving poor'.

5 Napoleon's decrees of 25 April 1807 limited the number of Parisian theatres to eight, plus the Cirque Olympique, and once again imposed restrictions on the genre they were to perform. This decree officially closed up to twenty-five theatres, though probably only eight of these

were operating regularly; Carlson, 'Epilogue', *Theatre of the Revolution*, pp. 285–7.

6 For detailed analysis of the O. P. Riots, see Baer, *Theatre and Disorder*; Gillian Russell, 'Playing at Revolution: The Politics of the O. P. Riots', *Theatre Notebook*, 44 (1990); Jane Moody, 'The Cultural Politics of Minor Theatre', unpublished Ph.D. thesis, Manchester University, 1995.

7 Barish, *Antitheatrical Prejudice*, pp. 299–307.

8 J. C. Trewin (ed.), *The Journal of William Charles Macready* (London, 1967), p. xvi.

9 The term *alienation* was applied in the eighteenth century to all kinds of insanity, while the study of madness 'had as yet no proper name, since the term "psychiatry" was not coined until 1808 (by Reil) . . . Since the term "psychosis" had not yet been defined in its modern sense . . . the first psychiatrists were unable to make the distinction commonly accepted today between psychosis and neurosis.' Theodore Ziolkowski, *German Romanticism and its Institutions* (Princeton, 1990), pp. 152–3.

10 Joel Kovel, *A Complete Guide to Therapy* (London, 1991), pp. 41–2.

11 Mario Praz, *The Romantic Agony* (1931; trans. A. Davidson, Oxford, 1933). Ziolkowski's chapter 'The Madhouse: Asylum of the Spirit', *German Romanticism*, pp. 138–217 provides a more balanced account of the Romantic obsession with madness.

12 Colley, *Britons*, p. 151.

13 S. Körner, 'On Rousseau's, Robespierre's and Kant's Criteria for Moral Action', *The Impact of the French Revolution on European Consciousness*, ed. H. T. Mason and W. Doyle (Gloucester, 1989), pp. 160–71.

14 Sadler's Wells, the leading pantomime house, introduced its new entertainments at Easter, when the summer season opened and artists moved back from their engagement at the Theatres Royal.

15 Mayer, *Harlequin in his Element*, pp. 5–8.

16 *Ibid.*, p. 24.

17 *Ibid.*, p. 56.

18 It is often suggested that Brecht's term *Verfremdung* is better translated as 'made strange', but the use of *alienation* does acknowledge his Marxist approach: Peter Brooker, *Bertolt Brecht: Dialectics, Poetry, Politics* (New York, 1988).

19 Marx, 'The Civil War in France', *Collected Works*, xi, 103–4.

20 G. Steiner, *In Bluebeard's Castle* (London, 1971), pp. 13–14.

21 *Ibid.*, p. 78. Steiner describes the development despairingly as 'post-Culture'. Since 1971 it has been more widely described as 'post-modernity'.

22 *Ibid.*, p. 94. Though Beethoven's destruction of the dedication to the Eroica Symphony shows that he at least thought his music was 'saying something'.

23 Carlson, *Theatre of the Revolution*, p. 256.

24 Kennedy and Netter, *Theatre and Opera in Paris*, pp. 47 and 50.

25 *Ibid.*, p. 50.

26 Carlson, *Theatre of the Revolution*, p. 264.

27 See chapter 1 above.

28 *The Catholic Encyclopaedia* (New York, 1909), vol. v: 'Berthier, L'Abbé de l'Epée, sa vie et ses œuvres' (Paris, 1852); Macdonald Critchley, *The Language of Gesture* (London, 1939), p. 33.

29 Maurice Descôtes, *Les Public de théâtre et son histoire* (Paris, 1964), p. 220, cited Frederick Brown, *Theatre and Revolution* (New York, 1980), p. 90.

30 For example: Brown, *Theatre and Revolution*; Frank Rahill, *The World of Melodrama* (Philadelphia, 1967); Clive Barker, 'A Theatre for the People' in eds., P. Thomson and K. Richards, *Nineteenth-Century British Theatre* (Cambridge, 1971); James L. Smith, *Melodrama* (London, 1973). For more sophisticated analyses of the politics of melodrama, see Peter Brooks, *The Melodramatic Imagination* (New Haven, 1976) and Bruce McConachie, *Melodramatic Formulations*.

31 Holcroft, *Cœlina* (London, 1802); Norma Parry, *Pixérécourt; Cœlina, ou l'enfant du mystére* (Exeter, 1972).

32 Shepherd and Womack, *English Drama*, p. 200.

33 *Ibid.*, p. 201. Shepherd and Womack cite James Kenney, *The Blind Boy of Bohemia* (1807) and Barnabas Rayner, *The Dumb Man of Manchester* (1837), but the difference in date suggests they may be reading the earlier plays in the light of later Chartist-inspired melodramas.

34 Brooks, *Melodramatic Imagination*, p. 36.

35 *Ibid.*, chapter 3, 'The Text of Muteness', pp. 56–80.

36 *Ibid.*, p. 72.

37 *Ibid.*, p. 201.

38 Dimond, *The Foundling of the Forest* (London, 1809), Huntington Library, Larpent MS: LA1617.

39 Brooks, *Melodramatic Imagination*, p. 79.

40 Kelly, *Reminiscences*, pp. 267–9.

41 The most productive authors 1800–1850, according to Allardyce Nicholl, *History of English Drama* (Cambridge, 1955), vol. iv.

42 Cited Brown, *Theatre and Revolution*, p. 94.

43 See Robin Blackburn, *The Overthrow of Colonial Slavery* (London, 1988) and *The Making of New World Slavery* (London, 1997) for the economic imperatives behind abolition.

44 G. Taylor, 'Anti-Slave Trade Drama'.

45 C. L. R. James, *The Black Jacobins* (London, 1938; 1994 edn).

46 A. McLaren, *The Negro Slaves; or, the Blackman and the Blackbird* (Edinburgh, 3rd edn, 1799) published, like McLaren's other plays, with a large list of subscribers, mainly of Scots nobility, but in this instance including the Duke of Devonshire. This suggests that although McLaren was seldom performed in London his work had some circulation.

47 If the story were based on fact, this kidnap would more probably have been by Creole maroons.

48 J. Fawcett *Obi; or, Three Fingered Jack*, Huntington Library, Larpent MS: LA1297, printed in *Songs and Prospectus* (Dublin, 1800).

49 *Kongo Kolo; or, the Mandingo Chief*, Huntington Library, Larpent MS: LA1644 – application by Philip Astley, 21 November 1800.

50 J. C. Cross, *King Caesar; or, the Negro Slaves*, printed in *Songs and Prospectus* (London, 1802).

51 See Said, *Orientalism*.

52 *Songs, Duets, Glees and Choruses of the New Grand Spectacle, Joanna of Surinam* (London, 1804).

53 For a discussion of John Gabriel Stedman, *Narrative of a five year expedition against the revolted Negroes of Surinam* (London, 1796), see the transcript of his original diary prepared by Richard and Sally Price (Baltimore, 1988) and R. Price, *Representations of Slavery: J. G. Stedman's 'Minnesota' Manuscript* (Minneapolis, 1989). The same story, taken from either Cross' burletta or Stedman's original, was given full comic opera treatment by Thomas Morton as *Freedom or Slavery* (Huntington Library, Larpent MS: LA1942), produced at Covent Garden as *The Slave* (12 Nov. 1816).

54 Backscheider, *Spectacular Politics*.

55 George Colman the Younger, *The Africans* (Huntington Library, Larpent MS: LA1553) and Cumberland edition, London, 1808.

REFLECTIONS TOWARDS A CONCLUSION

1 See chapter 1 above for the *Literary Journal* review of *John Bull*, p. 12.

2 Bagster-Collins, *Colman the Younger*, p. 202.

3 Joe Cowell, *Thirty Years Passed Among the Players* (New York, 1845), vol. I, p. 47.

4 *The Examiner*, 16 December 1810.

5 Frances Ann Kemble, *Record of a Girlhood* (London, 1878), vol. II, pp. 255–6.

6 E. P. Thompson, "History and Anthropology", *Persons and Polemics* (London, 1994), p. 223.

7 Paul, *William Godwin*, vol. I, p. 69.

8 Letter from William Tooke Harwood to Amelia Opie, Huntington Library, Larpent MS: OP4.

9 Hazlitt, *The Life of Thomas Holcroft*, ed. Colby.

Bibliography

Abrams, M. H. *The Mirror and the Lamp: Romantic Theory and the Critical Tradition* (New York, 1953).
Natural Supernaturalism: Tradition and Revolution in Romantic Literature (New York, 1971).
Ackroyd, Peter, *Blake* (London, 1995).
Adolphus, J., *Memoirs of John Bannister, Comedian* (London, 1839).
Altick, R. D., *The Shows of London* (Cambridge, Mass., 1978).
Arundell, Denis, *The Story of Sadler's Wells* (London, 1964).
Ashton, Rosemary, *The German Idea; Four English Writers and the Reception of German Thought, 1800–1860* (Cambridge, 1980).
Aspinall, A., ed., *The Correspondence of George, Prince of Wales* (London, 1963).
Backscheider, Paula R., *Spectacular Politics: Theatrical Power and Mass Culture in Early Modern England* (Baltimore, 1993).
Baer, Marc, *Theatre and Disorder in Late Georgian London* (Oxford, 1992).
Bagster-Collins, J. F., *George Colman the Younger* (New York, 1946).
Baine, Rodney M., *Thomas Holcroft and the Revolutionary Novel* (Athens, Ga., 1965).
Barbier, Patrick, *The World of the Castrati* (London, 1996).
Barish, Jonas, *The Antitheatrical Prejudice* (Berkeley, 1981).
Barker, Clive, 'A Theatre for the People' in Thomson and Richards, *Nineteenth-Century British Theatre* (Cambridge, 1971).
Baron-Wilson, Margaret Cornwall, *The Life and Correspondence of M. G. Lewis* (London, 1839).
Bate, Jonathan, *Shakespearean Constitutions: Politics, Theatre, Criticism 1730–1830* (Oxford, 1989).
Baugh, Christopher, *Garrick and Loutherbourg* (London, 1990).
Behrendt, S. C., ed., *History and Myth; Essays on English Romantic Literature* (Detroit, 1990).
Bell, Charles, *The Anatomy and Philosophy of Expression* (London, 1806).
Bennett, Geoffrey, *Nelson the Commander* (London, 1972).
Bindman, David, *The Shadow of the Guillotine; Britain and the French Revolution* (London, 1989).
Bingham, A. J., *Marie-Joseph Chénier: Early Political Life and Ideas* (New York, 1939).

Blackburn, Robin, *The Overthrow of Colonial Slavery* (London, 1988).
    The Making of New World Slavery (London, 1997).
Bloom, Harold, *Romanticism and Consciousness* (New York, 1970).
Boaden, James, *Memoirs of the Life of John Philip Kemble* (London, 1825), 2 vols.
    Memoirs of Mrs Siddons (London, 1827), 2 vols.
    Memoirs of Mrs Inchbald (London, 1833).
Bohstedt, John, *Riots and Community Politics in England and Wales, 1790–1810* (Cambridge, Mass., 1983).
Booth, M. R. *et al.*, *Revels History of Drama 1760–1880* (London, 1975).
Boswell, James, *Life of Johnson*, ed. G. B. Hill and L. F. Powell (Oxford, 1950), 2 vols.
Brooker, P., *Bertolt Brecht: Dialectics, Poetry, Politics* (London, 1988).
Brookner, Anita, *Jacques-Louis David* (London, 1980).
Brooks, Peter, 'Virtue and Terror: The Monk', *ECH*, 40 (1973).
    The Melodramatic Imagination (New Haven, 1976).
Brown, Frederick, *Theatre and Revolution* (New York, 1980).
Bryson, Scott S., *The Chastised Stage: Bourgeois Drama and the Exercise of Power* (Saratoga, Ill., 1991).
Burke, Edmund, *A Philosophical Enquiry into the Origins of our Ideas of the Sublime and Beautiful* (London, 1757; 1968).
    Reflections on the French Revolution (London, 1790; 1986).
Butler, Marilyn, *Romantics, Rebels and Reactionaries* (Oxford, 1981).
Callinicos, Alex, *The Revolutionary Ideas of Marx* (London, 1983).
Campbell, Thomas, *Life of Mrs Siddons* (London, 1834), 2 vols.
Carlson, Julie A., *In the Theatre of Romanticism: Coleridge, Nationalism, Women* (Cambridge, 1994).
Carlson, Marvin, *The Theatre of the French Revolution* (New York, 1966).
Chazin-Bennahur, J., *Dance in the Shadow of the Guillotine* (Carbondale, Ill., 1988).
Cobban, Alfred, *Aspects of the French Revolution* (New York, 1968).
Cole, Toby and Chinoy, Helen, *Actors on Acting* rev. edn (New York, 1975).
Coleridge, S. T., *Complete Poetical Works*, ed. E. H. Coleridge (Oxford, 1912; 1975 edn), 2 vols.
    Biographia Literaria, ed. J. Engell and W. Jackson Bate (Princeton, 1983), 2 vols.
Colley, Linda, *Britons: Forging the Nation 1707–1837* (New Haven, Conn., 1992).
Collins, Herbert F., *Talma* (London, 1964).
Comninel, George C., *Re-Thinking the French Revolution* (London, 1987).
Cone, Carl B., *The English Jacobins* (New York, 1968).
Conger, Syndy M., *Matthew G. Lewis, Charles Robert Maturin and the Germans* (Salzburg, 1977).
Conner, Patrick, *Michael Angelo Rooker* (London, 1984).
Conolly, L. W., *The Censorship of English Drama 1737–1832* (San Marino, Calif., 1976).

Cook, Dutton, *Hours with the Players* (London, 1881), 2 vols.

Cooter, Roger, *The Cultural Meaning of Popular Science* (Cambridge, 1984).

Copley, S. and Whale, J., *Beyond Romanticism: New Approaches to Texts and Contexts, 1780–1832* (London, 1992).

Cowell, Joe, *Thirty Years Passed Among the Players* (New York, 1845), 2 vols.

Cox, Jeffrey N., *In the Shadow of Romance: Romantic Tragic Drama in Germany, England and France* (Athens, Ohio, 1987).

'The French Revolution in the English Theatre' in *History and Myth: Essays on English Romantic Literature*, ed. S. C. Behrendt (Detroit, 1990).

Seven Gothic Dramas, 1789–1825 (Athens, Ohio, 1992).

Davis, Jim, *John Liston, Comedian* (London, 1985).

Deane, Seamus, *The French Revolution and Enlightenment in England, 1789–1832* (Cambridge, Mass., 1988).

De Bolla, Peter, *The Discourse of the Sublime; Readings in History, Aesthetics and the Subject* (Oxford, 1989).

Decastro, Jacob, *Memoirs* (London, 1825).

Descôtes, Maurice, *Les Public de théâtre et son histoire* (Paris, 1964).

Dibdin, Charles, *Professional and Literary Memoirs of Charles Dibdin the Younger*, ed. George Speaight (London, 1956).

Dickens, Charles, *Hard Times* (London, 1854; Oxford, 1955).

Dickinson, H. T., *British Radicalism and the French Revolution* (Oxford, 1985).

Donkin, Ellen, *Getting into the Act: Women Playwrights in London, 1776–1829* (London, 1995).

Donohue, Joseph W., Jr, *Dramatic Character in the English Romantic Age* (Princeton, 1970).

Theatre in the Age of Kean (Oxford, 1975).

Doyle, W., 'The Principles of the French Revolution', in *The Impact of the French Revolution on European Consciousness*, ed. H. T. Mason and W. Doyle (Gloucester, 1989).

Dugan, James, *The Great Mutiny* (New York, 1965).

Egan, Pearce, *Life in London* (London, 1821).

Emsley, Clive, *British Society and the French Wars 1793–1815* (London, 1979).

Epstein, James, 'Understanding the Cap of Liberty: Symbolic Practice and Social Conflict in Early Nineteenth-Century England', *Past and Present*, 122 (1989).

Evans, Bertrand, *Gothic Drama from Walpole to Shelley* (Berkeley, 1947).

Ffrench, Yvonne, *Mrs Siddons: Tragic Actress* (London, 1954).

Findlater, Richard, *Joe Grimaldi, His Life and Theatre* (Cambridge, 1978).

Fiske, Roger, *English Theatre Music in the Eighteenth Century* (Oxford, 1973).

Fletcher, Richard M., *English Romantic Drama, 1795–1843: A Critical History* (New York, 1966).

Foner, Philip S., ed., *The Life and Writings of Thomas Paine* (New York, 1993).

Furet, Fançois and Ozouf, Mona, ed., *The French Revolution and the Creation of Modern Political Culture* (Oxford, 1987).

Fussell, Paul, *The Rhetorical World of Augustan Humanism* (Oxford, 1965).

Gallagher, Catherine, 'Marxism and New Historicism' in *The New Historicism*, ed. H. Aram Veeser (London, 1989).

Genest, John, *An Account of the English Stage* (London, 1832).

George, M. Dorothy, *English Political Caricature, 1793–1832* (Oxford, 1959), 2 vols.

Girdham, Jane, *English Opera in Late Eighteenth-Century London* (Oxford, 1997).

Godwin, William, *An Inquiry Concerning Political Justice* (London, 1794; Toronto, 1946).

Goodden, Angelica, *Actio and Persuasion: Dramatic Performance in Eighteenth-Century France* (Oxford, 1986).

Goodwin, A., *The Friends of Liberty: English Democratic Movement in the Age of the French Revolution* (London, 1984).

Greenblatt, Stephen, 'Resonance and Wonder' in *Literary Theory Today*, ed. P. Collier and H. Geyer-Ryan (Cambridge, 1990).

Grimaldi, Joseph, *Memoirs*, ed. Charles Dickens (London, 1838).

Hare, Arnold, *George Frederick Cooke* (London, 1980).

Hazlitt, William, 'On Modern Comedy' in *Criticisms and Dramatic Essays*, 2nd edn (London, 1854).

The Life of Thomas Holcroft, ed. Elbridge Colby (London, 1925).

Hedgcock, Frank A., *David Garrick and his French Friends* (London, 1911).

Heriot, Angus, *The Castrati in Opera* (New York, 1974).

Herold, J. C., *Bonaparte in Egypt* (London, 1962).

Highfill, Philip, Jr., Kalman A. Burnim and Edward A. Langhans, *A Biographical Dictionary of Actors, Actresses, Musicians, Dancers, Managers, and Other Stage Personnel in London, 1660–1800* (Carbondale, Ill., 1973–93), 16 vols.

Hobsbawm, Eric, *The Age of Revolution* (London, 1962).

Holcroft, Thomas, *Alwyn, or the Gentleman Comedian* (London, 1780).

The Road to Ruin (London, 1791).

Anna St Ives (1792; ed P. Faulkner, Oxford, 1970).

Adventures of Hugh Trevor (1794; ed S. Deane, Oxford, 1973).

Memoirs of Bryan Perdue (London, 1805).

Holmström, Kirsten G., *Monodrama, Attitudes, Tableaux Vivants* (Stockholm, 1967).

Holzmann, Albert William, *Family Relationships in the Dramas of August von Kotzebue* (Princeton, 1935).

Howarth, W. D., *Sublime and Grotesque: French Romantic Drama* (London, 1975).

Huet, Marie-Hélène, *Rehearsing the Revolution*, trans. Robert Hurley (Berkeley, 1982).

Hunt, Lynn, *Politics, Culture and Class in the French Revolution* (Stanford, 1984).

Ihl, Olivier, *La fête républicaine* (Paris, 1996).

Inchbald, Elizabeth, *The British Theatre; or a Collection of Plays which are acted at the Theatres Royal, Drury Land, Covent Garden, and Haymarket . . . with Biographical and critical Remarks by Mrs Inchbald* (London, 1808), 25 vols.

Jacobus, Mary, 'That Great Stage Where Senators Perform': *Macbeth* and the Politics of Romantic Theatre', *Studies in Romanticism*, 22 (1983).

James, C. L. R., *The Black Jacobins* (London, 1938; 1994 edn).

Jameson, Frederick, *The Political Unconscious: Narrative as a Socially Symbolic Act* (Ithaca, N.Y., 1981).

Jordan, G. and N. Rogers, 'Admirals as Heroes: Patriotism and Liberty in Hanoverian England', *Journal of British Studies*, 28 (1989).

Keily, Robert, *The Romantic Novel in England* (Cambridge, Mass., 1979).

Kelly, Gary, *The English Jacobin Novel, 1780–1805* (Oxford, 1976).

English Fiction in the Romantic Period 1789–1830 (London, 1989).

Kelly, Linda, *The Kemble Era* (London, 1980).

Kelly, Michael, *Reminiscences of Michael Kelly of the King's Theatre and Theatre Royal, Drury Lane* (London, 1826, ed. R. Fiske, Oxford, 1975), 2 vols.

Kemble, Frances Ann, *Record of a Girlhood* (London, 1878), 2 vols.

Kennedy, Emmet, *A Cultural History of the French Revolution* (New Haven, Conn.,1989).

Kennedy, Emmet, Marie-Laurence Netter, James P. McGregor and Mark V. Olsen, *Theatre, Opera, and Audiences in Revolutionary Paris* (Westport, Conn., 1996).

Kovel, Joel, *A Complete Guide to Therapy* (London, 1991).

Kubiak, Anthony, *Stages of Terror* (Indiana, 1991).

Lacey, Alexander, *Pixérécourt and the French Romantic Drama* (Toronto, 1928).

Lamb, Charles and Mary Lamb, *The Works of Charles and Mary Lamb*, ed. E. V. Lucas (London, 1903–5), 7 vols.

Laver, James, *A Concise History of Costume* (London, 1967).

Littlewood, S. R., *Elizabeth Inchbald and her Circle* (London, 1921).

Liu, Alan, *Wordsworth: The Sense of History* (Stanford, 1989).

'Wordsworth and Subversion', *Yale Journal of Criticism*, 2 (spring 1989).

Loftis, John, *Sheridan and the Drama of Georgian England* (Cambridge, Mass. 1977).

The London Stage, 1660–1800, 5 parts in 11 vols., eds. W. Van Lennep, E. L. Avery, A. H. Scouter, G. W. Stone, Jnr. and C. B. Hogan (Carbondale, Ill., 1960–8).

Lonsdale, Roger, ed., *The Poems of Thomas Gray, William Collins and Oliver Goldsmith* (London, 1969).

Macready, W. C., *Reminiscences*, ed. F. Pollock (London, 1875).

Manvell, Roger, *Sarah Siddons, Portrait of an Actress* (London, 1970).

Marwood, James, *Life and Works of Richard Brinsley Sheridan* (Edinburgh, 1985).

Marx, Karl, *The German Ideology* (1846; ed. C. J. Arthur, London, 1977).

Collected Works of Marx and Engles (Moscow and London, 1974–89), 44 vols.

Mason., H. T. and W. Doyle, eds., *The Impact of the French Revolution on European Consciousness* (Gloucester, 1989).

Massin, Jean, *Almanach de la Révolution Français* (Paris, 1963).

Mayer, David, *Harlequin in his Element* (Cambridge, Mass., 1969).

McConachie, B., *Melodramatic Formulations: American Theatre and Society, 1820–1870* (Iowa, 1992).

McGann, Jerome J., *The Romantic Ideology: A Critical Investigation* (Chicago, 1983).

McGarr, Paul and Alex Callinicos, *Marxism and the Great French Revolution* (London, 1989).

Meizel, Martin, *Realizations* (Princeton, 1983).

Mercier, L.-S. *Le Déserteur*, ed. Simon Davis (Exeter, 1974).

Miles, Robert, *Ann Radcliffe, The Great Enchantress* (Manchester, 1995).

Moody, Jane, 'The Cultural Politics of Minor Theatre', unpublished Ph.D. thesis Manchester University, 1994.

Nalbach, David, *The King's Theatre, London's First Italian Operahouse 1704–1867* (London, 1972).

Nicholl, Allardyce, *History of English Drama* (Cambridge, 1952–9), 6 vols.

Nicholson, Watson, *The Struggle for a Free Stage* (Boston, 1906: New York, 1966).

Oliver, A. and J. Saunders, 'De Lontherbourg and Pizarro, 1799', *Theatre Notebook*, 20 (1965–6).

O'Toole, Finton, *A Traitor's Kiss* (London, 1997).

Oxberry, William, *Dramatic Biography and Histrionic Anecdotes* (London, 1835).

Ozouf, Mona, *Festivals and the French Revolution* (1976: trans; Alan Sheridan, Cambridge, Mass., 1988).

Paine, Thomas, *The Writings and Speeches*, ed. M. D. Conway (London, 1894–6).

Parker, Noel, *Portrayals of Revolution: Images, Debates and Patterns of Thought on the French Revolution* (New York, 1990).

Parry, Norma, *Pixérécourt; Cœlina, ou l'enfant du mystére* (Exeter, 1972).

Paul, C. Kegan, *William Godwin; his Friends and Contemporaries* (London, 1876).

Paulson, Ronald, 'Gothic Fiction and the French Revolution', *ELH*, 48 (1981).

Representations of Revolution (1789–1820) (New Haven, 1983).

Peck, Louis F., *A Life of Matthew G. Lewis* (Cambridge, Mass., 1961).

Pitou, Spire, *The Paris Opera, Rococo and Romantic* (Westport, Conn., 1985).

Playfair, Giles, *The Prodigy* (London, 1967).

Postlethwait, Thomas and Bruce McConachie, eds., *Interpreting the Theatrical Past: Essays in the Historiography of Performance* (Iowa, 1989).

Praz, Mario, *The Romantic Agony* (1931; trans. A. Davidson, Oxford, 1933).

Price, Cecil, ed., *Dramatic Works of R. B. Sheridan* (Oxford, 1973), 2 vols.

Price, Curtis, Judith Milhous and Robert D. Hume *Italian Opera in Late Eighteenth-Century London* (Oxford, 1995).

Price, R., *Representations of Slavery: J. G. Stedman's 'Minnesota' Manuscript* (Minneapolis, 1989).

Price, Victor, *The Plays of Georg Büchner* (Oxford, 1971).

Purinton, Marjean D., *Romantic Ideology Unmasked* (Newark, Del., 1994).

Quinlan, Maurice, 'Balloons and the Awareness of a New Age', *Studies in Burke and his Times*, 14. 3 (1973).

Rahill, Frank, *The World of Melodrama* (Philadelphia, 1967).

Ranger, Paul, *'Terror and Pity Reign in every Breast': Gothic Drama 1750–1820* (London, 1991).

Regnault-Warin, Jean-Joseph, *Memoires historiques et critique sur F. J. Talma* (Paris, 1827).

Reinelt, Janelle and Joseph Roach, eds., *Critical Theory and Performance* (Ann Arbor, Mich., 1992).

Reynolds, Frederick, *The Life and Times of Frederick Reynolds* (London, 1827), 2 vols.

Richards, Sandra, *The Rise of the English Actress* (London, 1993).

Richardson, Alan, *A Mental Theatre: Poetic Drama and Consciousness in the Romantic Age* (University Park, Penn., 1988).

Roach, Joseph, *The Player's Passion: Studies in the Science of Acting* (Newark, Del., 1985).

Robson, W., *The Old Playgoer* (London, 1847).

Rodmell, Graham E., *French Drama of the Revolutionary Years* (London, 1990).

Root-Bernstein, Michèle, *Boulevard Theater and Revolution in Eighteenth-Century Paris* (Ann Arbor, Mich., 1984).

Rose, J. H., *Cambridge Modern History* (1904; Cambridge, 1934 edn).

Rosenfeld, Sybil, *The Theatre of the London Fairs in the Eighteenth Century* (Cambridge, 1960).

A Short History of Scene Design in Great Britain (Oxford, 1973).

Temples of Thespis: Some Private Theatres and Theatricals in England and Wales, 1700–1820 (London, 1978).

Rostron, David, 'Kemble's Shakespeare' unpublished Ph.D. thesis, University of Manchester, 1976.

Russell, W. Clarke, *Representative Actors* (London, 1888).

Russell, Gillian, 'Playing at Revolution: The Politics of the O. P. Riots', *Theatre Notebook*, 44 (1990).

The Theatres of War (Oxford, 1995).

Sage, V., *The Gothick Novel: A Casebook* (Harmondsworth, 1995).

Said, Edward, *Orientalism* (New York, 1979).

Saxon, A. H., *Enter Foot and Horse* (New Haven, Conn., 1968).

Schama, Simon, *Citizens* (New York, 1989).

Scott, Walter, *Essays on Chivalry, Romance, and the Drama* (London, n.d.).

Shepherd, Simon and Peter Womack, *English Drama, a Cultural History* (Oxford, 1996).

Siddons, Henry, *Practical Illustrations of Rhetorical Gesture and Action, from J. J. Engel* (London, 1807: rpt. New York, 1969).

Sinfield, Alan, *Faultlines: Cultural Materialism and the Politics of Dissident Reading* (Oxford, 1992).

Smith, James L., *Melodrama* (London, 1973).

Soboul, Albert, *The French Revolution 1787–1799* (New York, 1975).

Southey, Robert, *The Life of Nelson* (London, 1809).

Steiner, George, *The Death of Tragedy* (New York, 1963).

In Bluebeard's Castle (London, 1971).

Storac, R. and K. McCreery, *Theatre as Weapon: Workers' Theatre in the Soviet Union, Germany and Britain 1917–34* (London, 1986).

Sutcliffe, Barry, *Plays by George Colman the Younger and Thomas Morton* (Cambridge, 1983).

Talma, François Joseph, *Reflections on the Actor's Art* (1825), Columbia University, Papers on Acting, 4 (1915).

Taylor, George, 'The Just Delineation of the Passions' in *The Eighteenth-Century English Stage*, ed. K. Richards and P. Thomson (London, 1972).

Plays by Samuel Foote and Arthur Murphy (Cambridge, 1984).

Players and Performances in the Victorian Theatre (Manchester, 1989).

'Anti-Slave Trade Drama in England, 1786–1808', *History of Theatre in Africa*, ed. Y. Hutchinson and E. Breitinger (Bayreuth and Stellenboch, 2000).

Thompson, E. P., *The Making of the English Working Class* (Harmondsworth, 1968).

Customs and Practices (London, 1991).

Persons and Polemics (London, 1994).

Tomalin, Claire, *Mrs Jordan's Profession* (London, 1994).

Trewin, J. C., ed., *The Journal of William Charles Macready* (London, 1967).

'The Romantic Poets in the Theatre', *Keats–Shelley Memorial Bulletin*, 23 (1969).

Turley, David, *The Culture of English Antislavery* (London, 1991).

Watkins, Daniel P., *A Materialist Critique of English Romantic Drama* (Gainesville, Fla., 1993).

Watson, J. Steven, *The Reign of George III* (Cambridge, 1960).

White, Eric Walter, *A History of English Opera* (London, 1983).

Wilkinson, Tate, *The Wandering Patentee* (York, 1795).

Willett, John, *Brecht on Theatre* (New York, 1964).

Williams, G. A., *Artisans and Sans Culottes: Popular Movements in France and Britain* (London, 1968).

Williams, Raymond, *Culture and Society 1780–1950* (London, 1958).

The Long Revolution (New York, 1961).

Marxism and Literature (Oxford, 1977).

The Sociology of Culture (New York, 1982).

Wilmeth, Don B., *George Frederick Cooke, Machiavel of the Stage* (Westport, Conn., 1980).

Winter, M. Hannah, *The Pre-Romantic Ballet* (London, 1974).

Wollstonecraft, Mary, *Maria; or, the Wrongs of Woman* (London, 1798: London, 1975).

The Works of Mary Wollstonecraft, ed. Janet Todd and Marilyn Butler (London, 1989), 7 vols.

Wordsworth, William, *The Poetical Works*, ed. E. DeSelincourt (Oxford, 1940).

Ziolkowski, Theodore, *German Romanticism and its Institutions* (Princeton, 1990).

Index